NO BULLET GOT ME YET

The Relentless Faith of Father Kapaun

NO BULLET GOT ME YET

The Relentless Faith
of Father Kapaun

JOHN STANSIFER

HANOVER
SQUARE
PRESS

HANOVER
SQUARE
PRESS™

Recycling programs
for this product may
not exist in your area.

ISBN-13: 978-1-335-00606-6

No Bullet Got Me Yet

Hanover Square Press
22 Adelaide St. West, 41st Floor
Toronto, Ontario M5H 4E3, Canada
HanoverSqPress.com
BookClubbish.com

Printed in U.S.A.

This book is dedicated to all the veterans of the United Nations forces who bravely served during the Korean War (1950–53) against overwhelming odds and prevailed in securing freedom for the grateful nation of South Korea. This was not a "forgotten war" but a forgotten victory. We give an especially heartfelt debt of gratitude to the Eighth Army's POWs who spent as many as three years in captivity enduring the worst conditions imaginable. About 7800 American MIAs remain unaccounted for. We thank you for your service and sacrifice. You are not forgotten.

Father Kapaun's Journey during Korean War
8th Regimental Chaplain, 1st Cavalry Division
July 18, 1950–May 23, 1951

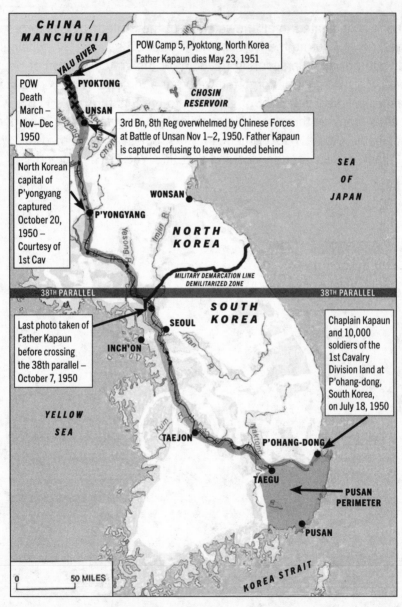

CHINA / MANCHURIA

YALU RIVER

POW Camp 5, Pyoktong, North Korea
Father Kapaun dies May 23, 1951

PYOKTONG

CHOSIN RESERVOIR

POW Death March – Nov–Dec 1950

UNSAN

3rd Bn, 8th Reg overwhelmed by Chinese Forces at Battle of Unsan Nov 1–2, 1950. Father Kapaun is captured refusing to leave wounded behind

SEA OF JAPAN

North Korean capital of P'yongyang captured October 20, 1950 – Courtesy of 1st Cav

WONSAN

P'YONGYANG

NORTH KOREA

MILITARY DEMARCATION LINE
DEMILITARIZED ZONE

38TH PARALLEL

38TH PARALLEL

SOUTH KOREA

Last photo taken of Father Kapaun before crossing the 38th parallel – October 7, 1950

SEOUL

INCH'ON

Chaplain Kapaun and 10,000 soldiers of the 1st Cavalry Division land at P'ohang-dong, South Korea, on July 18, 1950

YELLOW SEA

TAEJON

P'OHANG-DONG

TAEGU

PUSAN PERIMETER

PUSAN

0   50 MILES

KOREA STRAIT

NO BULLET
GOT ME YET

The Relentless Faith
of Father Kapaun

Pallas Athena now gave to Diomedes, Tydeus' son, the strength and courage that would make him shine among the Greeks and win him glory. Starlight flowed from his helmet and shield, as if Sirius had just risen from the sea. Before dawn in autumn, and the brightest of stars was blazing from his torso and face instead of from the sky, Athena aimed him to where the battle was thickest.

—*Iliad* by Homer

Somebody must be praying hard for us. No bullet got me yet although my pipe got wrecked and the day before yesterday a machine gunner sprayed us with bullets but we jumped into the ditch too quickly.

—Father Kapaun's last letter sent home

Table of Contents

Introduction

I am a Priest of the Diocese of Wichita, Kansas, currently serving as the Episcopal Delegate for the Cause for Beatification and Canonization of Father Emil Kapaun. Serving in this capacity, The Father Kapaun Guild has collected thousands of pages of interviews, articles, letters, and other pertinent documents regarding the life of Father Kapaun. These documents have been forwarded to the Congregation for Saints in Rome for use in the proof of Father Kapaun's life of sanctity and heroic virtue that will hopefully prove him worthy of the title Saint in the Roman Catholic Church. Some of these documents were provided to the US Army in their research of Father Kapaun's actions during the Korean War and helped corroborate Chaplain Kapaun's courage and heroism above and beyond the call of duty in 1950-51 that led to his being awarded the Medal of Honor in April of 2013.

The goal of the Diocese of Wichita is to pursue and promote Father Kapaun's Cause for Canonization as we continue to educate people of all faiths on the life and virtue of Father Kapaun as accurately as possible. The Catholic Church, like the rest of the world, strives for and admires perfection. It teaches that this perfection is achieved in following the example of Jesus Christ. The Church honors those the Church believes achieved that goal of perfection in following Christ by granting them the title of "Saint." My study of Canon Law taught me the processes of recognizing and naming a Saint. Canon Law sets rather strict standards for this process—one that is not taken lightly. Not only does the process provide for the title of Saint, but in turn, the Church is stating that this person has been granted that ultimate gift of eternal life in God's Kingdom. This perfection achieved through grace is the goal of all Christians.

John Stansifer first came to know Father Kapaun when he saw the Medal of Honor ceremony on live television, April 13, 2013. The story was of particular interest because John, a fellow Kansan, grew up about a hundred miles from Father Kapaun's hometown of Pilsen and his parents and grandparents were from Wichita. That day, John knew that he was to answer a call to do what he could to make the story of Father Kapaun known to a wider audience. He was compelled to bring Father Kapaun's story to life for those who had yet to hear of his heroism. Mr. Stansifer then spent nearly a decade reviewing thousands of pages of documents and doing interviews with those who knew Father Kapaun or served in the Korean War; many of whom had been held as Prisoners of War. He was happy to undertake this work because he recognized the state of perfection that is the life of Father Kapaun. He sought to share the story of this heroic priest and chaplain in a way that had not yet been done—first through an original screenplay biopic called "Father Kapaun's Valley," and next with a comprehensive examination of Father Kapaun's heroism in battle and unyielding faith with this biography entitled "No Bullet Got Me Yet," words written by Father Kapaun in one of his last letters sent home from Korea before his capture. This book is a compelling history that will inspire anyone looking to make sense out of suffering and through relentless faith continue to find inspiration and joy to all who seek perfection and recognize that perfection in others.

—Father John Hotze, Vice Postulator for Father Kapaun's Cause for Sainthood, Diocese of Wichita

Foreword

The chaplains of the US Army Chaplain Corps are men and women who selflessly serve God and those entrusted to their care. Their calling as servant representatives of America's many faith traditions is the strength of the army chaplaincy. Army chaplains are soldiers who sacrifice their personal freedom, like all of America's warriors, in order to support and defend the Constitution of the United States. Army chaplains provide for the religious liberty enshrined in the Constitution while delivering religious support and spiritual care to all the diverse members of the army family by nurturing the army's living, caring for the army's wounded, and honoring the army's fallen.

Chaplain Emil Kapaun stands out in the midst of the long line of many thousands of army chaplains who have supported our soldiers since the Army Chaplain Corps' inception in 1775, even before America became a country. After caring for America's soldiers during World War II, Kapaun served in the Korean War, where he ultimately continued his duties as a chaplain in a brutal Korean prisoner of war camp. His ultimate sacrifice in that camp, in 1951, is a continuing inspiration to me and to all my chaplaincy teammates currently serving in America's military services.

Kapaun's World War II training and experience empowered him, and his faith sustained him, right up to his final days. He fulfilled his calling as a Roman Catholic Priest and as an army chaplain by giving up his own life while caring for all the soldiers in the camp with him, regardless of their creeds or any other distinguishing factors. Kapaun exemplifies the very best of what makes us Americans, and of what makes US Army Chaplain Corps chaplains servants to their compatriots.

This book tells Chaplain Kapaun's story from the vantage point of Korean War soldiers who served alongside him. Their words reflect a man of God who loved everyone in his path, and who offered himself as a sacrifice so that others might live.

Chaplain Kapaun served as our nation's military chaplains do today—"For God and Country!" May we all follow his shining example.

—Chaplain (Major General) Thomas L. Solhjem, US Army (Ret.)

The views presented in this foreword are my own and do not necessarily represent the views of the Department of Defense or its components.

Prologue

A MAN OF GOD

Korea is a mountainous peninsula, about the size of Utah, jutting south from the Chinese mainland about six hundred miles. On the west is the Yellow Sea, and to the east, the Sea of Japan separates Korea from Japan. For centuries, Korean rulers did their best to remain isolated and steer clear of warring neighbors, earning the nickname "The Hermit Kingdom." But because of its strategic location, Japan brutally governed Korea as a colony from 1905 until its crushing defeat in 1945. With Stalin's iron grip over Eastern Europe leading up to the Cold War, news about Korea was sidelined, and thus the now diminished empire was hastily divided in half at the 38th parallel to appease the two strongest nationalists competing for leadership. In the South, Syngman Rhee, educated in America, wanted an independent government with support from the United States, while Kim Il Sung in the North was charged by Mao Zedong and Joseph Stalin to instill communism. Both sides wanted unification of the country, but with China embracing Communist rule in 1949, the border appeared permanent. An old Korean maxim says, "When whales collide, the shrimp in the middle is the one who suffers." Lacking an organized, well-equipped army, South Korea was now the "shrimp."

Perceiving the United States to be disinterested in protecting such a small country ravaged by war, the North Korean People's Army (NKPA) invaded South Korea in blitzkrieg-like fashion on June 25, 1950. Backed by Russian tanks and weapons, a 100,000-strong army stormed across the 38th parallel, forcing hundreds of thousands of South Koreans to flee to the port city of Pusan on the southernmost tip of the peninsula. This forty-by-forty-mile defensive area became known as the "Pusan Perimeter." President Harry Truman immediately authorized General Douglas MacArthur to lead the 8th Army, United Nations (UN) forces, and Republic of Korea (ROK) forces under the UN Command and defend South Korea from an aggressive Communist takeover, push the NKPA back over the 38th parallel, and if possible, unify Korea as a democracy. But while General MacArthur had great success in defeating the NKPA and even taking the North Korean capital of Pyongyang by October 1950, the Chinese entered the war soon after, sending hundreds of thousands of troops across the Yalu River. And they weren't coming for tea. The Battle of Unsan and brutal battles around the Chosin Reservoir in November and December essentially marked the second Communist offensive to take the entire Korean peninsula with the South Korean capital of Seoul changing hands several times.

In July 1950, the Marine Fighter Attack Squadron (VMF-312) were alerted for deployment, and the first aircraft flew in Korea providing air support for the First Marine Division. Known as the "Checkerboard Squadron," because of the black-and-white checkerboard bands painted on the cowling and rudders of the unit's aircraft, VMF-312 enjoyed an impeccable reputation among marine aviators. But while they ruled the air, the ground war was another matter, as the enormous Chinese Communist

Captain Gerald "Big G" Fink in his Grumman F6F Hellcat fighter plane, Pacific theater, World War II. Fink flew close-combat air support for the Marines in three wars. He was shot down on his first mission over North Korea and held as a POW for over two years. Though he was Jewish, he carved a sublime crucifix for use by the Catholic and Christian POWs in honor of Father Kapaun—a man he had never met.

Forces (CCF) doggedly brought the fighting back to the 38th parallel where it all began in the summer of 1951.

On August 11, 1951, Captain Gerald "Gerry" Fink, a marine reservist from Chicago, had partied all night in Tokyo. Gerry was one tough SOB who never backed down from a fight. Enlisting after the bombing of Pearl Harbor in 1941, he proved just how much of a fighter he was by flying combat missions in the Pacific Theater during World War II and ultimately in three wars. He was attending law school in 1951 when the Korean War accelerated, and as a reserve "weekend warrior," he volunteered to rejoin the Checkerboard Squadron stationed out of Itami, Japan, and aboard the *USS Bataan* to provide escort and blockade missions for the First Marine Division in Korea. At 0400 hours, he was abruptly awakened and sent to pilot an F4U Corsair on his first combat interdiction mission—attacking vehicles on a main supply route near Wonsan Harbor about eighteen miles from the east coast of North Korea. The Corsair had a top speed of 417 miles per hour and was armed with six .50 caliber machine guns, twin bomb racks, and attachments for air-to-ground rockets, making it one of the top fighter planes in aviation history. The troops of the NKPA and the CCF dreaded the vastly superior firepower of the close air support offered to US Marines and Army infantry. One well-piloted plane could turn an enemy convoy into scrap metal or eviscerate an onrushing enemy banzai charge.

Finding his target, Captain Fink came in low and unleashed a torrent of lead at an enemy convoy, ignoring the hail of small arms fire that rose to meet him. Some lucky shots hit his cockpit, and the throttle quadrant broke off in his hands. As he lost control of the plane, his last words over the radio were, "I'm hit… I'm on fire." Fink tried to bail out, but the damaged Plexiglas canopy was jammed. Plummeting fast, Fink desperately punched the canopy with all his strength until it blew off. By the time he bailed out, he was at such a low altitude that it only took three swings in his parachute before he hit the ground. Before he could get his chute pack off, North Koreans nearby opened fire, and a round struck Fink in the left knee. As enemy soldiers rushed in, he tried to draw his sidearm, but a North Korean soldier struck him in the mouth with the butt of his rifle so hard it knocked out his two front teeth. In the struggle, the soldiers also broke his arm, which Fink later had to set himself.

After being starved in a hole for three days, Fink was yanked out, hands bound, and his elbows bent over a tree branch across his back. His captors dragged him through several villages en route to Pak's Palace, a notorious interrogation camp near Pyongyang. When they stopped in villages and he lay helpless on the ground, a virtual procession of Korean women threw rocks, spat on him, and even squatted to urinate on him. At his lowest ebb, Fink felt that his survival was in the hands of God.

At Pak's Palace, Captain Fink was singled out for interrogation. The Communists were especially harsh on pilots in retribution for their superiority in the air and the ability to wipe out enemy troops with strafing runs and bombs, including napalm, which sowed terror in Chinese ground troops. Overall, the mistreatment and killing of prisoners of war by the Russian-backed North Korean and Communist Chinese armies during the Korean War were far higher than either the Nazis and the Japanese in WW2. Fully half of American POWs died or were killed in captivity between 1950 and 1953. Needless to say, the rules of the Geneva Convention were ignored by the communists.

"Why did you come to Korea?" an interpreter asked Fink.

"To kill all you goddamn commies!" was Fink's earnest reply, leaving the guards no doubt shocked at his audacity. The beatings continued, but after enduring days of interrogation, Fink only gave them information that was widely known or useless. After a couple of months, he and forty-five POWs were marched north 225 miles to Pin-Chon-Ni, North Korea, along the Yalu River, where Camp 2 was established exclusively for officers. Several men died along the way.

At Pin-Chon-Ni, Fink was again punished for antagonizing the guards. He soon met another Marine POW, a warrant officer named Felix McCool, who was just as brazen and confounding to the guards as Fink. McCool messed with their heads through confusion and chaos and took full advantage of the Chinese misunderstandings of much in the English language—especially mocking, joking, and replying to the guards with gibberish spoken with a straight face. Both Fink and McCool despised Comrade Sun, their abusive and intolerant English-speaking indoctrination officer at Camp 2, who was nicknamed "Screaming Skull."

The men had something else in common—they were both tough as nails. From Oklahoma, McCool had entered the Marine Corps in 1934 to get an education, but by the time his studies got underway, the world had plunged into a Second World War. He barely survived a last-ditch effort by the US Army and Marines to retake Corregidor Island in the Philippines in 1942 and clung to life as a prisoner of the Japanese for three and a half years after enduring the infamous Bataan death march. Now destined to spend nearly three more years as a guest of the Red Chinese, it's no wonder he stated later, "Twice I was born and twice I have died." He was able to provide cogent advice to his fellow POWs for whom he had great respect, saying Gerry Fink "was a giant of a man in stature, hard as nails physically, but a gentle nature who could do sculptures and wood carvings. He was knowledgeable in the humanities and conducted a school on it for us."

But what Fink couldn't understand when he arrived at Camp 2 was why the men were taking care of one another. That was unlike what he experienced at Pak's Palace. The despair and suffering in captivity led many a POW to become withdrawn, selfish, bitter, and even suicidal. Fink repeatedly asked why, and the response was always, "Father Kapaun… Father Kapaun…"

A proud Catholic, McCool told Fink that his faith in Christ's teachings helped him and the others survive. His faith had been further solidified by a POW he met—a chaplain from Kansas: "Then I met a man, a man of God, a Catholic priest. He was in one of the camps where we were held. His name was Emil Kapaun. A chaplain in the US Army, he ministered to all: Catholics, Protestants, Mohammedans and Jews. As I said, he was a Man of God. He would hold evening prayers, wash the clothes of the sick and hear confessions. Doing all this while he was slowly being eaten by disease, caused by lack of proper food, sanitation and clothing."

Fink was intrigued. McCool continued, "As a POW, it's the

simple things that count: air, sleep, kindness… If you don't help your fellow man like Christ taught, you don't survive." Before Fink's arrival, the Communist indoctrination classes had already begun, so the men worked out strategies for defiance like feigning ignorance or spouting just enough nonsense to not get seriously punished. Anything to pass the time and wait the war out, however long it took.

Fink had remarkable artistic and mechanical talents—especially as an amateur woodcarver. By scrounging in the camp, he fashioned homemade knives using the metal arch supports from worn-out boots and made drills out of pieces of barbed wire by hammering them into flat wedges. With a piece of gutter pipe and a wood handle, he was able to make sharp chisels, which he hit with a handmade mallet. He made stethoscopes from resonant wood and stolen tubing, which his fellow POWs who were doctors made good use of. Fink even fashioned an artificial leg for an Air Force major who had lost a limb when bailing out of his stricken plane over North Korea. The prosthetic was so well-constructed that he was able to play volleyball on it.

The gears started turning in Captain Fink's head. Like Mc-Cool, Fink was thoughtful and intelligent, yet subversive and brash against his captors. He was always thinking of ways to provoke the guards without getting punished. Now he thought about this army chaplain, the one with a Czech-Bohemian name, and the extraordinary influence he had on his fellow POWs even after his passing.

FUNGO

In Camp 2, each room had a light bulb dangling from a cord in the center and controlled by Chinese officials. Lights usually went out a couple of hours after dark. One night the Chinese guards became upset with the prisoners and turned off the lights early. The angered POWs proceeded to make a hellacious racket, yelling, whistling, banging on utensils, and stomping on the floor. A childish reaction for sure, but consciously conceived to aggravate the Chinese. At the height of the commotion, a POW alerted Lieutenant William Funchess to see the "big Carolina moon outside." William stepped out and gazed at the moon wondering if his wife, Sybil, in South Carolina, would be looking at the same moon hours later. They had married just before the war started.

Funchess, a South Carolina farm boy turned teacher, was an ROTC student at Clemson College and upon graduation in 1948 was commissioned a second lieutenant in the army infantry and began training recruits at Fort Jackson. Not long after he was transferred to the Twenty-Fourth Infantry Division in Japan, he received word on June 25, 1950, that North Korea had invaded South Korea. On July 4, his regiment set sail on four rusty landing ship tank boats (LSTs) and landed at Pusan the next day. They were one of the first fighting units to arrive as part of the ill-fated Task Force Smith. They took quite a beating defending the Pusan Perimeter, suffering 50 percent casualties before the First Cavalry Division would arrive. A smart leader, Lieutenant Funchess eventually fought hard all the way up to near the Chinese border until November 1950, when his unit was overrun nine miles north of Anju, North Korea, along the Chongchon River, and Chinese troops took him prisoner after he was hit. His life was saved by a quick-thinking officer, Mike Dowe, who was taken to the same POW camp.

With a bullet wound to the foot still slowly healing, Funchess went back to his room and found a flashlight shining in his face. One of the biggest Chinese guards grabbed him and yelled, "Come with!"

Funchess was taken to a house used for interrogation and ordered to stand at attention. Pacing back and forth, an interpreter repeatedly asked him, "Why you bark-a-like-a-the dog?"

Funchess tried to keep a straight face but finally cracked a smile.

"What so funny? Why you laugh?"

"I'm sorry," Funchess replied, but it was too late.

The guard was called back in. Funchess was pulled outside and surrounded by more guards, who beat him. He was thrown into the latrine and hours later pulled out, beaten again, and then thrown into "the hole." The hole was about four feet high, five feet wide, and three feet deep. The back and sides had been built up with stones, and the top was covered with logs and soil. The opening in front was about two feet high and made from metal cut out of fuel tanks from downed Russian MIG planes. Anyone deemed to be acting up or just looking at the guards the wrong way was tossed in this small, hot, and filthy cell to be isolated until such time as they "learned" their lesson and could be trusted to join the others. As if the confinement were not excruciating enough, prisoners were frequently ordered to "sit at attention" while serving their time and given less rations and water than usual.

Funchess curled up on the dirt floor covered with chicken droppings, and soon fell asleep. Sometime during the night, he was awakened by the sound of the guards opening the gate and shoving another POW right on top of him. As they settled into what little space they had, Funchess asked the man his name and heard, "Gerry Fink."

"I'm William Funchess. Welcome to the hole. It's a lot better than the latrine I was in earlier tonight."

Fink decided to nickname Funchess "Fungo" and called him that for the duration of their time together as POWs. Fink did all the talking, telling Funchess he had only one-half flight to his credit in Korea and that he had partied until the early morning hours when he was suddenly called to go on his first mission and got shot down. He reminisced about his childhood, his family, and Chicago until the sun came up.

Funchess was terribly sick and silent. Fink shouted, "Fungo, why in the hell won't you talk to me?"

Before he could answer, a Chinese guard banged on the metal door and yelled, "Sit at attention!"

Over the next two weeks in the hole, Fink heard more and more about Chaplain Kapaun.

"The chaplains were favorite targets of the communists. Father Felhoelter was captured near the Kum River and killed while praying over the wounded. Chaplain Hyslop was captured and killed by Chinese guards on the march north. Father Kapaun became one of their favorite targets. Father Kapaun was one of the greatest men I ever knew. Although I am Protestant, I loved him dearly. Father Kapaun offered comfort to the POWs all over Camp 5. A person's religious background made no difference to Father Kapaun as he administered to all. He offered last rights for anyone whenever he could. He participated in work details and was never too tired or busy to offer a prayer for a troubled POW."[1]

Fink also learned that the Chinese were in full control of the North Korean POW camps and that English-speaking indoctrination officers had been brought in to teach the POWs about the wonders of Communism and to reject capitalism and Christianity in every way possible. The guards refused to allow the POWs to conduct religious activities. They were even suspicious of anyone bursting into song and tried their best to prevent singing. "One of the [political] officers' favorite topics of discussion was what they termed 'The Myth of Christianity.' They used childish logic in their reasoning, harassing prisoners with such rhetoric as, 'Where is your God now? If you ever needed your God, you need him now. Why don't you ask your God to feed you? If you asked Stalin or Mao Tse-Tung to feed you, perhaps you wouldn't be starving.'"[2]

Not one POW asked for food.

Fink learned from Funchess about several occasions when the older civilians of Pyoktong showed a certain degree of compassion toward the POWs. Oftentimes they would give a slight bow whenever the POWs passed them on the road. Only if nobody was watching. Other POWs reported instances when some of the older North Koreans would whisper, "I am Christian." At least one Communist guard was kind to them, and under his shirt, despite the risk of great punishment, he wore a crucifix necklace. He too spoke highly of Father Kapaun. Had his superiors found this out, he would have been sent to the front lines or become a prisoner himself.

Fink realized the cross and crucifix, overt symbols of faith, were not only outlawed, but feared by the Communists. Even after outlawing Christianity, the Communists were deeply wary of pious clergy and Christian or Catholic chaplains and their use of the cross or rosary for prayer or religious services.

When Father Kapaun himself had become increasingly ill, the guards placed him in a room with Funchess, who told Fink tearfully, "There were no Catholics in my room, and I think that's the reason they put him in with us. They thought we would not take care of him. When they saw he was weak. They killed him. They took him from us."

But even after his death, the guards were still spooked by him. After getting out of the hole and back to the officers' camp, Fink continued his passion for woodcarving, and Funchess became more adept at creating useful carving tools. Funchess carved a makeshift pipe, which he drilled out of wood with flattened barbed wire. As soon as he finished, Fink carved an ornate *F* on the bowl with a crown above it. He handed the pipe to Funchess and said, "That stands for 'King Funchess.'"

Everyone complimented Fink on his carving abilities. At the same time, he discussed with his fellow POWs the need for a religious symbol in the camp. Fink wondered what it was about this mild, unassuming priest that had inspired such dedication on the part of these men. To them, Father Kapaun had "spoken, acted, and looked like Christ."

"He died in agony, the agony of Christ on the Cross," said McCool. "Before he died, he called me to him and said, 'When I die, say the last rites over my grave!' They never let me do this. He was spirited away before he died."

Because this priest from Kansas was held in such high regard by any and all prisoners merely in his presence, he became a very real threat to his captors. They were spooked by his kindness and faith in God, which only grew stronger as the guards did their best to humiliate, scare, cajole, even threaten and punish him physically. So in trying to strike fear into Father Kapaun, instead the Chinese captors only became more fearful of him. Here was a noncombatant in their midst and, despite all the screaming and sadistic torture these barbarians could muster, mild-mannered and soft-spoken speech delivered with purpose made Kapaun far more powerful than them.

Fink hated the Communists. He could sense that even months after his death, the guards were still spooked by Father Kapaun and his power to comfort and inspire men of all faiths. Fink saw that the Chinese were also offended by crosses—no matter what size. The Communists feared and hated any sign of non-Communist spirituality, and showed it no mercy. The Communists felt that the destruction of the church was symbolic of the destruction of Christianity. The "brain-washing" sessions were often held with the POWs sitting on the steps of a bombed out church. They felt that their battle was half won if the POWs believed Christianity was dead.

Lieutenant Ralph Nardella, a devout Catholic from New Jersey, told Fink that Father Kapaun told him and Mike Dowe personally to continue the services for the men after he was gone. What the services lacked was a crucifix to gather around. Nardella had Chaplain Kapaun's missal but not a physical symbol of Christ on the cross to serve as a reminder of the chaplain no longer with them as well as an essential element of Catholic devotion. Said Nardella, "When everybody else could think of nothing but self-preservation, Father Kapaun was thinking of everybody else. It was his actual deeds that gave the prisoners such a tremendous impact as they watched him living by God's law. In a few words, Chaplain Kapaun practiced what he preached." Through fellow prisoner Fezi Bey, a Turkish lieutenant and Mohammedan, Fink heard, "He is not of my religion, but he is a man of God."

It was clear to Fink that he had to honor this chaplain, so he decided he would carve a body (corpus) and cross for a large crucifix, something he had never done before. But first, he needed carving wood, and so his search began. Camp 2, as it was called, was simply the small village of Pin-Chon-Ni, on the banks of the Yalu River, appropriated by the Chinese, who forced most residents to make do on the outskirts so that housing would not have to be constructed for the growing number of POWs. Before it was a POW camp, it had been the target of US bombers who damaged most buildings and created rubble all over. It was from this wreckage that firewood was scrounged and after finding a chunk of scrub oak about four feet long, the Jewish Marine Corps fighter pilot from Chicago began carving. For the next two months, Fink worked in secret creating a religious symbol—against camp rules and against Communist doctrine—to honor Father Emil Kapaun—a man he had never met.

1

AD ASTRA PER ASPERA

When Kansas statehood was gained in 1861, a Massachusetts abolitionist named John James Ingalls proclaimed the state motto to be *"Ad Astra Per Aspera"*—a Latin turn of phrase reflecting the peoples' travails: "To the stars, through difficulties." Before Kansas was even a territory, it was simply the Great Plains in the lower center of North America—a mostly flat fertile landscape. And when the nights are clear, the sky looms larger than all the oceans—all the countless stars giving way to countless wishes. Is it any wonder a native of such a wide unending space would dream of reaching the stars, through countless difficulties, and living among them? As far back as 1541, word of magical cities of gold in Kansas led the legendary Spanish conquistador Francisco Vasquez de Coronado on an expedition along with three hundred Spanish soldiers and a thousand Indians to find this gold, without success. One of his missionaries, a Franciscan friar named Father Juan de Padilla, chose to remain with the Indians to spread the faith of Christ. Near what would become Emil Kapaun's birthplace nearly three hundred years later, Father Juan de Padilla was martyred by the Indians, becoming the first Catholic to shed his blood on Kansas soil. A monument in his name stands near present-day Council Grove, Kansas, where the Catholic Church gave him the title of Protomartyr of the United States of America. Fitting that hundreds of years later, young Emil Kapaun would write a lengthy paper in seminary school about the history of the Wichita Diocese and the expedition led by Vasquez de Coronado.

For nearly two hundred years after Coronado's expedition, the Spaniards searched for wealth in the southern part of North America while the French trapped and traded with the Indians in the north along the St. Lawrence River and the Great Lakes. In 1673 Father Marquette, a Jesuit, accompanied the French trader, Joliet, on an expedition to explore the Mississippi River. Father Marquette later ministered to a tribe of Indians, the Kanza or Kaw Indians, called the "People of the South Wind," and the name "Kansas" was born.

Most of present-day Kansas was part of the Louisiana Territory, which changed hands many times between Spain and France during the Napoleonic Wars. When the American colonies won their independence from England and Napoleon needed money to continue his conquests, he sold Louisiana to the United States for $15 million. The Louisiana Purchase of 1803 brought to the United States all of the Mississippi Valley, the Great Plains, and the land extending to the northwest across the Rocky Mountains to the Pacific and south of the Canadian border. By the 1820s, the Santa Fe Trail and the Oregon Trail both cut through Kansas, leading many settlers on the "great migration" west. But with cheap land and rich soil, many chose to remain in Kansas and give up any dreams of the coast.

"It is a curious anomaly," as Carl Becker noted in his essay, "Kansas," published in 1910, "that out of these diverse currents of migration, native and foreign, should have come not only the state of Kansas but the state of mind which makes the savannas of the east and the vast prairie of the west a place to which allegiance is sworn. It was not a region for those who feared space, for the limitless land met the limitless sky at the edge of the world, and over it all was a sunny silence... This was home. And so it was for those earlier peoples who found in the soil of Kansas the source of a new culture."

With the formation of the Kansas Territory in 1854, the government forced the Indian tribes into the Oklahoma Territory, thus draining Kansas of most of its aboriginal population. The Methodists, Presbyterians, Baptists, Quakers, and Catholics sent their missionaries and teachers into the territory under the joint auspices of the government and the various churches to minister to their religious and educational needs. That same year, the Kansas-Nebraska Act proclaimed that states could decide if they were to enter the union as a free or slave state. Missouri chose to become a slave state and as such, scores of Massachusetts abolitionists moved to Kansas to see it remain free. The fight became a decade of border wars with Missouri dubbed "Bleeding Kansas." Kansas ultimately settled as a free state in 1861.

BOHEMIAN BEGINNINGS IN KANSAS

Following the Civil War and the enactment of the Homestead Act, which gave free lands to Union soldiers, there came another mass migration to Kansas. Settling on the Santa Fe railroad lands were thousands of foreign-born settlers including Swedes, a Mennonite colony of German origin, Russian-Germans, Catholics, and groups of Bohemians mostly from Czechoslovakia and Germany. The growth of the Catholic Diocese was rapid, and on August 2, 1887, the Document of Rome was signed establishing Wichita and Concordia as Dioceses. The Catholic connection to the Bohemians dates back to the ninth century, when Saint Cyril and Saint Methodius brought the faith to the Bohemian provinces of the Austrian Empire.

So with the relaxing of its rigid emigration laws in the Czech Republic, some sixty thousand Bohemians crossed the Atlantic between 1850 and 1880 and settled all across the Midwest, with about 60 percent showing a distinct preference for farmland. On September 27, 1876, the first Bohemian Catholic periodical, the *Voice*, the mouthpiece of Catholic action for decades, carried the following proclamation:

> We, the Bohemian Catholics of America, are faced with a choice. Scattered and separated by great distances in this, our new country, we find it difficult to maintain our religious and national life. We neither manifest our strength nor utilize spiritually and materially, as we should, that advantage which naturally flows from a union of Catholic forces. The factors responsible for this failure are the dissipation of our power and the lack of a unified purpose in our social and religious activities. To attain more satisfying results to insure a firm foundation for our future, and to play an honorable role in this country of freedom as sons of a cultured and Christian nation, we must bring our ranks together.

This proclamation asserts some of the more urgent spiritual and social needs of Czech immigrants in the 1870s. It expresses the very real anxiety of a Catholic group trying to retain its ancestral faith in the New World, while simultaneously demonstrating the need of the Bohemian wage earner for a protective association of some sort as anti-Catholic and anti-immigrant bias were rampant. It is a document motivated by a spirit of democracy and pioneer neighborliness, and it shows how early the Bohemians learned to profess and practice independence and self-reliance, the very characteristics at the core of a newly arrived Bohemian's being. With this faith in their hearts, the first Bohemian settlers, around sixteen families, came to Kansas and founded the Community of Pilsen in 1874, named to honor the city of Pilzen (*Pilsen* in German) in Bohemia. Located in Marion County, Pilsen is close to the center of the state and near the geographic center of the continental United States—the literal "heart of America." Every year a few more families arrived so that by 1890, the settlement numbered forty-six Bohemian families with names like Franta, Rudolph, Vinduska, and Kapaun.

Enos Kapaun was born in Czechoslovakia in 1880 of German and Bohemian ancestry and was only seven years old when he made the trip from the Old Country to the New World with his parents. After a difficult ocean voyage, they took the train to Florence, Kansas, then settled in the Pilsen community. Fifteen years his junior, Elizabeth "Bessie" Hajek was born in 1895 near Wakeeny, in northwestern Kansas. Although Bessie's ancestry was Bohemian, she was the daughter of a railroad worker. She came with her parents to Marion County when she was three years old. By 1913, Bessie worked as a housekeeper for a local family. Before long, the teenage girl met farmer Enos Kapaun, and they married on May 18, 1915, with Father John M. Sklenar officiating.

The St. John of Nepomucene church in Pilsen was built in 1915 with Father Sklenar laying the cornerstone in 1914 and celebrating the first Mass on Sunday, September 26, 1915. It is a beautiful structure of Gothic architecture in which the service of God has taken place ever since. The steeple is 110 feet high and visible for miles around. Ten large stained-glass windows were imported from Munich, Germany, depicting several mysteries of the rosary and famous Bohemian saints. At the front of the altar is a large composition of the Last Supper. On the ten-acre parish plot stood five buildings: the 650-seat church, a two-story rectory, a school, a combination hall and gym, and a convent. There is also a well-kept cemetery. About one hundred families, mostly farmers, live today within the parish limits, an area of about ten by twelve miles.

COURTESY OF THE FATHER KAPAUN GUILD

The St. John Nepomucene Catholic Church is the heart of Pilsen, Kansas.

St. John Nepomucene, patron of the parish, was born in Bohemia around 1340 and takes his last name from Nepomuk, his birthplace. He is the patron saint of confessors and those who have been slandered. He is also the principal patron of Bohemia, where, in days of blessed memory, the people of that country prayed for his protection against floods and calumnies and for help in making a worthy confession. A life-size statue of the martyred priest stands above the high altar in the Pilsen church. His right index finger is placed against his lips as a reminder of his sacrifice in keeping inviolate the seal of the confessional, the solemn and serious responsibility of the priest never to reveal a sin heard in the tribunal of penance.

Like Enos, Father Sklenar had been born in Czechoslovakia and came to this country as a young boy. He was one of the first priests ordained for the Wichita Diocese in 1891 at just twenty-two. In 1901, Father Sklenar was installed as pastor at Pilsen—a post he would hold for thirty-eight years. Father Sklenar was a controversial figure, and the way he ran the parish was either defended by his followers or attacked by those who disagreed with him. He espoused the European tradition in which a social and educational barrier usually existed between the priest and his parishioners. He insisted that sermons and Mass be given in Bohemian over the objections of younger members eager to assimilate in the New World as English speakers. But his name became synonymous with the name Pilsen, and it has been remarked that a mention of Pilsen would be followed by the question, "And how is Father Sklenar?"

EMIL JOSEPH KAPAUN IS BORN

In a typical Kansas farmhouse, a couple miles southwest of Pilsen, and far from the World War that was ravaging their home countries, Bessie and Enos Kapaun welcomed their first son into the world on the morning of April 20, 1916. It was Holy Thursday, a day of joy that commemorates the ordination of the first Christian priests. On May 9, Father Sklenar baptized Emil Joseph Kapaun in the newly completed grand church.

FATHER KAPAUN GUILD

Enos and Bessie Kapaun holding a bundled-up baby, their firstborn son, Emil, eleven months old, in the open barn doors of an outbuilding on their acreage next to Pilsen, 1917.

Emil approximately age four.

The Kapaun farmhouse.

Enos Kapaun had built a two-story frame house in the middle of 160 leased acres including a barn, chicken coops, and a root cellar. Though not lavish, a strong spirit of family made the Kapaun home cheerful and comfortable. From the house there was an unobstructed view of the St. John Nepomucene Catholic Church in the middle of Pilsen, just a couple miles away.

With the language and culture in Pilsen predominantly Bohemian, Father Sklenar, who spoke English perfectly, had decided that the readings from Scared Scriptures, sermons, and the liturgical prayers should be recited in Bohemian. This was perfectly acceptable to the older generation since many of them spoke no English. The difficulty arose with the younger generation who were using English more and more. Before long, there were two opposing groups: one insisting that Bohemian should be the language for everything in Pilsen—including conversation in the family—and the other insisting that the process of Americanization should be helped along by using the English language for Divine Worship. The language problem in the Pilsen parish helps us to understand Emil Kapaun, because next to his parents he was most influenced by Father Sklenar. As a boy, he often remarked, "I want to be just like Father Sklenar." As a result, Emil rapidly became bilingual, embracing old and new.

But there was another language that Emil Kapaun learned early in his childhood—the language of love and faith. Young Emil was greatly influenced by the closeness of his loving parents and the atmosphere of religion that pervaded the home, which was adorned with simple prints and pictures—many of religious themes and Catholic icons. Emil did not have to wait until he went to school to learn his prayers; he learned them at his mother's knee. From early childhood he learned the fundamentals of the catechism and his parents took him to church from a young age. From their deep and natural piety, he caught what his mother thoughtfully described as his predominant characteristic, the trait that made him stand out, even as a boy: "He was always close to God."

Holy cards, prayer books, religious magazines, and newspapers were always at hand. Before he even learned to make out the words, little Emil indicated his later love for reading and study. He liked to look at holy pictures, especially when someone explained their meaning. His mother recalled the days when he was learning to serve at the altar. In spare moments he hurried out into the yard and knelt before a tree with folded hands. He would practice each gesture used by the servers over and over again. To serve as an acolyte, he wanted to be perfect.

His early prowess with the fishing pole was attested by a neighbor, Joe Meysing, who went fishing with his hired man in the creek near the Kapaun home. They had the best possible bait and fishing tackle. Little Emil happened to come to the same spot and join them. The men felt sorry for the boy, who had no modern fishing equipment. Confidently the lad dropped his line near the bank and soon after pulled out a beautiful three-pound fish, took it off the line, smiled and trotted home with his catch, leaving the experienced fishermen speechless.

One afternoon seven-year-old Emil was sitting on the bank, waiting patiently for a bite, when he noticed a long-legged king-fisher strutting along a shallow stretch in the creek. That evening, seated at supper, he surprised his parents with this remark: "Mom, I saw a stork this afternoon and I asked him to bring me a baby brother." With a smile his mother added, "A year later the stork did bring him a baby brother." Emil was eight when his brother, Eugene, arrived on March 10, 1924.

"On the Kapaun farm there was always something to be done, and young Emil never dodged work. He looked for it. Even when given a chance to relax, he would pick up a hoe and go to work in the garden or chop weeds along the fence rows, even in distant fields. For recreation he would take a dip in the stream that flowed nearby, or, with his fishing pole over his shoulder, he would seek out his favorite fishing spot. Running and play-

FATHER KAPAUN GUILD

Emil, age eight, poses with his new baby brother, Eugene, about 1924 or 1925.

ing in the fields, hunting, trapping, hiking, working or play-ing—he did everything earnestly and with vigor. He was skilled in repairing and building implements, a knowledge which, in his future ordeal, would prove vital.

From his parents he inherited the classic Bohemian tempera-ment. A kindly disposition coupled with tenacity and determina-tion. He was quiet, retiring, yet possessed of a keen sense of humor revealed by a wry but inviting smile. His parents bequeathed to their boy a spirit of sacrifice, an acceptance of things as they are, an ability to face facts and situations, and an abiding assurance that there is someone who directs the soul along the right path. One of the most admirable notes of country life, and especially of this

Emil Kapaun, age six, wears a beekeeping outfit tending to a beehive while mother Bessie works nearby, 1922.

community, was the close and affectionate association between parents and children. Above all, their Catholic faith was the warp and woof of their lives.

In appearance, Emil had an arresting grin, wide-set eyes, a strong nose, chin firm and deeply cleft, and an ever ready smile. He had a drawling, down-to-earth sense of humor. His mother recalled an amusing incident that happened to Emil when he was about ten years old. She was busy and asked him to attend to the milking of their cows. For some reason, one cow was jittery, and she would not stand still. Concluding that the cow missed the skillful handling of Mrs. Kapaun, Emil put on a dress belonging to his mother to fool the cow. The jumpy animal stood stock still while Emil milked her successfully!"[1]

On September 5, 1922, at the age of six, Emil began his formal education at the Pilsen School, which was staffed by three Sisters Adorers of the Precious Blood of Wichita, Kansas. His agile mind and retentive memory enabled him to complete the eight primary grades in six years, with little effort and almost perfect marks. His teachers testify that he grasped a subject at once.

"He was always ahead of himself. He certainly did not have to study hard," says Sister Coletta, who taught him in the eighth grade. At times the teacher called upon Emil to explain to his classmates some difficult problem in arithmetic. He was so unassuming that no one took offense. In religion class, Father Sklenar frequently asked him to explain points to the less adept. Most of this instruction was given in Bohemian, the puzzling language that young Kapaun was determined to read and write as well as speak.

"He was a real boy," Sister Coletta recalled. "Ever ready to tease and joke, an extremely clever mimic, imitating his teachers and classmates, but always inoffensively."

During his second year in school, Emil received his First Holy Communion on May 29, 1924. He had nearly perfect attendance during all six years of grade school, an astounding accomplishment, for the Kapaun home was three miles from school, the winters severe, and the roads often impassable. The lad also

FATHER KAPAUN GUILD

Emil Kapaun's first communion, May 29, 1924.

would arrive at church an hour before the others in order to serve Mass for Father Sklenar—even on his free days.

In the spring and fall he was often seen cycling to school with a load of wildflowers on the handlebars. These he had gathered for the altar, especially for the Blessed Mother, to whom he had a deep devotion. The Sisters of the Precious Blood didn't need much in the line of material conveniences and were devoted, well-trained teachers whose lives were dedicated to educating their young pupils. In this regard Emil was extremely fortunate, for the sisters realized that a boy as gifted as him should not be held back for his full eight years in grammar school, and they allowed him to finish early. Emil graduated from the eighth grade on May 18, 1928, and the next fall stayed in Pilsen, where Father Sklenar and the sisters had arranged a kind of two-year Catholic high school program in two rooms on the second floor of the school. In Kansas, or anywhere, to be a practical man and a student at the same time is a rare combination. Despite his simple surroundings, Emil's love of learning, languages, and writing developed early. By 1929 he had started a diary that gives a window into his growing and wonder-filled life at the time:

October 21, 1929: Dear Diary—Today we received our six week test grades. In Latin I received 100%, Science 98%. Business arithmetic 92% and in English 96%. Today we got our popular Science papers and it is blue Monday again because we do not know our lessons very well.

October 31, 1929: I was going to go to confession in the afternoon but I did not have any way of getting there but walk. And besides I had a lot of work to do.

November 1, 1929: Today is All Saints day therefore we attended High Mass and Benediction and I served the High

Mass. In the afternoon we did not work for today is a Holy Day of obligation but we celebrated it like Sunday.

November 2, 1929: Today is "All Souls Day" therefore we attended High Mass and after Mass we went in procession out to the Cemetery to pray for the souls departed. I also helped serve the High Mass and I carried the cross out to the cemetery.[2]

Not long after starting his diary, he notes the important Catholic holidays and sacraments. It is remarkable the roles and recognition given to various saints throughout Emil's life. From a very young age he studied the saints and the life of Christ without fanfare—just sheer devotion. The implications of these days in particular would prove clear during Kapaun's service in the Korean War as well as his recognition from Rome to follow.

On November 1, All Saints' Day is observed to honor and celebrate all the saints, both known and unknown, who have lived a life of exemplary holiness and virtue and are believed to be in heaven with God and a reminder of the communion of saints, the belief that all Christians, living and dead, are united in Christ and share in the same spiritual bond.

And on November 2, All Souls' Day is a day of prayer and remembrance for the souls of the faithful departed who have died and are believed to be in purgatory, a state of purification before entering heaven. Catholics pray for the souls of their deceased loved ones and for all souls in purgatory, asking God to grant them mercy and forgiveness and to reflect on the reality of death and the hope of eternal life in heaven. Quite simply, all Christians are called to be saints: people in heaven who lived lives of heroic virtue, offered their lives for others, or were martyred for their faith and thus blatantly worthy of imitation.

FATHER KAPAUN GUILD

Young Emil doing chores on the farm.

In Catholic doctrine, an official recognition of Sainthood is achieved through careful and lengthy study during an official Canonization process that demonstrates saints in heaven lived an exemplary life and standard of discipleship that the Church itself strives to achieve and imitate.

Many of Emil's diary entries are downright corny, but he displayed a keen point of view and an everlasting optimism about life that transcended his teenage Midwestern upbringing. He also wrote with a philosophical phraseology that was also deeply in touch with his spiritual being as well as an awareness of depression and "feeling blue" that he almost makes a game out of defeating.

Nov 11: Monday is back again and I suppose it will be blue for me again, for I do not know my lessons very good.

Nov 16: Today I got up about 4:30 for I wanted to husk corn with my father. I did my chores, ate breakfast, and got ready to go. We went out to hitch the horses and lo! it was raining which meant we had to stay home. It kept raining until about 9:00 it changed to snow. My! I could have ate my hat!!!!

Nov 18: Today is supposed to be blue Monday but it don't seem so blue yet. Maybe it will slip over by accident this time. "Boy!!! I sure hope it does." Don't you? Latin is getting harder right along but I sure hope we will have brains enough to get through it. "My! Wouldn't that be nice?"

Nov 26: At six o'clock came the voice from mother: "Boys get up!" It seemed rather dark and upon investigating we found it was foggy. Whoe! Yippy Lala! I bet we caught a muskrat. We hurried and sure enough we had caught a muskrat. We also caught an opossum and a skunk. That makes us eight furs. Only about ten dollars but I won't count my chickens before they are hatched.

Dec 1: Well only 25 days and good old Santa Claus will be crawling down the chimney. The atmosphere sure feels good these days.

Dec 10: Last night was foggy like on Dec. 9 but pooh! We did not catch anything anyhow. I guess I'll just have to commit suicide if this keeps on.

Dec 11: My Geminices! We did not catch anything again. Oh well! We all have our troubles.

Dec 12: Oh boy! I'm sure glad I did not commit suicide for
we caught a muskrat as you said we would. Thanks ever
so much for the hint.

DESIRE TO BE A MISSIONARY

In high school he had three great interests: his religion, the Latin
language, and mission magazines. He already had an awakened
desire that one day he might prepare for the priesthood, and
for this a good knowledge of Latin was necessary. His interest
in the mission magazines shows that he was already interested
in fulfilling the command of Our Lord before His ascension
into heaven when He said, "Go into the entire world and teach
all nations." Worried that his parents may not be able to afford
seminary school, Emil told his brother that becoming a missionary was exactly what he was going to do.

Emil's teacher in his sophomore year, Sister M. Vitalia, understood his early ambitions. She did not hesitate to speak about
the possibility of her student becoming a priest. She was naturally inclined to recommend the religious life for her favorite
pupil. In particular, she suggested writing to the Columban Fathers at Omaha, Nebraska.

The Columban Fathers were originally an Irish Mission Society but had established a number of houses in the United States
dedicated to foreign missions. If they would accept Emil as a
candidate, the entire financial burden would be removed from
his parents. But as soon as Father Sklenar heard about Emil's
plan to join the Columban Fathers, he became quite disturbed.
St. John Nepomucene Parish in Pilsen had existed nearly fifty
years but had not produced a single young man with a vocation to the priesthood. "Father Sklenar was confronted with a
practical difficulty. The Diocese of Wichita needed priests, especially priests who were born and raised in Kansas. The majority of priests working in the Wichita Diocese were either
Europeans or Americans from other states. While they took

care of the work in a marvelous way, there was still the difficulty of living in Kansas. No matter how much these outsiders loved Kansas, they did not have the advantage of having been born and raised here. So Father Sklenar advised young Emil that it would be better to study for the Diocesan priesthood. Since his parents could not afford to pay the expenses of a boarding school, he offered to advance the money. Father Sklenar helped many young farm boys from his community leave the farm to get a higher education. After talking the matter over with his parents, Emil Kapaun applied to Conception Abbey, a boarding school in Conception, Missouri, just north of Kansas City. He was accepted and enrolled on September 1, 1929."[3] Most of the students did not go on to the priesthood, according to Father Edward Malone, a professor. He writes:

I well remember Father Kapaun as a student. Thinking of him now is somewhat like thinking of a mystery story after you have read the ending. Had you been more observant you might have spotted the clues which would have led you to guess the ending before you reached the last page. So it was with Father Kapaun. Now one remembers little things about him which were not significant then, but which might have let you know what sort of man he would be when the going was difficult, had he become involved in a crisis. Only one would hardly have suspected Emil Kapaun of becoming involved in a crisis. He was quiet, almost shy, just a nice boy to have around...

But when you think of him now, you begin to remember things—the way he played football, for example. He lingered around the edges without anyone's suspecting his being there. He was not a particularly muscular or rugged boy and hardly had the physique to make a regular berth on a football team, even one as anemic and battered as ours was. But he did play, and you would usually find him crawling out from under a pile-up, and you wondered how he happened to be there at all. He sort of reversed the formula of another great soldier, "he got there fastest with the leastest." Of course you can't win wars that way. You can't even win football games that way, and we didn't win many. But there was a certain toughness and pertinacity in the man that always seemed to get him into the midst of things no matter how hopeless the struggle. I imagine it must have been much the same with him in the last grim game he played along the Yalu River. The game was hopeless, but he stuck to his job.

Father Malone concluded Kapaun seemed to "work himself to the top like a large stone in a bucket of sand."[4]

Another professor at Conception College, Father Walter Heeny recalls:

He was the most normal man I ever met. When it was time to study, he studied. When he had to play a game, he would always be on time. He played his game and left. He liked to read for he was a brilliant student. His classmates would gather in his room before philosophy class and ask for his help since he knew Latin and Greek very well. He was witty in his way, but there was nothing flashy about him. He gave one the impression of a clean-cut fellow, around who one would never tell a dirty joke or story.

His main job was in the sacristy. One would find him working there, or in the chapel praying. It was his custom to make a visit before and after his work. He was always congenial and ready to help in any way. He was an exceptionally good student, who always knew the answers but never made a display of his knowledge. He was consistently on the honor roll. Emil was active in dramatics, in the Blessed Virgin Sodality, and in the Polyphonic Choir. His favorite sport was handball. He loved to walk, often

FATHER KAPAUN GUILD

High school senior photo, 1932.

hiking out to the grotto of our Blessed Mother two miles from the Abbey. His devotion to Our Lady was exceptional.

Amidst all this formal education, one thing that distinguished Emil was his power of remaining undistinguished. He was in no way an extremist. His brother Eugene echoed the observation: "Emil wanted to join the priesthood for as long as I can remember and he always took his religious studies seriously. Yet he never argued to convince anyone of his own beliefs. Instead he had a way of humorously suggesting their merits—an attitude that was not only more convincing but which made him well liked."[5]

In the fall of 1929 the Great Depression began a decade of drought and dust storms that dropped Midwest farm productivity nearly in half—especially Oklahoma and Kansas which were dubbed the "Dust Bowl." But you would hardly know such a calamity befell the Kapaun family or the hardworking Bohemians of Marion County—they toiled away undaunted and helped one another out. Emil helped as well when he returned for visits, and hardship and bad luck seemed to be only mentioned in jest.

When Emil returned to help with the harvest one hot June, a neighbor, Martin Klenda, noticed that Emil was not wearing gloves. His hands were blistered and raw. When asked why he worked with bare hands, he replied in a matter-of-fact tone:

'I want to feel some of the pain our Lord felt, when He was nailed to the cross.'"[6]

The back-breaking and exhausting labor of the fields was salted with humor, sometimes with horseplay and practical jokes. The Kapauns had hired a man whose prize possession was a battered Model T Ford. One day young Kapaun shut off the gas line on the ancient jalopy. The hired man drove out of the yard to the main road. The car stalled. He cranked and cranked until his hands were blistered. Finally, Emil sauntered over and suggested that maybe he was not giving it enough gas!

Although his board and tuition were covered by scholarships, the young seminarian had to have a few extra dollars for travel and incidentals. To meet these expenses, he raised chickens. His mother would start them off in the spring while he was away at school. To visitors she pointed them out as 'Emil's chickens.'

No matter how busy the day promised to be, Emil went to Holy Mass and Holy Communion every morning and generally served at the altar in place of the boys assigned who were often irregular during vacation. He was already attending Conception when his younger brother, Eugene, started in the first grade. They made up for the months of separation by full days of hunting, trapping, and ice-skating during the Christmas holidays.

"I remember," Eugene recalls, "when Emil mildly shocked one of his schoolgirl friends by wiring her seat to the ignition!

FATHER KAPAUN GUILD

Emil Kapaun working the wheat harvest. He is second from left, kneeling.

He wasn't above playing a good joke, so long as it didn't really hurt anyone."[7]

On September 11, 1936, Emil Kapaun began the study of theology at Kenrick Seminary in Saint Louis, Missouri, a Roman Catholic seminary established in 1818 providing education and formation to seminarians for ordination to the sacred priesthood. A classmate and close friend, Father Vesecky, recollected their time there:

He was loved by everyone, young and old, and he loved all people. His studies always came before recreation or sport. But he was always devout and had a warm smile for everyone. When permitted he would go fishing in the little lake on the seminary grounds. What fish he caught he gave to the Sisters in the kitchen. A memorable characteristic of his manner of speaking was the constant usage of the word "peoples" instead of people.

Emil's private spiritual life was a case of still waters running
deep; he tried to keep his piety hidden. As a seminarian, of
course, he followed the minimum practices of daily Mass and
Communion, a visit to the Blessed Sacrament, saying the stations and reciting the Rosary in honor of Our Lady. His love of
our Blessed Mother was deep and heartfelt. Proof is offered in a
leaflet found in his prayer book with the title THE PRACTICE
OF THE THREE HAIL MARYS, in honor of the Power, Wisdom, and Mercy of the Blessed Virgin Mary. It has the well-
worn edges and the thumbed pages that betray frequent use and
includes the prayer:

> PRACTICE: Recite, morning and evening, the Three Hail
> Marys in honor of these three great prerogatives, with this
> concluding invocation:

> In the morning, 'O my Mother, keep me from mortal sin
> during the day.'

> In the evening, 'O my Mother, keep me from mortal sin
> during this night.'

Emil completed his last two years of college work at Conception with special emphasis on philosophy. Up until the candidate for the altar enters upon the study of philosophy, his work
is considered preparatory. Following that, two years of philosophy and four of theology are the minimum requirements for
the priesthood. Like every student for the priesthood, at times
he was beset with doubts and fears concerning his worthiness
for so exacting a calling. Even as a seminarian, when friends
mentioned that he might someday be a priest, he almost always
answered, 'Sometimes I think the sun will have to rise in the
west before I could ever be priest.'

He honestly thought that the dignity and responsibilities of

Christ's official representatives were too high for him. Here and there in his letters, even in those penned in a lighter vein, he expressed his high esteem for the honors to which he was called and in contrast his own profound unworthiness. Once on a Saturday night, a time when farmers often congregate in town to shop and gossip, Emil was sitting with several friends on the steps of the Marion courthouse. To them he expressed his very serious doubts about his vocation. When they insisted on the immense amount of good he might do, his drooping spirits revived, and he was greatly encouraged."[8]

Sister M. Virgila recounted to Reverend Arthur Tonne in 1954 a time when her dad and brother visited when she was a postulant in the novitiate and ran into Emil and asked him if he had decided to enter the seminary. When Emil gave his coy, demure answer, "When the sun rises from the west," Sister Virgila's dad was ready: "Well, Virgie, this is the reason why we came. He wants to tell you something." Emil then told them he was entering in the fall and wanted special prayers to become a whole priest and not a half.[9]

Sister Virgila later said, "Emil Kapaun ever since always asked for prayers and trusted much in my feeble one up to the time of his First Mass. Since then Father Kapaun has depended much on my promise of prayers and sacrifices for his intentions."

This very sentiment was spoken of repeatedly by Father Kapaun and was especially poignant in his explanations for his good fortune in surviving numerous deadly attacks on him during the Korean War, which he shrugged off with the simple answer that God had his hand on him and that he wore "God's armor." His future letters home from those battlefields reflected several times that the prayers of loved ones helped him escape grave danger. From a young age, really since birth, Emil Kapaun carried with humility the aura of someone who was truly a servant of God. Father Bede Scholz wrote to Reverend Tonne in 1954 after the Korean War:

Emil Kapaun was once ready to give up. After letting him
tell everything I told him to go on. His piety was of such
depths and yet such simplicity that I was convinced the little
difficulties would not stand in the way of reaching his goal.
In spite of the many duties performed quietly such as sac-
ristan or head librarian never kept him from praying most
every day in chapel. This piety he had before he came but
developed a great love for the Mass. Throughout the day
he would again and again come back to the Mass. This he
kept even when he returned for the retreats, the Mass was
truly the center of his life. At one of the retreats he had
me correct the ceremonies of the mass which he might be
careless about for as he stated this is most important.[10]

EMIL IS BECOMING A PROLIFIC WRITER

In 1938, Emil wrote a lengthy paper for his studies entitled
"Modern Church History," and in 1939 he wrote a paper entitled the "History of the Diocese of Wichita" that gives great
details about Francisco Vasquez de Coronado's Spanish Expedition and their search for the Seven Cities of Gold. Emil must
have been fascinated to learn that the first missionary to set foot
on Kansas soil was Juan de Padilla, a Franciscan friar, whose role
was similar to that of a military chaplain. But after splitting with
the expedition to remain as a missionary, he was killed around
the area that would become Kapaun's birthplace, becoming the
first Christian martyr in Kansas. Emil obviously had deep interest in this research as the paper is well detailed. The com-
parisons to Chaplain Emil Kapaun just twelve years later are
uncanny and prophetic.

Kapaun's closest friend remained his cousin, Emil Melcher. It
is about this period when Emil's diary entries gave way to pro-
lific letter writing. At just twenty-two years of age, he displayed
not only a deep sense of history but also an acute awareness of

world affairs and the growing fear of war in Europe. In a letter
to Emil Melcher and his wife, Vicky, in October 1938, he wrote:

> It looks like Czechoslovakia is having her troubles too.
> Hitler seems to be getting his "share of the cake" and he
> takes it without anybody doing anything about it. I'd hate
> to be living over there now. Just so that war spirit doesn't
> get over here. Did you pay any attention to the Big Series?
> I listened to the 4th game yesterday and I sure was dis-
> gusted with the Cubs.

Hitler annexed a huge portion of Czechoslovakia in 1938, resulting in Nazi occupation and control of the ancestral homeland
of virtually every citizen of Pilsen, Kansas. Emil's glib response
to not getting "that war spirit" was typical of most Americans
at the time. Kapaun gives a more vociferous opinion to the
Melchers a few months later:

> Dear Emil and Vicky, In regard to Hitler making us all ex-
> cited I am afraid we are being fooled a little. Hitler seems to
> be getting a raking over the coals lately. But I do not think it
> is as bad as we are told it is. England and France would like
> to rope in America again so that Americans would gener-
> ously do the fighting for them at our expense of both lives
> and money—and then England and France would nicely
> rake in some more territory etc as they did in the last world
> war. England cleverly gobbles up Australia, Madagascar,
> India, colonies in Africa and several islands in the ocean.
>   Germany was unjustly robbed of its rights and territory
> by that Versailles treaty and now when Hitler wants to take
> what Germany was robbed of, England and France make a
> big howl about the "dangerous" Hitler. The real danger to
> us Americans is England, France and Russia. By propaganda,
> they are trying to fool the American people again. The con-

trolled newspapers picture one side of the question and the
other they leave. We found that out in the war that was recently going in Spain. In America we heard of Franco as a
"rebel" dangerous and destructive. The actions he made were
always pictured in a bad light. But now we are beginning to
understand that we were not told the whole story. The sad
part of it is that some Americans went over there to fight for
the Communists against the Christians and they were practically wiped out. I wonder when the Americans will learn
to not fall for all that propaganda. Oh shucks—I should not
be writing stuff like this.

These two letters are extremely telling of the times back in early
1939. What Emil is learning from the news is the widespread attitude of Americans at that time termed "appeasement," a diplomatic policy of making political or material concessions to an
aggressive power in order to avoid conflict. Most notably it was
the policy of the British prime ministers towards Nazi Germany
and fascist Italy between 1935 and 1939. Early on, these concessions were widely seen as positive due to the trauma of World
War I, second thoughts about the treatment of Germany in the
Treaty of Versailles, and a perception among the upper classes that
fascism was a healthy form of anti-Communism. Emil's letter directly reflects the naïve feelings of what much of the international
community was fed by the press and the actions of the British
leadership. It is with great irony that Emil states, "By propaganda,
they are trying to fool the American people again"—because he
now believes other propaganda, saying Franco was "pictured in a
bad light" and Hitler was "unjustly robbed" of his rights and territory. The rest of the world simply did not see the massive Nazi
war machine being built and the plans being made for the Third
Reich. Appeasement for Americans meant simply not getting involved and certainly not "joining the fight," as the fascist/Com-
munist clash in Europe was not ours. How wrong America and

Kapaun were became apparent just a few months later when Hitler, believing that the democratic nations would not oppose him, invaded Poland and Norway and turned public opinion against Prime Minister Neville Chamberlain, forcing him to resign and giving rise to Winston Churchill. Emil's letter practically runs the gamut of appeasement policy and perceptions at the time.

THOU ART A PRIEST FOREVER

By Christmas 1939, Deacon Kapaun, home for the holidays, received permission to preach at the Midnight Mass. "Picture the delight of the congregation, the swelled chests of relatives, the thrill for Father Sklenar, when this son of the parish began to speak fluently and eloquently in Bohemian. His dear mother's eyes sparkled when she recalled that night. She even repeated some of the points he emphasized. She smiled when relating how

Kenrick-Glennon Seminary portrait, St. Louis, Missouri, 1940.

FATHER KAPAUN GUILD

some of the relatives leaned over to her and asked, "Is that really Emil up there?"[11]

And in April 1940, Emil Kapaun can barely contain his excitement in another letter to the Melchers—he is being called to the priesthood:

Man alive!! I sure got behind on this one. You got to excuse me for being so slow. Yessir—I just didn't get around to writing. What with a lot of studying to do and a lot of writing to get things set for the "Big Day" and going into the City getting things lined up I just failed to write.

You know, Emil & Vicky, I feel like the dickens. Maybe you do not realize fully what it means to be a priest, but I tell you—after I have studied all these years I am more convinced that a man must be a living saint in order to dare to take that step. And that is where my worries come in. Gee whiz, I have a feeling that I am far, far from being a saint worthy to receive the Priesthood. Think what it means!! To Offer up the Living Body & Blood of Our Savior every day in Holy Mass—to absolve souls from sin in Holy Confession and snatch them from the gates of hell in which they would suffer for all eternity. These and a hundred or more duties and responsibilities make a person realize that the Vocation to the Priesthood is so sublime that the angels in heaven were not given a vocation to the Priesthood, no, not even the Blessed Mother who was never stained with sin— even she was not called to be a priest of God—and here I am called!! I hope you will be at the Ordination. And write me a letter—you fell down as bad as I did. Maybe I won't get to write from now till then, so don't forget, June 9th. Yours sincerely in Christ, Emil

Father Kapaun's many friends were remembered at his First Solemn High Mass celebrated in his home parish on Thursday,

Father Kapaun delivers his first Mass at the Pilsen church.

June 20, 1940. At 9:30 a.m., a long procession started from the rectory to the church, led by Eugene Kapaun, brother of the celebrant, and two acolytes with torches. Then came fourteen priests, thirty-two flower girls, members of the Knights of Saint George and the Catholic Workmen Societies, five pages, two brides of honor, the bride, her veil bearer, four Mass servers, subdeacon, deacon, archpriest, and lastly, the celebrant. The two marching bands of Pilsen escorted the procession to and from the church.

Before the Mass, Sister M. Virgila remembers these words from Emil: "I am on the way to Calvary with Christ and there I shall draw all men to Him." After Mass, the celebrant and his classmates, Father Preisner and Father Vesecky, gave their priestly blessing to the entire congregation. A banquet was served at noon and in the evening to more than 1,200 guests, and the parish presented a short program in honor of its first priest. *The Marion Record* concluded a June 27, 1940, article on Father Kapaun's First Mass with this prophetic observation:

> Rev. Kapaun is not only the first young man to attain priesthood in the Pilsen Parish, but the first in Rev. Sklenar's years

FATHER KAPAUN GUILD

Father Kapaun in a virtual halo of blue poses with his family and Father Sklenar and various children from the community during his first Mass.

of service which number forty-nine. Not many young men are taken through life by the same Rev. Father. Congratulations are given to both and to the parents who have offered their son to help others as He has helped. Rev. Kapaun's many friends are happy and proud of this young man who has offered his life to God. It is a great sacrifice and a holy one and as Father Kapaun goes on, may the problems that he will confront, be easily met, burdens be lighter and sunshine obscure the dark day. Many in his group will lighten the path that leads us to eternity. God bless him, his parents, brother, his Pastor.

Ten days later the newly ordained was appointed assistant in his home parish. The aging pastor needed a helper who could speak Bohemian. The kind, capable, and energetic assistant threw himself into the spiritual, social, and material activities of the parish. He worked particularly with the children and youth. Every recess, when he was not occupied with other duties, he was out on the

Father Kapaun's blessings being given after his first Mass, June 20, 1940.

playground. The little ones adored him. A photographer caught Father hitting a home run while he was wearing the Roman collar. Father wore it at all times in humble deference to the wishes of Father Sklenar, who was a stickler for his own version of clerical decorum; he later dubbed as a "cowboy priest" any Catholic clergyman who appeared anywhere without his Roman collar.

"Kapaun did a tremendous amount of manual labor in the churchyard, mowing around the buildings and in the cemetery, cleaning up rubbish and trimming trees. One afternoon the energetic assistant was filling in a low spot between the church and the rectory. The wheelbarrow was a creaky affair with a steel-rimmed wheel. Crunching noisily over the stones and sidewalk, it disturbed the siesta of the aged pastor, who was never slow to express his likes and dislikes. After a few moments of deliberation, Father Emil hurried across the street and asked George

Father Kapaun, hand over heart, poses with the young boys of Pilsen. Almost all of them are wearing overalls.

Father Kapaun playing baseball while wearing his Roman collar.

Vinduska for an old bicycle tire, cut it the proper length, wired it round the steel rim, and continued his labors quietly enough to permit the pastor to get his rest."[12]

On June 21, 1941, Father Sklenar celebrated fifty years as a priest and thirty-eight years as pastor of Pilsen. Father Kapaun directed preparations for the grand occasion and put many weeks of research into writing a forty-four page "GOLDEN JUBILEE BOOKLET" honoring Father Sklenar. Father Kapaun had also written a paper entitled "PRACTICES AND CUSTOMS AT ST. JOHN NEPOMUCENE PARISH, PILSEN, KANSAS." These papers are a veritable gold mine of information about the early days of Pilsen and the parish setup. In the conclusion of the booklet, Father Kapaun writes:

> With the spirit of war tearing the countries of Europe and Asia, the United States of America proceeded to organize forces of defense. After a nation-wide registration of youth of military age, volunteers were received, and soon the draft system selected young men for training and service... Father Sklenar and the Community of Pilsen are proud of these young men. In their sacrifices and work shines forth the everlasting truth that all men were placed in this world to serve God. And to serve God adequately men must be loyal and patriotic to their country, a country of freedom, righteousness, and justice of God.
>
> When men are called upon to do their duty to God or to God's country, their allegiance shows itself in their response. Today men are being called to the army of our country. Fifty years ago a man, Father Sklenar, was called to the army of Christ. He responded whole-heartedly. He waged the battle through years of suffering and self-denial. Today he is a proven soldier—a Soldier of Christ.

2

FOR GOD AND COUNTRY

That June of 1941, *The Marion Record* carried a full front page account of the career of Father Sklenar, written by Father Kapaun. Three months later, the elderly pastor received the honored title of Monsignor. At the suggestion of Father Kapaun, Mrs. William Rudolph baked several cakes representing the sacred vessels and symbols of Holy Mass—a chalice, a lamb, a sheaf of wheat, a bunch of grapes, and a missal. The Mass book appeared so real that a visiting priest walked up to it resting on the table and tried to open it. Father Kapaun was in high glee at the surprise of the padre and commented with a chuckle, "I just knew some priest would do that!"

How quickly events would change. Soon after Father Kapaun's words about serving God and country as a soldier of Christ, the duty of serving God's country would test everyone in America. The solemnity in Father Kapaun's next diary entries speaks volumes:

November 2, 1941: All Souls Day. I said all three Masses at the side altar, and the pastor had High Mass at 9. No sermon. After blessing of the catafalque, we went to the cemetery. At the cross, Monsignor led the Litany for the Poor Souls in Bohemian.

December 7, 1941: vigil of Immaculate Conception. Japan declared war on the United States. As I listened to the Catholic Evidence Hour from Salina, I was shocked to hear the program interrupted by a special announcement of war hostilities.

December 8, 1941: Feast of the Immaculate Conception. The people were greatly disturbed over the war. At noon today Congress declared war on Japan. Such a way to honor the Patroness of our country.[1]

WORLD WAR II BEGINS

Though world war had been waging across the globe for years, the Japanese bombing of Pearl Harbor on December 7, 1941, grabbed the attention of every American and the United States was finally driven into the war. Legends were born daily and rushed to the press. One story quickly emerged from the raid on Pearl Harbor involving the Pacific Fleet Chaplain, William Maguire. Just as Chaplain Maguire begun offering Mass on the deck of the USS California, a swarm of Japanese planes appeared and started bombing every ship in their sights. Stopping the Mass (the story goes), the chaplain yelled, "Praise the Lord and pass the ammunition!" He then manned an anti-aircraft gun and gave the Japanese a dose of their own medicine.

"The story originated in the mind of a popular young song-writer. Shortly after the strike on the harbor, the American composer Frank J. Loesser, moved by the tragedy of the event, began work on a song with the title, 'Praise the Lord and Pass the Ammunition.' It described the exploits of a heroic but un-named chaplain (whom he called 'the sky pilot') who fought back against the Japanese using not only prayer and homily but bullet and gun barrel as well." The ballad became the first of the war's great fight songs, and it made its author an instant celebrity.[2]

Such legends must have had an impact on Emil Kapaun, a newly ordained priest and a red-blooded patriot. By February 1942, he was already signaling his desire to join the fight and writes Bishop Winkelmann on February 18:

Since the day of our Junior Clergy Examinations at which you appealed to the Junior Clergy for volunteers as military chaplains, I have been considering seriously the importance of such a step. I consulted Msgr. Sklenar about the matter, and asked him what he would do if he were in my position. He reminded me that one must be capable of fulfilling such a responsible position, also that one should feel inclined to such work before attempting it. He added no words of discouragement nor any more words of encouragement, except that all of us have the patriotic duty to serve our country.

On one hand I feel very much obligated to Msgr. Sklenar for all that he has done for me, and I have been trying my best to repay him by obedient and satisfactory service as Assistant to him here at Pilsen. On the other hand I wish to be entirely obedient to you, dear Bishop, my superior, and to respond whole-heartedly to the needs of our Diocese. And therefore I leave the matter entirely to your prudent and considerate judgement, assuring you that I am most eager and willing to be at your service whether that be as a "chaplain of the colors" or as a minister in our "home lines."

I remain, Your Excellency's most humble servant, Rev. Emil J. Kapaun

A couple days later, Reverend Kapaun receives Bishop Winkelmann's reply, which denies Kapaun's request to join the Chaplain Corps but ironically notes that he should redouble efforts to instill "high ideals" and "supernatural values" and to stimulate "patriotic loyalty to our country" to those at home not serving overseas. This kind of service seems more "chaplain" than "priest":

Dear Father Emil:

Grateful acknowledgement is herewith made of your February 18 communication. The sentiments expressed in your letter are deserving of the highest commendation and I am truly happy to note your willingness to join the armed forces for the benefit of our people.

In view of the fact that you placed the decision entirely in my hands, I do think that under present circumstances, as assistant to our beloved Monsignor, we need your services here in the diocese. Were I to permit you to leave, I would be at a loss for an assistant for the good Monsignor. You realize as well as I that we may not at his age expect additional burdens. He is no longer a young man and he needs your faithful and loyal cooperation. After all, during this period of terrible dislocation in all phases of human activity, the religious forces must redouble every effort to keep before the faithful high ideals and, above all, supernatural values. For these reasons, I believe it would be best if you would continue as you have in the past, assisting the good Monsignor and at the same time doing whatever you can to stimulate devotion and patriotic loyalty to our country.

Tendering the Monsignor and you my very best wishes for health and happiness, and praying our Eucharistic King to shower on both of you an abundance of this holy season's graces, I remain

Yours very sincerely in the Lord, Bishop of Wichita

THE STORY OF THE MACCABEES

Just a week later, Father Kapaun presided over the funeral of a young woman taken from this earth before her time. Mary Rudolph, whose family was one of the founders of Pilsen, was stricken with a debilitating illness and bedridden by late 1941. By February 1942, doctors could do nothing further, and she was expected to die within days. Last Rites were administered at her home, and she passed away soon after. She was only thirty-one. Her funeral was held on February 27, 1942, and Father Kapaun prepared a thoughtful and profound homily. Though many of Father Kapaun's homilies are thankfully preserved, this one stands out for an exceptional reason. In it, Father Kapaun relates the story of the Maccabees, which teaches that sometimes it is God's will that we die young. From his hand-written sermon:

"The King of this world will raise us up, who die for His laws, in the resurrection of eternal life." (II Machabees VII 9) God, our Creator, our Keeper, and our Rewarder has again claimed one of His children. By the hand of death He has taken her from us. Death, as it were, severs us from this world, and takes us to the throne of God to be judged by Him. But death does not treat all people alike. He finds some people who shrink from him as from the powers of hell itself, because those people know beyond death not all will be well with them. He finds some people who are prepared to die, who do not fear him, because to them death is not a tormentor, but a gentle guide on their road to happiness.

Oh today, as we gather about the remains of Mary Rudolph, we are reminded that when death took her, he found a victim who was not afraid. She had no reason to fear. She was prepared to die, for she had received a long warning that death was gradually consuming her life away. She did not give up to discouragement, for her holy Faith told her that after this life of suffering there awaited her a life of greater joy.

Young hate to think of death. But death often reminds us that he takes the young too. It is a blessing to live a long life: but it might be the will of God that we die young."

Antiochus's brutal efforts are ineffective. Death has lost its power in the face of obedience to the laws of the ancestors and belief in God's mercy and resurrection of the dead. Resurrection cancels fears of earthly death for faithful Jews and Christians. Vengeance and vindication belong to God alone—not the earthly king, Antiochus. At the end, she is crying out of happiness, not the king's brutality, because her sons are going to a place of happiness.

Father Kapaun's use of the term "a happy death" means that if you are prepared to die, then you should be happy in your last moments because you lived as you should have—free from evil and prepared to die at any age. Yet another profound premonition, prophecy even, was infused in the young priest, who would be faced with this very prospect at the hands of his captors.

KAPAUN MENTIONS "OUR BOYS"

Kapaun carried on a faithful correspondence with the boys of the parish who were in service. His letters were newsy and spiced with humor and affection. He wrote Private Gerald Franta in October 1942:

How are you by this time? From what your mother told me and the snapshot of you and your pal, you must be getting along pretty well. We are surely glad to hear that. And I suppose they are keeping you pretty busy. Where would you rather, in the Air Corps or at home? (Please excuse the typing mistakes.) By typing letters to you boys, I can make a little headway. This is number five tonight. If I wrote all of them in longhand, I soon would have to carry my arm in a sling.

The next month he again writes Gerald Franta reflecting the power of prayers:

You mentioned that I should keep the cold winds over here in Kansas. But I surely had my hands full lately. I could not control it all. The wind was coming from Texas a sort of "hot wind." I guess you fellows began to whoop it up or something, and the hot wind just naturally began to spread around. When you get to feeling blue or things don't go so well, just think of your friends on the "home front" who are praying for you. Every week a holy Mass is said for you and your folks. May God bring you back again healthy and safe and victorious. Write again!

From a soldier of Christ, Father Emil Kapaun

KAPAUN BECOMES AN AUXILIARY CHAPLAIN

Father Kapaun had his first taste of military service when he was accepted as an auxiliary chaplain at the newly built Herington Army Air Field (274th AAF) just under thirty miles north of Pilsen. He performed this service from January 5, 1943, until July 12, 1944. With the rapid expansion of the army air corps before becoming the air force in 1947, bases sprang up all over the country, and Wichita became a major production factory for our bombers. The Twenty-First Bombardment Wing out of Topeka Army Airfield used Herington as the Sixth Heavy Bombardment Processing Headquarters—a satellite field to train heavy bombardment crews and stage bombers for shipment overseas. What a sight to behold, seeing B-24 Liberators and B-17 Flying Fortresses take off and land all day.

DEPARTMENT OF DEFENSE (DOD)

Father Kapaun celebrates Mass as an auxiliary chaplain at Herington Army Air Field, Kansas, 1943. Most of the men in the pews are wearing the classic fleece-collared bomber jacket.

KAPAUN WRITES PRIVATE GERALD FRANTA

We have fellows scattered all over. The last boys drafted from Pilsen are my brother Eugene Kapaun and Leonard Lentz. Eugene is in a tank division, presently in the desert of California. He writes that it is a tough place. If the army wants more men, I guess some more Pilseners will have to go. They called recently for 4,000 chaplains. Looks like we young priests will get a chance for some army action. During the winter I did you a favor by keeping the cold up here, so now you do me a favor and keep that strong wind in Texas.

Every Sunday about midafternoon, Father Kapaun and Albert Stika, postmaster, would start out from Pilsen with Albert driving and Father reading his Breviary. Along the way they picked up servicemen as they approached the base. The first Mass Father offered at Herington was on April 11, 1943, in a recreation room reeking of tobacco smoke and decorated with cigarette and cigar butts, burnt matches and ashes. A more devotional setting was provided later. After the Mass at 5:00 pm, they drove home, eating the lunch provided by the good Sisters at Pilsen on the way. Father also said Mass at the base on Monday and Tuesday. On every trip, he also visited the jail and the hospital.

"I LOVE THAT WORK"

Kapaun writes Bishop Winkelmann in 1943:

> I am sending you a copy of the report which I already have sent to the Military Ordinariate. So far I am saying Holy Mass at the Base every Sunday. I enjoy the work with the men very much. I visit them in the hospital. They certainly are glad to see a Catholic priest. I brought some Catholic magazines to read, among them our Advance Register, and am making arrangements to bring them the Sunday Visitor for their reading room. In short, dear Bishop, I love that work.[3]

THE GOOD SHEPHERD

After three years of humble and obedient assistance to Father Sklenar, Father Kapaun was appointed as administrator of the St. John parish, effective when Monsignor resigned on November 2, 1943. Father Kapaun took his added responsibility seriously. That he had won the hearts of the people in his home parish is attested by a petition sent to Bishop Winkelmann, November 7, 1943:

> We the undersigned committee of the St. John Nepomucene Church in Pilsen humbly petition your Excellency for this favor: We would greatly appreciate and consider it a favor if your Excellency would leave Rev. E.J. Kapaun,

our present administrator, as a permanent pastor of our
parish unless your Excellency has already made a different
assignment. There are peculiar circumstances and needs
of our community which require proper handling of our
people. We consider this appointment would rebound to
our parish's good and to the service of the whole diocese.
In the name and wish of our parish membership we have
undertaken this step. We assure your Excellency of our filial
respect and obedience to whatever your decision may be.
Signed Adolph Holub—Joseph Steiner—Alphonse E. Bosh
George Vinduska—Church Committee

In February 1944, this rather odd internal letter from Herrington Army Air Field administrators ended up being forwarded to Bishop Winkelmann for his consideration to remove
Father Kapaun from his chaplain duty at Herrington in order
to "keep Holy the Sabbath":

The matter with which this letter is concerned, may or
may not be connected with your office, but, inasmuch as
it may, in one aspect, be considered as a suggestion for the
good of the men of this field, I am taking the liberty of dis-
cussing it with you. Because of a recent letter that you sent
me concerning a suggestion for more sidewalks around the
Base Theater, that appeared in our column, the "Medics
News," I believe that you are an officer that has a definite
interest in the men of Herington Army Air Field.

Many say that the afternoon Mass on Sunday more or
less spoils the entire feeling of "Keeping Holy the Sabbath."
Not Father Kapaun's fault as he has to drive 40 miles but
they want their own Catholic chaplain to hold Mass in the
mornings. Father Kapaun is a wonderful priest and we all
have a deep feeling of indebtedness to him for all the ef-

forts that he puts forth in our behalf. Despite all this, the fact remains, that if we had our own Chaplain, not only would these complaints be overcome, but also, it would present new interests for the Catholic personnel of this field and served to increase our attendance.

What a pickle Father Kapaun found himself in. Having been told to remain at his home parish to assist Father Sklenar, he was denied the opportunity to enlist in the army as a chaplain. While serving in his small parish, the newspapers and the radio programs were brimming with news of the war. Father Kapaun constantly mentioned his desire to serve in the military. Kapaun was then allowed to volunteer as an auxiliary chaplain at Herington Air Base, a thirty-mile drive north, but only after morning Mass was given in Pilsen first. In November 1943, Monsignor Sklenar resigned, and Father Kapaun was appointed as administrator to St. John's church in Pilsen. A few days later, the St. John's church committee petitioned Bishop Winkelmann to make Father Kapaun their "permanent pastor." Then, three months later, a letter was written to the Special Services Office at Herington with the most unusual wording one can imagine about Sunday services in a relatively small chapel—a complaint that because Father Kapaun must drive forty miles ("not Father Kapaun's fault") then Mass was held in the afternoon, rather than the morning, and that "more or less spoils the entire feeling of 'Keeping Holy the Sabbath.'"

The request was then made that Herington Air Base should have their own chaplain to "increase attendance" in a direct attempt to boost morale. They wanted more attendance and more chaplain accessibility to keep their trainees' minds focused on the dangerous job at hand. They wanted the men to be right with God. And that meant Mass is given in the morning of the Sabbath, not the afternoon. This tug-of-war disturbed Kapaun's conscience more and more as he felt the call to serve God and country in its hour of need over the demands of his local parish, who he felt certain would be just fine with a new priest.

The next few letter exchanges between Kapaun and the Bishop of Wichita are utterly fascinating looks into the mind of a patriotic priest who knew what God intended for him—serving the much larger parish of the US Army. The date of Father Kapaun's letter to his bishop is June 8, 1944, just two days after the D-Day landing at Normandy and the largest amphibious invasion in military history that showed Germany the United States and the Allies were "all in." But exactly how he expressed who should replace him in Pilsen is sheer intellectual genius that can only be described from his own words:

A STRANGE BOHEMIAN PRIEST

Most Reverend and dear Bishop, I am writing to you for the sake of clearing my conscience. When I received my first appointment as assistant in my home parish, I realized the situation would be very delicate. I understood you to remark that you were making me pastor of Pilsen, my home parish. Since then, my conscience has been bothering me because, in regard to the salvation of souls, several things should be considered.

As assistant, I was determined to do my work solely for Christ. I show no favoritism to anyone. In fact, I treated my relatives and friends coldly (with no special affection). Some people seemed to be scandalized at that, but I am sure all of them realized I was trying to be a good priest to all. The people told me that they do not want me to go, but I assured them that the Bishop knows what is best and that the will of God is expressed through his decision. The people know that. And if they get a good, holy priest, they will be as attached to him in a short time as they have become attached to me. This part does not worry me, but the following fact does. I was raised in this parish. There are people here, relatives and friends, who are superior to me (in age, in school, etc.). Some find it difficult to look up to me as their spiritual superior. They do not say anything, but from the way they act and the way they perform their spiritual obligations, I know they find me a great moral obstacle. If they had a "strange" Bohemian priest, that obstacle would no longer exist. The people here at Pilsen must have a priest who can hear confessions in Bohemian. He must also give sermons occasionally in this language of the majority, although most understand English.

Those who want to keep me here are the good, faithful members. If they received another good priest who works with them in their language, they will be as faithful and zealous under him as they were under good Monsignor Sklenar and me; and the other people, those who find me to be a moral obstacle, will be assured that with a "strange" priest they will not have that trouble. I am sure you realize what I mean.

It is in consideration of these people who will not complain or say anything but who really need a "strange" Bohemian priest that I am writing this letter. My conscience tells me to do it because their souls are at stake. Some of those people feel that I still remember and hold against them things they did in former years. I could tell them a hundred times that all is forgotten—yet they will not be assured but will hold back and be afraid. That is the human element, and it creates a serious moral obstacle. To remove it I try to be humble and kind as possible. Your Excellency, I am sure you understand that I am most anxious someone be given them who can be, as St. Paul describe it, "All things to all men." When I was ordained, I was determined to "spend myself" for God. I was determined to do that cheerfully, no matter in what circumstances I would be placed or how hard a life I would be asked to lead. This is why I volunteered for the Army and that is why today I would a thousand times rather be working, deprived of all ordinary comforts, being a true "Father" to all my people, than be living in a nice, comfortable place but with my conscience telling me that I am an obstacle to many. I had wished to mention this to you a long time ago. But I trust this is not too late and that now my conscience will be at peace in this regard.

Wishing you God's blessing and trusting in your kind benevolence toward Pilsen Parish, I remain

Your Excellency's humble Servant, Rev. Emil Kapaun

"Bishop Winkelmann was fond of referring to Kapaun as an "anima candida," a candid soul. The bishop understood that here was a young priest who was so earnest in his duties that he felt he could do better work somewhere else. Bishop Winkel-mann showed the letter to his chancellor and vice-chancellor. The vice-chancellor was home that summer from his studies of Canon Law at the Catholic University in Washington, DC, and knew nothing about the Pilsen parish. However, Monsignor Morrell, the chancellor, was well-acquainted with it and knew that Pilsen was a difficult parish. Nevertheless, it was his recommendation that the bishop should consider the request of Father Kapaun."[4]

THE MILITARY ORDINARIATE

Prior to the bombing of Pearl Harbor, there was never an issue of enough priests, rabbis, and ministers wanting to become chaplains. But the call to serve against the evils of fascism drew many, young and old, straight into our armed fighting forces, leaving the Chaplain Corps numbers low and needing to be increased proportionately. Thus was founded a special "Military Ordinariate" that supervised the training and work of the Catholic chaplains. The need was so urgent that the Cardinal Archbishop of New York, Francis Spellman, assumed the position of the chief military chaplain and pressured all the Catholic bishops in the country to be very generous in permitting young priests to volunteer for the armed forces. The requirements for entry into a chaplaincy? Applying to your denomination's endorsing board with a certification of ordination and evidence of two years of successful work in their active ministry, followed by completing the same six weeks of basic training required by all enlisted service members.

"Filling every vacancy became increasing difficult as the war spread across the globe. Further complicating an equitable distribution of chaplains was the failure of some denominations to contribute enough candidates to the services. Among the religious bodies represented in the two corps (thirty-seven in the navy, forty in the army), the worst offender in this respect was the Roman Catholic church, as it never filled its informal 'quota.' With the church itself, the Archdiocese of Philadelphia and the Society of Jesus (the Jesuits) contributed the smallest percentages, sending a smaller proportion of their available priests than the other archdioceses, dioceses, and religious orders. Judaism, by contrast, sent the military chaplaincies half of all the rabbis in the United States.

Throughout the war, most chaplains ministered nearly as often to men of other religions as to those of their own because the armed services, laboring under a chronic shortage of chaplains, could assign only one chaplain to every 1,200 servicemen. With less than a third of the soldiers, sailors, and airmen calling themselves 'Catholics,' a priest-chaplain soon found himself acting as a kind of 'universal minister' who took care of everyone's religious and personal needs as best he could."[5]

★ ★ ★

Finally, by June 15, 1944, the bishop's reply to Father Kapaun
is decidedly different:

Dear Reverend Father:
Aware of your ardent desire to become an Army Chaplain,
and realizing that the Military Ordinariate is in dire need
of additional chaplains, I am today recommending you to
the Military Ordinariate and have penned a letter of recommendation to His Excellency, the Most Reverend John F.
O'Hara, C.S.C. My reason for not granting this request earlier was due to the fact that I felt that your health would not
permit you to stand the strenuous ordeal of camp and army
life. But when I saw you last week during the retreat and noticed your fine physical condition, I immediately concluded
that you were fit in every way to enter the armed service.

I am deeply grateful to you for offering your services for
this most important service, and I am sure that the good
people of St. John Nepomucene, Pilsen, will rejoice that
their administrator is now rendering this service for God
and country. In a few days Bishop O'Hara will undoubt-
edly favor you with some instructions and then the Army's
official additional instructions will be forthcoming. Your
successor at Pilsen will be announced at some future time.
With all good wishes, and assuring you of my prayers,
I remain Yours very sincerely in the Lord, Bishop of Wichita

Though the number of priests available to do the work in the
Wichita Diocese was insufficient, apparently Bishop Winkelmann
had a great love for men in uniform. So on July 12, 1944, the bishop
relieved Father Kapaun from his jobs of pastor in Pilsen and auxiliary chaplain in Herington. He was free to go to chaplains training school and become a full-time military chaplain. On August
23, Father Kapaun finally said goodbye to his parents. They took

FATHER KAPAUN GUILD

Father Kapaun poses with his mother, Bessie.

a lot of pride in their son not only being a chaplain, but an officer in the US Army. Father Kapaun left his car at home and traveled by train to Chicago, where he had friends and relatives. Upon arriving there, he wrote a postcard to his parents which stated, "This morning I offered Mass in the Bohemian Church of Blessed Agnes. It seems everyone is Bohemian in this part of Chicago. I will write more later. Emil." From Chicago he continued by train and finally reported at the Chaplain's School at Fort Devens, Massachusetts.

FOR GOD AND COUNTRY

Father Kapaun officially began his military career in August 1944 in a class of 145 prospective chaplains. At the training school at Fort Devens, clergymen of many faiths prepared for duty in all theaters of wartime operations. Becoming a chaplain in the service of an army is by no means a cowardly avoidance of combat. It is steeped in tradition and requires spiritual leadership during times of war. "Across the centuries, religious services on the eve of battle and prayers for divine help in crises have been trusted as powerful aids to victory. For as long as armies have existed, military chaplains have served alongside soldiers, providing for their spiritual needs, working to improve morale, and aiding the wounded. The priests of Ammon-Ra accompanied the armies of Pharaoh into battle thirty-five centuries ago. The Hebrew prevailed while Moses held up his hands in blessing. As Christianity became the predominant religion of the Roman Empire, Christian chaplains administered to Roman soldiers."[6]

The US Army Chaplain Corps is one of the oldest branches of the army, dating back to July 1775, when the Continental Congress and General George Washington authorized one chaplain for each regiment of the Continental Army, with pay equaling that of a captain. Since then, dozens of chaplains have made the ultimate sacrifice, living up to the Chaplain Corps motto, "*Pro Deo Et Patria*"—"For God and Country."

"When a clergyman enters the military chaplaincy, he or she takes their orders from their commanding officer, just like everyone else in the armed forces. Instead of entering boot camp, however, he reports to the Chaplain School where he learns the essentials of his new trade. The highly programmed (and by general consensus, almost fatally boring) course of studies taught all the fledgling chaplains the same subjects: laws governing the services, customs, drill, the use of equipment, physical fitness, and history of the corps. Above all, they learned how to work in close cooperation with chaplains and servicemen of other denominations."[7]

CHAPLAIN SCHOOL, FORT DEVENS, MASSACHUSETTS

On September 10, 1944, Father Kapaun wrote Gerald Franta:

Here at Chaplain's School I am like a bug in a rug. Strapped down to a rigorous routine of classes and besides that we drill like master troopers. They want to toughen us up in a hurry, and I really enjoy it. Soon we will be crawling through the infiltration course, under machine gun fire, etc. I guess you know what that is. We have a few fat fellows here and I don't see how they will squeeze under the bullets. They are fairly worried. Haha. We have about 150 Chaplains here. 40 of them are Catholics. All of us say Mass together in a building which has 40 altars. That is better than a Cathedral.

"During the week of training at Fort Devens and later during his active duty at Camp Wheeler, Georgia, and in India, Father Kapaun was faithful in sending a copy of any report he made to the Military Ordinariate to his own bishop in Wichita. A carefully drawn-up letter always accompanied these reports. In their style, these letters show a marked difference from the letters he sent to his parents, relatives, and friends. He would use a more formal way of writing to express the deep respect that he had of his ecclesiastical superiors. The main theme of these letters was the observation that there were not enough Catholic chaplains to do the great deal of work, but that it was very satisfying work. His only regret was that his many duties kept him from accomplishing more for his own spiritual life."[8]

"The chaplain holds a unique position in the American war machine. That is to say, they had one foot inside the military and one outside. As commissioned officers of the army and navy, they occupied official positions in the military, but as ordained clergymen, they were, in a sense, outside the command structure. Even though they obeyed orders from superior officers and followed the laws governing the armed services, they still maintained an allegiance to their own religious bodies, to which almost all of them would return after the war ended.

"This unique position meant that the chaplains had an opportunity to observe both the working of the military command

structure and the lives of the enlisted men who had submitted to it. Often bonded by close ties to their fellow officers and
the enlisted personnel, they nevertheless stood apart from both.
They had a special vantage point from which they could see the
successes and achievements of the military people they served,
their sufferings and ordeals, and their religious and psychological states of mind. From the chaplains' reports, letters, and oral
recollections, one can piece together a description of the life of
the foot soldier that is available nowhere else. These men of God
become men of war had an independent viewpoint, and their
harrowing and sometimes deeply moving descriptions of what
they saw seem worthy of serious examination."[9]

"Shortly after his arrival at the Chaplain's School, Bishop
Winkelmann sent him a 'Mass kit' that had been provided by
the Wichita Chaplains Aid Society, a group of Catholic ladies
who collected money, books, and magazines to help Catholic
priests working in the armed forces. The Mass kit was an in-
genious arrangement in a sturdy black suitcase of all the things
needed by a chaplain to set up a temporary altar. It contained
an altar stone, the cards for the permanent Mass prayers, a missal, the linen for the altar, the cruets for wine and water, a simple chalice, an alb (a full-length vestment with sleeves), and a
chasuble (the outermost liturgical vestment) that had a twofold
use. One side was black for a requiem Mass, and the other side
white for other Masses."[10] Father Kapaun wrote back to Bishop
Winkelmann:

Most Reverend and dear Bishop, I wish to express my sin-
cerest thanks for the Mass Kit forwarded to me through the
Chaplain Aid Association as a donation from you and the
"Faithful of the Diocese of Wichita." There are nearly 40
Catholic priests in a class of 145. Holy Mass is my great-
est consolation. We priests offer Mass together in a special

building. We have Rosary in common in the morning. We
must find time to say our office privately. I am very happy.
Classes are interesting and practical. And might I add that
the drills and marches give a person a tremendous appe-
tite. In appreciation to Chaplains' Aid, I am sending them a
check of $150.00 Without help, the Association would not
be able to do its wonderful work. Again I thank you for
the kindness, and I hope to pay you a visit after graduation.

Bishop Winkelmann replied:

I am sure that the Chaplains' Aid was surprised when you,
in turn, sent them a munificent donation of $150 to pro-
mote their work. This gesture on your part reveals your
noble character and disposition. I am sure that God will
abundantly bless you and that your work will be most successful, no matter where your assignment.

"Father Kapaun apparently had an easy task of getting acquainted with his fellow priests and ministers. After introduc-
ing himself, he tried to give the impression, "I am a nobody,
pay no attention to me. I will gladly stand in the background."
A few days were usually sufficient to convince everybody that
this young priest from Kansas was indeed somebody. His unassuming ways were the result of a personality fueled by charity
and humility. Whenever anything had to be done, or a problem came up, he could forget his natural modesty and solve it."[11]
A week later he reported to Bishop Winkelmann that early in
the morning the forty priests would say Holy Mass and would say
the rosary together, but the Breviary was said in private. There
were classes to attend, rigorous exercise and marches, regular
meals and occasional recreation. He noted that the army food
was quite good and that, ironically, it was prepared by German
prisoners of war. He wrote that the water "tastes awful, but I

solved that problem. I light a cigar and take a smoke so I cannot taste anything. In the army we have to figure out all kinds of things."

Both the army and the navy viewed religious conflict as highly destructive and inculcated the virtues of collaboration and teamwork. The chiefs of the two corps would quickly call a fractious chaplain to account, telling him to get along or get out. Following a slogan of "cooperation without compromise," the two schools tried to make collaboration a practical matter by treating Catholics, Protestants, and Jews as one group. Although each denomination received time during the day for its own religious services, everyone ate, slept, drilled, and shared recreation time together, and members of differing denominations were mixed up as much as possible. Many Catholic priests found that for the first time in their lives, they had the experience of talking to Protestant and Jewish counterparts—and vice versa.

In a later period, this kind of meshing would come to be known as "ecumenism," one of the most revolutionary developments in recent American religious history. The wartime chaplaincy gave the idea an enormous impetus by making it a principle for every chaplain to follow wherever he went, whatever work he undertook. During the war, it was a matter of the simplest possible expediency, a result of necessity rather than of a progressive theology within the churches themselves. In the postwar decades, theologians from Catholic, Protestant, and Jewish ranks would develop the idea.

"On October 4, 1944, Kapaun finished his work at the training school and was assigned to Camp Wheeler, Georgia. The cowboy priest from Kansas, now commissioned a lieutenant in the US Army, came to Georgia a soldier priest. His chief duties were to say Holy Mass for the soldiers, administer the sacraments, and counsel those who came to him. He was still young enough

US ARMY

Army portrait of newly commissioned officer Emil Kapaun, second lieutenant.

to understand and sympathize with the problems of the soldiers, many of whom were away from home for the first time. His good health made it possible to meet all of his obligations in a cheerful, efficient way. Every day brought new challenges, and he, the great realist, met them as they came. In matters of faith and morals, he steadfastly defended the principles of God and the teachings of Jesus. There was no compromise or dilution of divine doctrine. Times of war can bring a relaxed attitude toward morals, but Father Kapaun was too much a priest to give in to temptations. Kindness and understanding, yes; watering down of principles, no."[12]

To Bishop Winkelmann again, Chaplain Kapaun wrote, "I

have a lot of things to learn about army life. But with the strain of it all comes the consolation of doing some little good for men who are willing and worthy."

Before Kapaun received orders of his next transfer, he received notice of the passing of Mrs. Henry Jirak of Pilsen. With typical thoughtfulness, he wrote a letter of condolence that poetically touches upon the Communion of Saints:

Dear Mr. Jirak and Children:
With these few lines I wish to express to you my sympathy and sorrow on reading that death has struck in your family. I wish to mention that I have remembered her in Holy Mass today and will continue to pray that God will grant her that happy home in heaven which is in store for those as faithful as she was. It is a wonderful thought to know that in the "Communion of Saints" we are in touch with the Saints in heaven and the souls in Purgatory, and to know that our loved ones are in the Communion of Saints.
May God's blessing be upon you.

Chaplain Kapaun may have had a lot to learn about army life, but his devotion to God and absolute conviction of Catholic ideals was that of a patient, strong, and learned man of God. This was made clear in a sermon of his published in the "Chaplain's Corner" of *SPOKE*, the Camp Wheeler newspaper, on January 25, 1945, entitled "The Chaplain and Personal Opinion":

A chaplain in the US Army does many things in his line of duty. He gives his time, his strength, his patience, to encourage soldiers to fulfill their duties to Almighty God. He provides the means and the opportunity for men to worship God. In this, he stands for what is most sacred and most necessary. However, in this duty, the chaplain often finds hindrances and enemies which ruin his work. One of these enemies is personal opinion.

How much harm personal opinion has done is difficult to judge. A soldier, after hearing a zealous talk concerning the holiness of God's name, walks back to his barracks and says: "That was a good sermon, but I do not agree with what was said. I have my own opinion. I feel free to use it the way I want to." As far as that soldier is concerned, the chaplain and his sacred work are worth nothing.

At another time, the chaplain gives a stirring instruction on the Sixth Commandment which is: "Thou shalt not commit adultery." He tells in pointed language that any sign of impurity and indecency is a terrible offense in the sight of God. A soldier remarks: "I don't think it is that way at all. Why, my idea about it is this: I live only once. So why not get every pleasure out of life?" That soldier has his own personal opinion, and he dares to commit sins of impurity. To him the chaplain and the chaplain's work are worth nothing.

If personal opinion is to guide our lives, then we might as well throw away all laws, even the laws of God, and proceed to live our lives by personal opinion. There is, however, one serious drawback to this procedure: We have a Master who is checking up on us. And this Master is most strict and exact. He is the one whom the chaplain is trying to represent to the soldiers and officers. That Master is God.

3

ABOVE THE CLOUDS

In February 1945, the army transferred Kapaun again. His travels began after a ten-day stopover in Miami, where he received cholera and other inoculations. On March 4, he and four other clergymen took off in a military transport, not knowing at first where they were headed. Only after the aircraft was over the Atlantic did they learn that they were traveling to the China-India-Burma (CBI) Theater of wartime operations. This being Kapaun's first travel overseas, the newly commissioned officer was fascinated by what he could see below, which included Bethlehem. He wrote to Bishop Winkelmann, "Imagine the thrill to be up in the clouds where the angels of the Nativity had sung. We could see a part of Jericho and the Jordan emptying into the Dead Sea. The grazing land and white rocks looked beautiful from the high skies."

One of the other passengers was Chaplain William S. Bowdern, who would later become rector at the future Chaplain Kapaun Memorial High School in Wichita, Kansas. Chaplains Bowdern and Kapaun served together for about two months after they reached their destination and never met again due to the nature of the chaplain's work spread over thousands of miles of travel. Bowdern praised Kapaun's work in caring for the religious needs of the American soldiers and in 1962 wrote this President's Message to the student body of Chaplain Kapaun Memorial High School:

> It was my privilege to serve with Father Kapaun as a fellow chaplain in World War II. Little did I ever think then that I would be the president of a school dedicated to him and the things for which he died. His way of life and the things he fought so hard for should inspire all you men of Kapaun. The ideals that he had always lived by became evident to the world only under the pressures of the North Korean prison compound. However, even before his ordeal, he had lived each day inspired by the same kind of high ideals. At Kapaun High School we hope that these same high ideals will become part of your way of life. Only God knows whether you will be called upon to display the same type of heroism as Father Kapaun.

THE CBI THEATER

Officially established in June 1942, the CBI Theater is often referred to as the Forgotten Theater of World War II. Of the 12,300,000 Americans under arms at the height of mobilization, only about 250,000 (2 percent) were assigned there, making "CBI Veterans Are Unique" more than just a slogan. Initially important to the Allied war effort because of plans to invade Japan from China, the goal became keeping China supplied and in the war. Because of the rugged terrain, the massive airlift operations were called flying "the hump" and by war's end had brought to the region over thirteen thousand aircraft—many of them sold as surplus to become American airliners and establishing the United States as the world's airline leader. Also of

Father Kapaun (left) poses with chaplain staff Roman Blaz, Father Francis Quinn, CSSR, and Father Bowdern in New Delhi, India, March 1945. Decades later, Father Bowdern's exorcism of Roland Doe in 1949 would become the basis for William Peter Blatty's bestselling book The Exorcist.

vital importance to our fighting forces was the ability to travel over rough terrain and roads with a durable four-wheel-drive vehicle. Thus the jeep was introduced in 1941, and by 1945, over 650,000 were manufactured. Jeeps played an essential role in US Army Chaplain Corps history by making chaplains mobile and accessible to soldiers in the field. Without a jeep, the ability to provide ministry for soldiers would have been greatly challenged. During World War II, a jeep and trailer were authorized for each chaplain. The hood of the jeep was commonly used as an altar. The chaplain kit, a portable organ, bibles, prayer books, and hymnals were stored inside the trailer when traveling. Most pictures taken of Father Kapaun in theaters of war had either a jeep or his pipe shown—making both items essential tools in this wartime chaplain's Mass kit.

★ ★ ★

The majority of Americans in the CBI Theater worked to bring lend-lease supplies to China. The Flying Tigers fought the Japanese in the air over China and Burma, and the army air forces flew supplies over the hump from India to China. Merrill's Marauders and the Mars Task Force fought through the jungles of Burma so the army engineers could build the Ledo Road to open a land supply route. This work was mostly completed by the time Chaplain Kapaun arrived, but the devastation in the wake of the Japanese occupation left plenty of work to do: rebuild the isolated communities and missions, and convince countless civilians and refugees that Japanese imperialism was defeated. Father Kapaun's trip landed him in New Delhi, India, for two weeks, where he visited the large palace of Shadahan and the world-famous Taj Mahal in Agra. He then went on to Bhamo and Lashio in Burma for permanent assignments. The Kansas native found out quickly how hot the weather was in Burma and even hotter in the jungles. He found the Burma natives to be very kind, and many were Christians.

Father Kapaun came in contact with the priests and sisters who worked as missionaries in India. In grade school he had read about the Columban Fathers. Now he met them in their field of activity. Their way of living and their work for the poorest of the poor made a deep impression upon the American soldiers. Some of them were so impressed that they decided to study for the priesthood upon their return to the United States. And thus, besides his work as a military chaplain, Father Kapaun found himself giving instruction in Latin to a young military chaplain, a seminary professor, and a lieutenant in the 198th Ordnance Battalion.

On April 12, 1945, the news of President Franklin D. Roosevelt's death shocked the globe. Allied troops conducted memorial services throughout the world, including a ceremony in Burma on April 15. Father Kapaun delivered the invocation before a crowd of nine thousand people, including Chinese and US troops. No one imagined on that solemn occasion that within a few years, the armies of the two countries would be fighting one another. Father Kapaun's handwritten memorial prayer reads thusly:

Almighty and Eternal God, Creator and heavenly Ruler of all peoples and nations, to you we bow our heads in humble sorrow on this occasion, the memorial solemnity in honor of President Franklin Delano Roosevelt. We, the citizens of the United States of America, together with our Allied Friends here present, render our thanks to you, O God, our heavenly Father, that you did bless us with such a capable and understanding ruler, and international friend, as President Franklin Delano Roosevelt. To him we pay every honor and respect as a grateful people united and dedicated to the principles of democracy, that all people are created equal, with inalienable rights to life, liberty and pursuit of happiness.

It is our humble prayer to you, O God, in this time of world crisis, that you continue to bless our democratic nation with power and valor, with unselfish leaders and people. We pray that the hope of President Roosevelt, a true peace among all nations, be realized and preserved. In this hope may all nations live and have a continuous memory to the one whom we mourn today, President Franklin Delano Roosevelt.

Classic photo of Father Kapaun riding a bike in New Delhi, India, 1946. Here he is displaying two of the iconic activities he was most known for in one picture: smoking a pipe and riding a bicycle.

US ARMY

Classic pose of Chaplain Kapaun holding his pipe, with Columban missionaries and Catholic sisters in Burma, 1945 or 1946.

"JUST LIKE OUR OWN FATHER"

Father Kapaun found his work extremely gratifying. A man of many hats, he was interchangeably an army officer, a military chaplain, a Catholic priest, a teacher, and now a Catholic missionary—blessed not only to see the efforts many natives made to go to Holy Mass and the Sacraments but also to give his men the opportunity to see how the Catholic missionaries live. He remarked that the heroism of the missionaries during the Japanese occupation "puts us to shame." One experience he had explains why:

Father Kapaun met two Catholic Sisters from Italy who the Americans found still living in a cave in the hills with several native people, including children. It was Good Friday. They had no news of the war and had to be reassured that the Japanese Army had been driven out, because just fifteen months prior, they were forced into hiding after Japanese soldiers sacked their mission and took their priest away. When the Sisters fled, they took everything from the church that they could including vestments, the chalice, and the like, and they hid them in a jungle cave nearby with an entrance not much bigger than a rabbit hole. Now safe, they lowered a native child by rope into the cave to retrieve the items, piece by piece, as no adult would fit. The Americans then brought them all out of hiding to live in a nearby dwelling while their mission was being restored, and an American Chaplain named Father Flavin said Holy Mass for the Sisters and the natives on Easter Sunday.

Soon after this experience, on May 8, 1945, the United States declared victory over Europe, which was monumental news to all our forces in the Pacific Theater. It must have signaled to the Japanese that the US fighting forces were not going away and in fact were growing stronger in their resolve to stop Japanese occupation and imperialism. Father Kapaun makes no mention of the end of fighting in Europe but carries out his mission relentlessly, traveling as much as 2,500 miles a month by air and jeep to have Mass for the troops in chapels, mess halls, recreation rooms and theaters and taking confessions, giving communions and performing baptisms. And though he had written Bishop Winkelmann before about the rescue of the Italian Sisters and their mission, he mentions it again in greater detail and really expresses a profound love of his work and heartfelt desire that the Catholic Diocese of Wichita and all Catholics see the impact of true missionary work around the world. On June 1, 1945, he writes:

Our work with the soldiers is sometimes strenuous, sometimes dangerous, but nearly always with the realization that it is worth the effort. My outfits are scattered over long distances of jungles and mountains. I travel mostly by aeroplane, making a round trip of 500 miles every week to reach my units during May. Once my pilot and I escaped a very serious accident by about 30 seconds. I am sure we both would have been killed. After that, my Guardian Angel really received a hearty thanks, I tell you; and our work continues as ever, thanks be to God.

Chaplain Kapaun (right) with Chaplain Stuart at Pangsau Pass along Ledo Road (later renamed Stilwell Road), 1945 or 1946. It was a bumpy and dangerous road through the mountains from Ledo, India, into Burma, built by the Allies to transport troops and supplies in the fight against the Japanese Imperial Army.

Chaplain Kapaun (right) with his ever-present pipe in mouth, poses with a sergeant and another Catholic chaplain, 1945 or 1946, while assigned to the CBI Theater during World War II.

I believe in my last letter I mentioned something about the Missionary Father and Sisters out here. For the Sisters, our Catholic soldiers built a church and school. Imagine the gratitude of those good Sisters who had been up in the mountains hiding in a cave for nearly three years. They did not have a priest or Holy Mass for 15 long months. Now the priests are returning again to their Missions. They had been interned by the Japanese and were treated fairly well. However, many of them have scars to give away their past experience, and one of them was killed while saying Mass. We soldiers got together and gave the good Sisters a gift of some $1,100.00, and again we pitched in and gave the Missionary Fathers a gift of some $1,700.00. No doubt our Catholic soldiers took those Missionaries by such a surprise that they hardly knew what to say. We took the Sisters to our Mass in the Army Chapel. When they saw it jammed with Catholic soldiers, and the Communion railing filled with about 100 Communicants, the Sisters were so impressed that they began to cry. The native Catholics, too, can see that the Catholic Church is very much alive in other countries.

One day after I had said Mass in the village, the children who had attended Mass came to Sister and said to her: "Why, the American Father says Mass just like our own Father." Yes, one cannot help but be impressed that the Catholic Church is one and the same the whole world over; even little children are able to notice that.

I wish that the good people in the Wichita Diocese could see face to face the work that the generous Missionary Fathers and Sisters are doing out here. Surely our Catholic soldiers who see this and then return to the US will appreciate so much more the struggling Missions and their faithful priests and Sisters. I think we can appreciate a little more the great work of the Society of the Propa-

gation of Faith in the Diocese of Wichita. When one sees
the devout and well-behaved children attending Mass out
here, with their parents kneeling in devout prayer, many
of whom are very poor and have only the bare necessities
of life, it makes a person think back to things at home and
remember too that at home there are many such holy parents
and children. Surely one is as precious in the sight of
God as the other, whether in Missionary lands or in well-
established Dioceses. My letter has reached already an unusual length. May God shower His blessings upon our good
Catholic people.

I remain, Your Excellency's humble servant, EMIL J. KAPAUN,
Chaplain (1st lt)

A chaplain born in Slovakia but raised in Ohio, Father John
Cyril Jablonovsky served in the CBI Theater from 1943 to 1946
and later as a chaplain from 1950 to 1953 mostly in Germany.
He met Father Kapaun only once but was so struck by his presence, he wrote about the visit years later:

> I was serving as XO in New Delhi, India, in the Chaplains
> HQs office. Job to check up on chaplain's needs. I found
> him to be not only a personable and cheerful man, but
> a truly humble Christian gentleman. I congratulated Fr.
> Emil on the splendid reputation he established as a priest.
> He brushed off the compliments with a remark, "Yes, they
> have been good to me."
>
> I half expected to hear some complaints about things in
> general and criticisms about the behavior of some of the of-
> ficers in particular. But nothing of the sort came from his
> mouth. I was reminded of St. James' observation that if a
> man offends not in tongue, he was a perfect man. Strange
> that this Scripture text came to me on that visit and has
> stayed with me. I was grateful for the inspiration, then, and

I cherish the memory now. Nothing else comes to mind about that one visit—except the euphoria I felt at this truly priestly man who obviously was happy in his vocation and pouring out his concern and compassion on his men.

While still serving in Burma, Father Kapaun and the rest of the world learned that on August 15, 1945, the Japanese surrendered, marking the end of World War II. Celebrations of answered prayers erupted everywhere. Then on Sunday, September 2, it seemed as if the Battleship Missouri, anchored in Tokyo Bay, momentarily became the pulpit in a world cathedral as General Douglas MacArthur delivered a homily like no other—a great liturgy of peace:

> We have had our last chance. If we do not now devise some greater and more equitable system Armageddon will be at our door. The problem basically is theological and involves a spiritual recrudescence and improvement of human character that will synchronize with our almost matchless advance in science, art, literature and all material and cultural developments of the past two thousand years. It must be of the spirit if we are to save the flesh...

MacArthur then spoke perhaps the most memorable lines of his career:

> We are gathered here, representatives of the major warring powers, to conclude a solemn agreement whereby peace may be restored. The issues, involving divergent ideals and ideologies, have been determined on the battlefields of the world and hence are not for our discussion or debate. Nor is it for us here to meet, representing as we do a majority of the people of the earth, in a spirit of distrust, malice or hatred. But rather it is for us, both victors and vanquished,

to rise to that higher dignity which alone befits the sacred purposes we are about to service, committing all our people unreservedly to faithful compliance with the understanding they are here formally to assume.

It is my earnest hope, and indeed the hope of all mankind, that from this solemn occasion a better world shall emerge out of the blood and carnage of the past—a world dedicated to the dignity of man and the fulfillment of his most cherished wish for freedom, tolerance and justice.

The significance of the Allied victory over Japan can never be understated. For every American who died fighting Japan, about nine Japanese perished. An estimated seventeen million people died at the hands of the Japanese, many of them noncombatants. But for General MacArthur to live up to his monumental words, there was no other choice but to give him the unprecedented title of Supreme Commander for the Allied Powers in the Pacific, leader of the United Nations Command and the de facto ruler of Japan during the postwar reconstruction. He effectively became the most powerful American in history even as the US Army shrank from 8.3 million to about 1.3 million by the end of 1946. Chaplain Kapaun would be one of those returning home to civilian life. Meanwhile, the threat of further military aggression by Russia and China in the Korean peninsula was grossly underestimated.

KOREA DIVIDED AT THE 38th PARALLEL

During World War II, the Soviets were brutal to the Japanese and Koreans, capturing at least two million people, of which about four hundred thousand or more perished. With the US Army occupying Japan, it was pretty clear to Russia and China that Japan would not be able to be turned into a Communist regime. But because Korea was no longer occupied by the Japanese and the Soviets were only able to grab the Kuril Islands in the north, all Communist leaders set their sights on taking the entire Korean peninsula. Russia had declared war on Japan as well and defeated their troops in Manchuria in 1945, leaving many Russian soldiers along the border and inside North Korea. The US took for granted that the hastily drawn border along the 38th parallel would hold long enough for an official border resolution to come in the future. With bigger issues going on in Europe and elsewhere and with the United Nations being rapidly formed with long-lasting and consequential decisions being forged, the war-weary Koreans were left to fend for themselves until the clash of ideologies prevented a civil reunification.

POSTWAR PERIOD

After the war, the Chief of Chaplains office was swamped with requests for release from active duty. By mid-1946, even General Eisenhower, then the Army's Chief of Staff, attempted to discourage the rapid departure of chaplains:

> ...today, with the fighting over, the need for [the chaplains'] continued service is undiminished. Our soldiers the world over, with more time on their hands, anxious to go home and conscious of the problems facing them on return to civil life, are urgently in need of the counsel of these men who served them so well in battle... It is my earnest endeavor to release as rapidly as possible every individual not actually required in accomplishing the Army's mission. In the meantime, I must repeat, the opportunity for service by the Army Chaplain is as great, or greater, than it has ever been.[1]

Despite such an impassioned plea from General Eisenhower, the army chaplains' ranks diminished in proportion to all offi-

cers and enlisted eager to return to civilian life. Chaplain Kapaun's original unit dissolved, and he was left to serve with an
ordnance battalion that was also completing its tasks in the CBI
theater. He continued his work over an enormous amount of
rugged territory but no doubt saw the writing on the wall—with
the vast majority of our military departing Burma and India,
the work of priests and missionaries would fall to church groups
and not to military chaplains. Kapaun's letter to his parents on
October 26, 1945, reflects that his obvious love for serving as
an army chaplain will be perceived as "goofy" when returning
to civilian life:

> Eugene is now a corporal. Guess he will be pretty well dec-
> orated when he gets home. Well, he sure deserves it after
> all he has been through.
>
> My, it will be tough to get back to work again in a par-
> ish or what not. I don't know what the Bishop is going to
> do with us Army Chaplains. He can imagine that we got
> all kind of diseases, that we are spoiled by the rough life
> of the Army, that we will be hard to handle, that we will
> be all worn out, and have all kinds of ugly habits. Sure
> would hate to be the Bishop. And on top of it all he can
> figure that some of us Chaplains out in the hot countries
> will probably be "goofy." I guess some of us are goofy al-
> ready. Haha. But I like the work, get along well with the
> soldiers & natives & learn a lot of things. You can see by
> the picture of my tent how nice a place I have. And the
> road is like a highway. What better could a fellow expect?

Chaplain Kapaun's next letter in November to Bishop Winkle-
mann is more matter-of-fact about his work despite the bishop
quashing any ideas he had of reenlisting in the army. But Kapaun
can't help describing the wonderful sensation of being "above
the clouds" in an army jeep:

The work of the Catholic priest among the soldiers still continues even though the war is over. I enjoy my work very much, in fact, I have been very happy ever since the day you told me you were releasing me for the Armed Forces. The officers and men have been most cooperative, so that I have no complaints whatsoever. God in His Goodness has favored me with good health; He has protected me from dangerous accidents several times, and He has given me many friends among the soldiers, and especially among the good Catholic Chaplains, and our good Missionaries. I have always been free to do my work, and I have been furnished most obligingly with all the things I need to do that work. Every week I travel the Stillwell Road (Ledo Road) over the mountains from Ledo to Myitkyina, a distance of 268 miles one way. It is a grand sight and a wonderful sensation to be driving in a jeep in the clouds and above them. In fact from Pangsau Pass we can look northward and see the high snow-capped peaks in the Himalaya range.

Today is All Saints' Day, but here it is not a holy day of obligation. However, we encouraged the soldiers to attend Mass today and are giving them the opportunity of attending Mass also on Sundays. We have only 3 holydays of obligation here; Christmas, Ascension Thursday, and the Feast of Our Lady, Aug. 15. That seems very strange to one used to the holydays in the USA.

The Army is making a great effort to get our soldiers back to the US as soon as possible. It is a gigantic problem, especially with all the equipment which must be properly disposed of. Many units are already on their way home. Surely it will be a happy Christmas for them.

KAPAUN'S MONTHLY CHAPLAIN REPORT

Our personnel are being shipped out rapidly so that the units here have small numbers of men. Hence, in covering long distances we really reach only a few. However, the few are as precious as many, and I believe that a priest who would refuse to go out just for a few would be seriously neglecting his duty. My farthest unit was 170 miles from my office.

On January 3, 1946, Kapaun wrote his bishop after finally being promoted to captain:

In regard to becoming a Regular Army Chaplain, I would hesitate to assume such a burden, especially since the type of life itself is filled with so many "unclerical circumstances" and one is so hampered in trying to lead a normal priestly life. However, someone surely has to take up the burden; and, if you should decide that I ought to do so, I would accept it as the will of God and try to make the best of it. Perhaps it is entirely unpriestly of me to look upon such a difficult life with hesitation, for surely a priest should be anxious to take up any cross for his love of God.

With his promotion, Captain Kapaun was asking himself whether or not to make permanent his military career. His work had become lighter since the soldiers were leaving this theater of war, but he hesitated because becoming a regular army member would bring him too many nonclerical occupations. Father Kapaun was foremost a priest; his greatest desire was to be a spiritual man of God. The many duties that were not strictly priestly obligations he was willing to tolerate only during the war, but not otherwise. At the end of his army tour, he expresses this succinctly in a letter to Bishop Winkelmann on March 1, 1946:

The number of our soldiers is gradually getting less and less, much to the happiness and hope of all the American personnel. However, in our short stay here in India, I feel that I have become somewhat attached, especially in experiencing the great spirituality and humility of the Missionaries working here. It certainly is a great field for true Christian charity and sacrifice.

"Father Kapaun sailed from Calcutta, India, May 3, 1946, and arrived at San Francisco on May 30. On June 4, he was discharged from active service. Before returning to Kansas, he went to his old school in Conception, Missouri, to make a private retreat. Before starting the normal life of a Catholic priest again, he wanted to make a spiritual renewal of finding himself in God."[2]

4

THE CATHOLIC UNIVERSITY OF AMERICA

When Father Kapaun reported for duty to the Wichita Chancery Office in July 1946, he found Bishop Winkelmann showing signs of sickness and had to limit his activities. Nobody knew how serious his illness was. But he had plans in mind for Father Kapaun other than bouncing him around from one small Kansas parish to the next—he wanted his luminous priest to be in graduate studies at The Catholic University of America in Washington, DC.

Higher education for his clergy was Bishop Winkelmann's constant dream. He realized the great demand put on the Catholic educational system. He understood that the Catholic higher education had to expand, and he wanted his priests to participate in this program. In order to do this, they must pursue graduate studies and obtain academic degrees. Now, here was a wonderful opportunity. Father Kapaun had good marks all through high school and college as well as at Kenrick Seminary, and the government was willing to pay for his higher education through the GI Bill. At first there were some difficulties. Even before leaving the Mayo Clinic, Bishop Winkelmann had instructed his new chancellor to obtain a place for Kapaun at The Catholic University. But Father Kapaun himself was uneasy about this whole business of graduate studies. In his private conversation with the bishop, as well as in his correspondence, he expressed his serious doubts as to whether he was qualified to pursue graduate studies—in effect saying that his army career left him little opportunity for books and rigid study. Was he just being too hard on himself, or was he subconsciously expressing a deeper desire to continue service in the army?

"But the bishop himself had made the decision, and Father Kapaun was too obedient a priest to oppose his wishes. As always, he was determined to make the best of the situation. Before leaving for Washington, he had a long talk with the chancellor of the diocese, who had spent three years at The Catholic University and had only recently returned. He was very frank about the whole business. He thought The Catholic University had a very fine faculty and demanded a great deal from the students, but the physical accommodations were lacking. Poor accommodations didn't bother Father Kapaun. After all, he had just finished two years as a military chaplain, having undergone all kinds of hardships and survived them with relative ease.

He arrived in Washington, DC, on October 1. After settling down, he began his graduate work in the field of education. Around the same time, Bishop Winkelmann decided to leave his residence on Belmont Avenue in Wichita and live at St. Joseph Hospital on the east side of the city. He would never leave the hospital again. On Monday evening, November 18, 1946, Bishop Winkelmann quietly slipped into eternity. On Ash Wednesday in 1947, the news reached Wichita that Rome had appointed as successor the Most Reverend Mark Carroll, also from Saint Louis, Missouri. Father Kapaun did not travel to Saint Louis for the consecration of the new bishop, nor to Wichita for the in-

Father Kapaun rides a bike while attending Catholic University, 1947.

stallation as Ordinary of the Wichita Diocese. Instead, he sent a carefully worded letter of congratulations.

In regard to his studies, all his fears that he would not be able to undergo a strenuous program of graduate studies proved wrong. He was a very good student, and within a few weeks after arriving in Washington, he found the systematic program of study very appealing. In his master's dissertation, he tried to investigate how many grade school districts in the United States gave credit for courses in religion. In preparation, he collected a tremendous number of notes through a great deal of correspondence. All in all, Bishop Winkelmann was more than justified in sending him to The Catholic University."[1] By August 1947, deep into his dissertation work, Father Kapaun had an interesting choice of words when writing to his parents:

My, I hope you do not feel bad that I did not come to visit you this summer. But I am sure you understand, especially since it is such a long trip and pretty expensive too, and nowadays I am just living off what I saved up while in the Army. God knows how long that will have to last me. Our summer school ended on August 9. From August 11 till August 13, we had the Cana Institute here, a series of talks about protecting young boys and girls from the many evils of our day. In this system, the fathers and mothers are instructed in what to do to protect their growing children. That is a tremendous problem, especially in the cities. I hope that someday I will be able to do some good in this life.

Bishop Carroll gave me permission to remain in Washington this summer to work on my Dissertation. To get a Master's Degree in Education, all are required to write a detailed study of some problem in education. I have chosen the topic: A Study of the Accrediting of Religion in the High Schools of the United States. I am covering all 48 states and some possessions like Alaska, American Samoa, etc. That means much research, then writing the Dissertation, and getting it bound. In the office of the National Catholic Welfare Conference here I can find a lot of information. The last few days I have been working from early in the morning until 1:30 next morning. But yesterday I was very tired so today I am taking a rest. If I get this project finished and have enough money, I might visit you for a few days in September. Just a pleasant thought. I will promise nothing at this time.

Glad you liked the pictures. How much do you think I weigh, just looking at those pictures? Well, the scales go down to 175, so I cannot say I am doing much suffering here. That is the most I ever weighed. So Eugene has a girlfriend. Well, that is really fine. I have been wondering just how long he would try to remain a "bachelor." He is 23 years old now and should be deciding. I surely hope he

has a wonderful girl and a good Catholic. Maybe someday before too long we will be privileged to celebrate their
"great day," just as we celebrated mine seven years ago. I
bet you had a great time with them at Sunday dinner. I
surely wish them happiness.

When Father Kapaun's dissertation is completed in February
1948, he writes this conclusion:

In an ideal Catholic State which would give religion its
true evaluation, the Catholic schools would not have any
difficulty in giving just credit in courses of religion. The
student would be shown in a concrete and practical way
that the most important subjects are rewarded as the most
important. However, as facts really exist here in the United
States, the Catholic schools find themselves in a situation
which is not ideal. In fact, the Catholic schools meet many
difficulties especially since they must coordinate their educational practice with a secular system of education which
has adopted a "hands-off" policy toward religion. However, the Catholic schools are trying to do the best they
can under the circumstances.

...After all, the Catholic schools are not intended to be
merely "credit-anxious"; they intend to turn out students
properly prepared to be successful in this life and to save
their souls.

"The studious side of Father Kapaun's nature is betrayed in
his thesis, the first attempt to discover how many school districts gave credit for religion. Since religion in education is a
daily news topic, his study was very valuable. His serious and
scholarly approach to his dissertation can be realized by the fact
that part of his notes and voluminous correspondence in this
project fill more than half a trunk. With his development as a

scholarly graduate student, one begins to notice a subtle change in his spiritual direction. He slowly formed a sincere conviction that the Master, whom his arduous soul desired to serve so completely, was calling him to labor in a particular vineyard. As the young priest himself said so frequently during his last few months on earth, "God moves in strange ways." Strange indeed. His advanced studies, in which he acquitted himself brilliantly, seemed to convince him of the need for greater simplicity in order to expend himself for the salvation of humble souls."[2] He writes to his former teacher in ninth grade at Pilsen on December 26, 1947:

Dear Sister Euphrasia:

I wish to thank you for the lovely Christmas Greeting Card. I see you are still using your gift of art to make others happy, as indeed your card made me happy and brought back pleasant memories. After attending the University I have begun to realize what a tremendous task it is to be a teacher. Surely God must have a very rich reward for those of you who have dedicated your lives to such a work. I hope and pray that God will never inflict upon me such a task, for it would be calamitous to expect an ungifted person to assume such responsibilities. I am happily convinced that God put me in the class of people who can admire teachers but not hope to imitate them.

5

THE WILL OF GOD COMES FIRST

In February 1948, after the acceptance of his dissertation, Father Kapaun received a master's degree in education and was ready to leave Washington. But before he did, he used his army earnings to buy a secondhand car, which he intended to drive back to Wichita. The car never made it. On a highway in Missouri, not far from the Kansas border, Father Kapaun, with two priests as his passengers, faced an oncoming car head-on that was trying to pass two cars. To avoid a collision, Kapaun swerved into a ditch that bottomed out so hard all three priests were ejected out of the car. Although the car was demolished, none of the priests received a scratch. Divine Providence had other plans for Father Kapaun. He had to take a bus to Wichita.

"During the four years that he had been away from Pilsen, a lot of things had happened. Father John Vesecky, upon taking over the parish in July 1944, had set out to bring to Pilsen a gradual Americanization. From now on the sermons were given in English, and all the prayers were said in English. Father Vesecky made use of the Bohemian language only for confession. There were constant delegations going from Pilsen to the Wichita Chancery Office, either to the bishop or the chancellor, to complain about the pastor or to counteract the complaints and praise him."[1]

On April 9, 1948, to quiet the Pilsen parish, Bishop Carroll installed Father Clupny, a Bohemian-speaking priest, as their pastor and appointed Father Kapaun pastor of Holy Trinity Church in nearby Timken, Kansas, another predominantly Bohemian parish. There he labored until called back into service as a chaplain on October 9 of the same year. In that brief period, he captured the hearts of the people just as he later won the esteem of the fellows in the foxholes of Korea. Everyone with whom he came in contact—businessmen, farmers, priests—attested to the warmth his sunny nature evoked.

"Joe Fiala, owner of a bowling alley, threw up his hands in surprise when asked if he remembered the priest. "Do I remember him? He used to bowl with me and the boys. The Father was a man's man and one of the best sports I have ever known. I'm not a Catholic, but that did not make any difference," Fiala added. "Everybody around here, Protestant and Catholic, liked him."

As Father Clupny summed it up: "He was the most wonderful man I ever met," adding, "A saint is the best possible description of Father Kapaun I could give. A go-getter... No, I would rather say he was a go-giver. That would better describe his spirit of service to others."[2]

THE RISE OF COMMUNISM

The late 1940s were very tumultuous worldwide. Because of the increasing troubles in Europe, the United States was withdrawing its forces in Korea to bolster occupation in Japan. In 1946, the Iron Curtain between East and West Germany went up, effectively starting the Cold War. The Marshall Plan of 1947 was the start of a massive rebuilding of Europe that Stalin wanted no part of. The Soviet Union then instituted the Berlin Blockade, which blocked all supply routes into Eastern Europe despite many Western supporters still trapped on the wrong side, and the US "Berlin Airlift" was put in place for an entire year until the Soviets lifted the siege. All these events demonstrated the "rise of Communism" was well underway and scaring Americans, including Father Kapaun, that Communism was worse than the Axis of Evil in World War II. In 1949, the North Atlantic Treaty Organization (NATO) was formed with General Dwight Eisenhower named as its first commander. With all this going on, Korea was divided in two with the north favoring Communism and the south favoring democracy. It was a powder keg left with a short fuse that led some experts to exclaim that Christianity and Communism were about to be in a life-and-death fight.

In 1948, Dr. Hyungki Lew, a leading educator and author, praised the hard work of US occupation personnel and American missionaries but maintained that they were being 'out-talked' by the Communists:

"What first came to a head on the battlefields of Korea was a growing antagonism between two political systems, an antagonism that had started decades earlier. Soviet Communism versus Western democracy was always far more than an argument between politicians or a simple disagreement on the more efficient form of government. The deep chasm between them was formed by a variance in their very philosophies of man. Preached with a religious enthusiasm, Soviet Communism made bold advances following World War II. It was not surprising, therefore, that this considered threat to democracy caused concern among many Americans over the defense and continuance of their old ideals. To a certain extent, that concern was instrumental in developing new trends in the United States Army Chaplaincy."[3]

Although Father Kapaun seemed happy in Kansas, he had the growing conviction that his services, again, were of much greater need in the army than on the home front. He felt the current events could lead to a major conflict challenging the readiness of the US Army. He made his point clear in a letter to Bishop Carroll in September 1948:

> Most Reverend and dear Bishop:
> The reason that I am willing to go back into active duty is the same reason that Bishop Winkelmann permitted me to join the reserves, namely—that we would have priests who are trained to go into duty immediately when the need came. As Cardinal Spellman described in his letter, the need of Catholic Chaplains is great, especially if our vacancies would be taken by non-Catholic Chaplains. If the choice depended only on personal desires, I would never wish to relinquish my work here in Timken for work in the Army. But in matters such as these, I believe a priest should be desirous of offering himself even though he personally would much rather remain in the Diocese. During my short term here at Timken I have grown to love these people very much, but even so, in conscience, I believe I should offer myself for work in the Armed Forces, especially in this crisis.

After thinking this matter over for several days, Bishop Carroll gave Father Kapaun permission to reenlist for military service. Before he left, he went home to visit family and his friend Father Joseph Goracy, who had recently been appointed Pastor at Kapaun's hometown. Father Goracy had been in Pilsen only a few days, wondering how to get acquainted with his new field of work. Then one afternoon, the doorbell rang, and upon opening the door, there stood Father Kapaun in the uniform of a captain in the US Army, quite a sight to behold. He was thirty-two years of age and dressed in a neat-fitting uniform. Upon taking off his cap, he showed a fine shock of blond hair. His face was still youthful-looking, but that of a man and an experienced Army officer.

BACK IN THE SERVICE

On November 15, 1948, Father Kapaun was assigned to the 502nd Anti-Aircraft battalion at Fort Bliss, Texas—real desert country. Kapaun described his surroundings thusly: "We can see at least forty miles to the next mountain range. Not even grass will grow here, just cactus, and a sort of sickly-looking weed. It is very dusty as the desert sand sometimes blows so hard that it takes the paint off my car." Many fine military training grounds that had been built during the war in haste and at vast expense had been deactivated. By 1948, the ever-expanding threat of Communism caused many of these training camps to be reactivated. Father Kapaun's first interest, as a chaplain, was naturally the chapel. The chapels at Fort Bliss had not been used for two years. Like the other buildings, they had deteriorated tremendously and were badly in need of cleaning and renovation. At first there was not even an office available, only a little shack that served as both his living quarters and office. In his first letter to his friend Fred Tuzicka, he writes,

This letter is coming from a desert in Texas near El Paso, at the foot of a mountain from the "boy" in khaki. The wind is blowing hard and the sand is beating my shack so hard that I wonder how the roof stays on. We are not organized yet, in fact that is part of our work. In about 6 weeks we expect 35,000 soldiers to be here to be trained. Then there will be plenty of work for us 2 Catholic Chaplains. I am very happy to be back in the Army. The soldiers need priests very badly. Right now I do not even have a chair so I'm writing this on my knee as I sit on my cot. It is a rough life—but I like it rough. That makes the priest-hood very interesting. The soldiers have a high regard for Catholic Chaplains.

During Father Kapaun's many returns home to Kansas, he consorted frequently with fellow pastor Father Joseph Goracy. In his unpublished biography of Kapaun, he goes into lengthy but profound examinations of Father Kapaun's psyche and spiritual awareness that no other friend of Kapaun could ever hope to achieve. Father Goracy was deeply affected by this man:

"Human beings are capable of high development, but most men and women reach only a part of their potential. In attainment in the physical order, such as athletics, we can train ourselves to a high point of efficiency, and then middle age will inevitably slow us down. This is not true in the intellectual field. Any linguist who will learn a few new words and one or two grammatical rules a day will become a great specialist in languages over the years. A philosopher or scientist who keeps on working in his chosen field can achieve great intellectual development, and instead of the accumulating years interfering, the progress of years gradually changes the ordinary assimilation and knowledge into the much-desired quality of tranquility that we call wisdom. In spiritual achievements, the possibility of constant progress is even greater because middle age and old age can realize a great help. The Bible history and catechism that the child learned becomes a strong conviction when he is a young man, but the real achievement comes only when the conviction becomes a way of life. To grasp intellectually the beauties of the doctrine of the New Testament and to live according to them as a spiritual conviction are two different things. A Scripture scholar may know every detail of the Eight Beatitudes, but his life may be far removed from their ideals. A truly religious man will not be satisfied with intellectual curiosity concerning his religion. He will want to go farther and put all the Commandments and all the counsels of the New Testament into his way of living.

Father Kapaun was already a very spiritual man of God. After eight years in the priesthood, he was a man who worked and lived according to his religious convictions. Everyone who made contact with this young Levite was impressed by his earnestness in spiritual matters. He not only studied the life of Christ as a part of his theological studies, but his leading religious motive was to follow Christ, who says, "I am the way, the truth, and the life... He who follows me can never walk in darkness."

Yet there was nothing super-pious about him. He smoked his cigar and his beloved pipe, and he would not hesitate to offer alcohol to his guests, even though he rarely took a drink himself. He was able to tell a good joke and laugh heartily when he heard something really funny, as long as it was not at the expense of someone else. He was a practical man who did not hesitate to mow the lawn, trim the trees, make minor repairs, and do whatever else might fall within the scope of parish administration. He never hesitated in meeting any problems that came up. Father Kapaun was also accomplished in amusements. From his boyhood he knew all the games and sports that young Americans like. In his home parish at Pilsen, he had seen how people could entertain themselves by simple means, such as cakewalks, parties, meals and dances. His deep spirituality did not keep him away from these things—just the opposite. They developed his personality and made him sociable and friendly. He was a person with whom everybody liked to associate.

The armed forces needed spiritual leaders: rabbis for the Jewish boys, ministers for the Protestants, and priests for the Catholics. The army realized that true discipline could not be had unless the young soldiers, many of whom were away from home for the first time, remained steadfast in their accustomed spiritual activities. The army was generous in providing special training schools for the military chaplains as well as in building simple but devotional chapels where the chaplains could conduct divine services. Every military chaplain was meant to have his own office where young soldiers could come with confidence to find help and advice or just to shoot the breeze a little and break the monotony of camp.

There are always a few chaplains who have entered a military career simply because they were not successful at home. Possibly they had a small parish and were not very successful, and then, more or less as a way out, they volunteered for the armed services. Happily, they were much in the minority. The majority of our chaplains were fine men, whose volunteering for the armed service meant a great personal sacrifice."[4]

JANUARY 30, 1949—LETTER TO FRED TUZICKA

Dear Fred, Boy, you sure did make up for lost time in the last letter you wrote—such a nice long letter. Of course, needless to say, I might add that that is the kind of letters which are really worthwhile. By the time you receive this letter your exams will be over; you will have celebrated a victorious jubilation, and perhaps you will be in retreat all ready. In that event, you probably will not receive this letter till after retreat. Well, I am sure you will have received the best from it. Your description of the dread of exams, of the "numb" feeling, of being tired and not caring if the roof falls in—all this brings back memories of what I once went thru. The worse of all is the waiting and wondering if everything turned out all right. Maybe your dogma Prof will be touched by some special grace from God and surprise all of you fellows. I hope so.

You mentioned about Ft. Bliss being a "misnomer." Sometimes I wonder. However, it is not so bad. It is the best set-up I have ever had in the Army, and I am one happy fellow. The work of course is the same. It is a wonderful work though because we have the young soldiers to work with, young fellows who have a lot of life and who are trying to make this a success. I have to smile sometimes at their ignorance and their innocence. They are a nice lot to work with. I believe you will find that out too when you get to work as a priest with the young people. They look to the priest for example and courage. Thank God we have something real to give to them.

Well, I am in need of a GI haircut myself. Guess I'll just drop over to Conception. Haha. I can imagine how busy you are. Of course you would not be happy unless you were busy. They say that the days in the Seminary are the happiest days. I just wonder who ever said that. Since I have been out of the Seminary I have been just as happy, in fact, much more so because we are doing the real work of the priesthood. There are no Seminary "walls" to protect us or to restrain us. But who wants Seminary "walls" anyway? As long as a person follows the footsteps of our Savior he needs no walls at all. That reminds me of Father Bede. If he knew I made a crack like that he would say: "Why, that ungrateful &%$#()★." (The symbols are subject to private interpretation.) (If an old Army Sergeant would read this and put his version on &%$#()★ Father Bede's face would get rather red. But I know you will not put on such a version.) Anyway, many thanks to Fr. Bede for his kind remembrance of the fellow who caused him a lot of headaches. Of course I still contend that in his Greek course we fellows knew more Greek than he did, but, of course, he did not think so, and whenever there was a dispute of any kind he always was right because he was the professor. Just an example of how the "under-dog" has the disadvantage. My, if you tell this to Fr. Bede he will be fuming. But really I want to congratulate him on being elected Superior. I hope someday again to come to Conception for a visit. It is the sort of a "home" to me, with a lot of friends there,

and with the staunch, true, Catholic atmosphere there. I
believe you will see that someday even more clearly than
you see it now, Fred.

Well, Fred, I am wishing the best for you, and remembering you in my prayers. I hope that tomorrow, Tuesday
and Wednesday will not be too strenuous on you.
As ever in Christ, Fr. Emil Kapaun

"MY, THAT IS A THRILL"

"Father Kapaun became acquainted with the commanding general in a very strange way. Upon arrival in El Paso, he felt so
dusty that the first thing he needed was a shower. He had to
use the common shower since it was the only one that was
working. There he met another officer, and when he had introduced himself as one on the new chaplains, the other officer
introduced himself as the commanding general. A week later,
the general became better acquainted with this chaplain from
Kansas. Complaining about certain things that did not proceed
quickly enough, he thought that Father Kapaun had not done
his full duty. Father Kapaun wrote about it thus: 'At the end
of my first week here, my Commanding General a very fine
man, who takes an exceptionally keen interest in the work of
his chaplains, told me that I had not done my duty. I disagreed,
and told him so in no uncertain terms. Ever since he has been
wonderful to me.'"[5]

At some point after Kapaun had written about his Commanding General, he was given an opportunity to fire a huge anti-
aircraft gun that weighed about thirty-five thousand pounds.
"My, that is a thrill," he exclaimed. "We shot at targets about 5
miles away pulled by an airplane." Kapaun became a frequent
visitor of the troops on the firing range, wearing a pistol belt
with only his canteen and first aid kit but was allowed to practice on the rifle range like anyone else.

The story of the army chaplain offered an opportunity to fire such a powerful weapon is telling of Chaplain Kapaun's character. How many chaplains would jump at the chance? From the witnesses to Emil Kapaun's childhood and coming-of-age in rural Kansas, he was well-known to be a trapper of animals but not known as a hunter with a rifle. This is probably because of the expense of the rifle, not an aversion to firing a gun. During basic training, a noncombatant chaplain is not required to qualify with a rifle, but does participate in a live fire adjustment course where every soldier starts downrange from a machine gun (fixed to fire about five feet above the ground) and must crawl a distance to the platform the gun is firing from. The training is effective. It teaches you what bullets sound like whipping near you, and most importantly to keep your head and your "brain bucket" down under fire.

"But matters such as these were not his foremost concern as a Catholic chaplain. It so happened that Fort Bliss had a high percentage of Catholic boys, running between 50 and 60 percent of the base. At first there were only two Catholic chaplains, but later a third came from Boston. By January 1949, the number of soldiers being trained at Fort Bliss was expected to be as high as 30,000, and for this number, only three Catholic chaplains were available.

At The Catholic University, Father Kapaun had taken a special course entitled "Youth and Character," which he admitted was a great help to him in consultations he had with the young soldiers. In chapel he conducted all the services that his boys were accustomed to at home. He was always available to hear confessions, say Mass, preach sermons, and distribute Holy Communion. He also had special devotions to the Blessed Virgin Mary, and during every day in Lent, Stations of the Cross. Several of the young soldiers were immigrants from Ireland. Father Kapaun did not hesitate to arrange special devotions in honor of St. Patrick for them. After all, the parents of one of the boys had sent him some real Irish shamrocks.

By October 1949, this particular group of soldiers had finished their training and were ready to be sent to different posts. At first Father Kapaun thought that he would stay at Fort Bliss and began to get ready for an entirely new group of soldiers, but things turned out differently, and he was alerted for overseas duty. His soldiers had orders to leave Fort Bliss by December 8, 1949, and he himself had orders to report at the Port of Embarkation at Seattle, Washington, not later than January 2, 1950, for shipment to Yokohama, Japan."[6]

HOMECOMING—CHRISTMAS 1949

"He was able to leave Fort Bliss by December 12 to spend a short vacation with his parents at home. Again, the Pilsen pastor was privileged to enjoy the company of this fine military chaplain. His sense of clerical discipline was so acute that he did not stay with his parents but asked the hospitality of the rectory. There was no particular law that required him to live there, but he had learned from Monsignor Sklenar that this was the better thing to do. The first thing he would do in the morning was say Mass and finish his Breviary for the day. Only then would he go out to visit his parents, relatives and friends as well as find plenty of time to help with the duties of the parish.

At the children's Christmas party, he played the part of Santa Claus. At the Altar Society's Christmas party, he would have a talk about his experiences with the boys at Fort Bliss. With special pride he pointed out to the ladies that their sons were well cared for, that parents did not have to worry about their physical and spiritual welfare. To emphasize the success of a chaplain's work, he pointed out that only last year at Fort Bliss, four boys had confided to him that as soon as they had finished their military service, they would begin studying for the priesthood. Two others were determined to join religious communities as Brothers. This talk was a great consolation to the ladies, many of whom were mothers of boys who were about to be drafted.

FATHER KAPAUN GUILD

Chaplain Emil Kapaun in dress uniform poses with his proud parents, Enos and Bessie Kapaun.

Mrs. Kapaun's ducks and chickens had a rough time. If Father Kapaun did not eat at home, she would send these delicious dinners to the rectory. Evidently Father Kapaun had no weight problem. He could eat what he wanted and remain slender, something that could not be said of the Pilsen pastor. Although he was officially on vacation, he was active in getting the church ready for the celebration of Christmas. He used his car to drive the pastor anywhere he had to go. During the Midnight Mass, he assisted in the sanctuary. The next morning he said his three

Masses, which are a special privilege of the day, and spent the rest of the holiday with his parents. After eleven years, it is rather difficult to describe exactly the atmosphere of his last vacation in his home parish in Pilsen. Father Kapaun was joyful, cooperative, and sensitive, as always, but there was also this added atmosphere of solemnity, similar to that which surrounded the Last Supper. Even before the outbreak of the Korean War, the atmosphere was heavy. The possibility that open warfare would break out anytime in the world was almost a certainty. To report for overseas duty necessarily included a willingness to be ready for anything, even possible death. Father Kapaun was too sensitive a man not to feel this. He could not help but leave Pilsen with a heavy heart. But on December 26, 1949, on the feast of St. Stephen, the first martyr, Captain Emil J. Kapaun left his home for the last time to travel to the West Coast and, following orders, ship out."[7]

From San Francisco, Father Kapaun continued to Fort Lawton in Seattle, Washington. From there he went to the Port of Embarkation in Seattle, and was processed for overseas travel. On January 22, 1950, he left Seattle aboard the *USS General M.M. Patrick*, a troopship bound for Japan. Father Kapaun and his parents had always been very close, but now they were somehow closer than ever before. Time would not stand still for them, but the proud parents of this military chaplain knew they made the best use of every hour they spent with their firstborn son. Nobody mentioned the possibility that this could be his last time spent at home and even the last time they would be together here on earth.

In 1954, Sister Mary Loyola wrote a letter to the first Kapaun biographer, Reverend Arthur Tonne, and said how proud she was seeing Kapaun on the day of his departure. She even kept a snapshot of him taken the same morning. The end of her letter reads:

Father Kapaun played Santa Claus for the children's Christmas party the year he left. He certainly brought out the Christian idea of the Christ-Child and the real significance of Christmas. Perhaps you remember I am the little nun who has dedicated "life" for the priests and have your name among my priest friends. Well, when I asked Father Kapaun for his signature in my book and told him I would remember him in a special way on a certain day of the week. He replied, "Sister, that will be most wonderful, but don't worry about me, just remember my boys."

6

OCCUPIED JAPAN—1950

The trip aboard the *USS General M. M. Patrick* from Seattle to Yokohama took from January 23 until February 7, 1950. Evidently, Father Kapaun was not acquainted with the newly discovered Dramamine. He mentioned in one of his letters that he was quite ill for the first few days. After he had recovered from the worst of his seasickness, he was able to say Holy Mass every morning. Jim Draskovich remembers meeting Kapaun aboard their troopship:

"I was on KP being only a private when given a short time off to attend mass. When I reached the upper deck area, Fr. Kapaun was ready to say mass. I served for him. After mass, he asked me to stay and talk. I told him I was on KP and would be in big trouble if I did not return. He wrote a note and told me to give it to the officer in charge. Thus I was no longer on KP, I was his assistant. Days on the ship started with mass. With Father we talked about several things. I had full run of the ship with no duties other than serve mass.

"On a Sunday—the small area was crowded with GIs. Fa-

DOD

Chaplain Kapaun on the USS General M. M. Patrick *transport ship en route to Japan, February 1950.*

ther took a small basket (I don't know where he got it.) I passed the basket, it was over filled. After mass the ship PX was open. Father told me to get to the PX as it would not open again. I told him I had no money. He reached into the basket full and gave me about $10. Needless to say it made my day—I needed several items. After 14 days at sea—Father always looked neat in his uniform, with shoulder patch from his WWII days patch of India-Burma-China. When we reached Yokohama we exchanged addresses. I never saw Father Kapaun again."[1]

OCCUPIED JAPAN—1945–1950

The US occupation of Japan began on August 28, 1945, and was led by General Douglas MacArthur, who was appointed as the Supreme Commander of the Allied Powers. He was also the defacto ruler of Japan, making him one of the most powerful leaders on the planet tasked with dismantling the Japanese military and its war machine so that they would never again become a military threat to the world. At the time, the Japanese Armed Forces numbered over 6.9 million men. Of this number, 3.5 million were located in the home islands. They were supported by hundreds of ships and over six thousand combat aircraft. The occupation also aimed to democratize Japan and promote sweeping economic and social reforms. To achieve these things, as many as one million troops and subcontractors rotated through Japan in seven years.

World War II had decimated Japan and its people to say the least. The Japanese, wary of Americans, were surprised by the generosity of the American soldiers. Such humane acts went above and beyond ensuring a peaceful transition to a more democratic, and as MacArthur hoped, a much more Christian nation. This hope was succinctly expressed at the time by retired Admiral William Halsey, one of the most decorated naval commanders in WW2, who wrote: "It is very apparent that the Japanese associate democracy with Christianity."

By the time of Father Kapaun's arrival in 1950, the American occupation was nothing less than one of the marvels of the twentieth century in the Far East. MacArthur was Japan's first foreign ruler since the age of Christ and boldly placated Emperor Hirohito's autocratic rule into an impotent token figure and installed a democratic government to be led by the will of the people participating in free elections. For centuries, the Japanese practiced the Shinto religion, which focused on ritual behavior rather than doctrine. But by 1912, Japan's nationalist leadership formed State Shinto, which strongly encouraged citizens to worship the emperor as a kami, or spiritual being whose edicts were to be followed precisely. Along comes General MacArthur, a god warrior in his own right, and Shinto practice is disavowed and officially separated from the state. It was clear to MacArthur that Shinto never held strong in the daily life of the

Japanese and it was a political tool by design needed to motivate a strong imperialist army. MacArthur believed what saved
the Philippines was Christianity and democracy—his plan now
for Japan.

"The determination of MacArthur to bring the combination
of Christianity and democracy to Japan was emphasized repeatedly during his command... By the late 1940s MacArthur encouraged a mass distribution of Bibles in Japan. He referred to
efforts in this program as a 'demonstration of practical Christianity' which met the 'heart-needs' of the Japanese by giving
them the Scriptures 'which reveal the knowledge of God and
His love through Jesus Christ.' As late as 1950 he commented to
a visiting American churchman: 'Please send ten missionaries for
every one you now have in Japan. We must have ten thousand
Christian missionaries and a million Bibles to complete the occupation of this land.' It's no wonder that one chaplain in Japan
referred to the General in a letter by saying, 'He has done more
than any other man to further Christianity in Japan.'"[2]

However, this didn't stick long. Despite the wins and losses
on the world battlefields, the battle for the hearts and minds of
the survivors was now ramping up between Communism and
capitalism and between Christianity and atheism—especially in
Japan and Korea. So imagine what lay ahead for a well-traveled
army chaplain from Kansas who had reached the "Christly" age
of thirty-three.

Just a couple of months after his arrival, Father Kapaun delivered a homily chosen from the Beatitudes from Matthew's Gospel on the Armed Forces Radio Network broadcast throughout
Japan and as far away as China:

In the sermon on the mountain Christ gave to us the eight
Beatitudes. In the list of eight he mentioned first "Blessed

are the poor in spirit, for theirs is the Kingdom of Heaven." This beatitude is very important, for on another occasion Christ had said: "Therefore do not be anxious saying 'What shall we eat' or 'What shall we drink' or 'what are we to put on', (for after all these things the Gentiles seek): for your Father knows that you need all these things. But seek first the Kingdom of God and His justice, and all these things shall be given you beside."

When Christ walked on this earth with His apostles, He made use of many things which people had in their way of living. His dress was that of a common man: He ate food— even took part in banquets and feasts; He used the peoples' means of transportation, their fishing craft and their beasts of burden. He accepted the hospitality of the people and visited with them in their homes. He used money and in- structed people to pay their debts and to pay the laborer a just wage in return for work performed. He used a cross of wood on which He died to atone for the sins of mankind. In none of these things was Christ extravagant, haughty, or proud. He made use of earthly things in a modest way— He did not let earthly things make use of Him, to make Him proud, or unjust, or selfish. He gave the example of the truly "Poor in Spirit."

O God of Heaven and earth, who placed us into this world, to use it properly, modestly, humbly, and honestly, and who gave us the example of how to use it as a stepping stone to heaven, grant that all of us may appreciate your blessing and follow your example. "Blessed are the poor in spirit, for theirs is the Kingdom of Heaven."

THE 1st CAVALRY DIVISION
"THE FIRST TEAM"

When Captain Kapaun checked into his new unit, he was as- signed a leadership role as the 8th Regiment Chaplain in the

1st Cavalry Division. The 1st Cavalry was formally activated in September 1921 at Fort Bliss, Texas, with early duties patrolling the Mexican border and rough-riding with horse-mounted soldiers. Their activation to duty in World War II, Korea, Vietnam and Iraq have earned them the moniker "the First Team." Led by General Douglas MacArthur, the 1st Cavalry were first into Manila in February 1945, and in September, the First Team led occupational forces into Japan's capital, earning the distinction of "First in Tokyo." Father Kapaun had arranged to have his car shipped from the United States to Japan. With a car he could be freer in his movements. At first he was stationed in the city of Tokyo itself and later in the suburbs of the city. Units of the 1st Cavalry were dispersed around the Kanto Plain on the main Japanese island of Honshu, but the division headquarters were outside of Tokyo at Camp Drake. One of its officers remarked critically that an assignment there "…served as a place to give senior officers a 'going away present' before they went home and retired." This was no place for any 1st Cavalry officer to retire as soon enough, in about seven months, Chaplain Kapaun would find himself along with this unit to be "First in Pyongyang," the capital of North Korea. How befitting for this now experienced army chaplain to serve in a leadership role among one of the most storied US Army units in history, always leading the way.

Serving alongside Kapaun in the 8th Regiment were Chaplain Arthur E. Mills, an Adventist Christian, and Donald F. Carter, a Progressive Brethren. Mills wrote later that his best friends among the "sky pilots" were Chaplain Kapaun and Chaplain Donald Carter. When Mills was alerted to accompany a unit to Korea, he picked the 8th Regiment so he could be with the two of them.

Assigned to be Chaplain Kapaun's assistant was Private Patrick J. Schuler. From Cincinnati, Ohio, Schuler joined the army on January 5, 1949, and served until July 1, 1951. Before entering the service, he was a brakeman for the Indiana Division of the New York Central Railroad. In Kapaun's monthly report, he stated he was assigned a 1/4-ton truck (standard jeep) and trailer, and lists "Pvt. Patrick J. Schuler-drives and maintains vehicle-assists in all Masses." Private Schuler stuck by Chaplain Kapaun's side through thick and thin when they were sent into battle a few months later.

"Many chaplains are very poor letter writers. Their mani-fold duties can distract them from answering correspondence for weeks or even months, and when they finally get to it, they write as little as possible. At home in Wichita, Bishop Carroll was a man who prided himself in answering promptly all corre-spondence with newsy letters to his chaplains in service. Father Kapaun followed the example of his bishop. He was regular in sending his official report to the Military Ordinariate in New York and a second copy to his home diocese of Wichita. Be-sides this official report, he always included a letter with any news that was not restricted militarily. He also showed an ad-mirable willingness and readiness to write to his parents, rela-tives and friends. The style of these letters was always in perfect harmony with the person to whom he was writing. He could write very formal letters to his superiors, but when writing to his parents and friends, he could be just as homey in narrating news as any farm boy.

His seriousness in correspondence can also be seen in the fact that he acknowledged every postcard, letter, and package sent to him in May 1950 from the new pastor of Pilsen who was with the pilgrimage from Wichita in Rome for the celebration of the Holy Year. In one of the offices in Rome, he found a special Holy Year letter composed in Latin to be sent to priests. He took one of these form letters, signed his name to it, and addressed it to Chaplain Kapaun. He hardly arrived home in Pilsen when he received a letter of thanks from Father Kapaun expressing his great joy at having been remembered during the Holy Year."[3] Kapaun wrote Bishop Carroll in February 1950:

There are many interesting things in Japan. I was very much impressed by the attitude of the people. They seem to be clean and neat and courteous. Yesterday, four officers and myself were walking to our headquarters. An old Japanese stepped off the street into the gutter and bowed very graciously. We did not like so much ceremony, but I guess he wanted to show us courtesy. We bowed back and greeted him. Other people on the street greet us with a slight bow of the head. I guess they do not know how to say "hello" or "good morning" in English, and we do not know how to say it in Japanese, but we accomplish in actions what we would like to say in words. I see now that I am going to be studying the Japanese language! A fellow at least should be able to exchange the ordinary courtesies.

Most officers and many soldiers also kept army trunks at the base where they were stationed. After the Korean War ended, Captain Kapaun's trunk was shipped back to his family in Kansas. Many interesting items were inside, and sure enough, one of the books he had was a guide to speaking the Japanese language. Although he expected to be stationed at least two years in Japan, he had an examination in the Czech language (passing with a good grade), which could have meant that the army contemplated sending him eventually to Europe. In his short life, this scholar studied and learned Bohemian, German, English, Greek, Latin, Czech, Japanese, and some Hindi as well.

FEBRUARY 24—KAPAUN LETTER HOME

Dear Dad and Mom, I bet you think I got lost. How are you? I am fine and getting fatter every day. It freezes here, but the days are warm and sunny.

I am assigned to the Cavalry Regiment, but we do not have any horses. We are just plain infantry—you know—walking and marching. We are located right in the city of Tokyo, the third largest in the world. The Japanese do not mark their streets. A newcomer can get lost very easily. The streets run in every direction. It will take me some time to get used to them. The people drive on the left side of the street, and the policemen have the Japanese way of conducting traffic...

"Father Kapaun was very impressed by the people of Japan. He found them both courteous and industrious. Born on a farm, he was interested in the native agriculture. He wrote to his parents that the fields owned by individual farmers were no larger than the garden around their house at Pilsen. The wheat was planted in rows about twelve inches apart. He noted how everything was done by hand, and how the women of Japan had an active part in cultivating the ground as well as in harvesting. He found the planting of rice a very difficult and messy affair, the rice plants being first raised in greenhouses and later transplanted into very muddy ground. A man raised in the city would not be as interested in these things, but Father Kapaun had learned to handle farm machinery at an early age. While he found a great deal of industrial progress in factories, railroads, and automobiles, he was very much surprised that mechanical progress had not yet been adopted in the agriculture of Japan.

From his arrival in Japan on February 7, 1950, until June 25, when North Korean forces invaded South Korea, only a few months were to pass by. The soldiers who were under the care of Father Kapaun during that period were not occupational soldiers but actual combat soldiers who were kept in constant readiness for any eventuality. General MacArthur was quite conscious that there could be an outbreak of Communist hostilities anywhere

at any time. For that reason, a number of combat units were
kept in constant readiness."[4] As early as March 1, 1950, Kapaun
writes Bishop Carroll with a warning of war:

> Most Reverend and dear Bishop:
> Lenten greetings to you from the Chaplain from the Wich-
> ita Diocese who is in Japan.
>
> At last I am located in a Chapel and with a unit of soldiers.
> (None of this letter is for publication as it might be alarming.)
> Our Division is a combat training unit. We are not occupa-
> tion forces as the other units are in Japan. We are training
> for battle, and will be called on in event of war in this part
> of the world. We go on maneuvers in a couple of months.
>
> Kyoto, where I have been told the Sisters of St. Joseph
> are, is south from us. I do not know how far. It is difficult
> to travel by auto; the highways are wide, but bumpy, and
> traffic is heavy. It takes about an hour to drive 20 miles.
> Train service in Japan is very good, but for a person who
> is not acquainted with the cities nor the language of the
> people, it is best not to attempt to travel too far.

Robert G. Wixom, who like Kapaun enlisted in the 1st Cavalry Division at Fort Bliss in 1948, and was also stationed in
Japan by 1950, remembers seeing Chaplain Kapaun: "In Tokyo
he would come up to the barracks to see us and wondered why
we were not coming to Mass. We said we had to get to the mess
hall for breakfast, however, he said he would take care of the
mess hall if we started showing up in the Chapel!" During his
service in Korea, Wixom received two Purple Hearts and was
awarded the Bronze Star.

MARCH 10—LETTER HOME

Dear Dad and Mom, How are you? I hope you are well
and that you did not blow away in the March winds. Our

paper said yesterday that the Middle West had some very strong winds and dust storms. It freezes at night, but the days are fairly comfortable. A fellow can wear an overcoat with comfort through the whole day. Before long, spring will be here. Some of the trees are starting to bloom already. I want to see the famous Japanese cherry trees bloom. They are very pretty. Since I have been here we have had three earthquakes. My, the earth can surely jump around. One lasted twenty minutes. The earth just kept moving and trembling and jolted back and forth. It is an awful feeling. I guess we will have to get used to it. Some of the Japanese just "freeze" in their tracks from fright, and cannot move or talk. They become white as a sheet. Last year some old buildings collapsed in an earthquake. The soldiers tell me that before I came here they had an earthquake which tossed them right out of bed. About forty miles from here is Mount Fuji, a volcano, the highest mountain in Japan. We can see it on a clear day, as it towers above the clouds. My soldiers will keep me plenty busy, especially after we go out on maneuvers. That will mean a lot of traveling and I will get to see a lot of the country. I do not get much chance to drive around, except on Sunday afternoon. My car comes in handy. I would have to do a whole lot of walking without it. Today is Eugene's birthday. I guess he will have a big celebration.

LETTER TO MR. AND MRS. JOSEPH MEYSING

My dear friends, I want to thank you for the nice letter you sent me and the description of your trip from San Francisco. I am glad that you enjoyed it and that you got to see a lot of things. You saw one thing that I did not get to see—the Golden Gate Bridge. Although I drove over it, I could not see it—the fog was so thick. Isn't that something? I have to laugh every time I think of it.

I have a job with a unit of soldiers which will mean a lot of traveling. I like to knock around that way. I am going to buy a camera and color film. The sights are beautiful and if I get them in color I will have some priceless remembrances of my visit to Japan. I saw the Emperor's grounds. No one is permitted to go in there. They are surrounded by a high wall and a moat (canal of water). Right across the street from this canal is General MacArthur's Headquarters building, and the American flag is gracefully flying on top of it. It really is an impressive sight. It makes a fellow think too. If I had been here 5 years earlier I probably would be in some prison. The Japanese are hard workers. They have to work hard if they want to live on such a small piece of ground."

"The percentage of Catholics in Father Kapaun's care was not as high as in Fort Bliss, Texas. But in spite of the few Catholic soldiers, he was kept busy due to the constant movements of his troops. Father Kapaun was never a man who would stay behind while his soldiers were out on maneuvers. He could have excused himself easily, but he was too conscientious to do that. When work had to be done, he always faced it."[5]

MARCH CHAPLAIN REPORT

List Factors Affecting Religious Work: I gave 6 mixed marriage instructions and 2 convert instructions.

General Remarks: According to a very recent survey our regiment has 65% Protestants, 23% Catholics, 1% Jews, and 11% No religion. In the whole Regiment I have nearly 400 Catholics. I was amazed to discover how many of these soldiers had not been going to the Sacraments for years. They are just as neglectful about attending Mass.

Suggestions: A number of Catholic soldiers are very faithful and are ideal Catholics. Other Catholic Chaplains have told me the same thing. It seems that the soldier we have today comes from families who had been neglectful. This situation, on the surface, looks discouraging, yet we Catholic Chaplains have a large field to work in to bring back these "straying sheep." It is a great joy for me to be instrumental in bringing at least a few of them back into the fold.

At the same time Chaplain Kapaun is expressing his enthusiasm for bringing the lapsed Catholic soldiers back into the fold, he expresses to his friend Fred Tuzicka sheer happiness and blessings from God that the Japanese, too, are going to receive the true faith, and that he is a missionary in a "pagan land": "It really is a peculiar thing—the way God permits such great changes. I never dreamed (when I was in Timken) that at your ordination I would be in Japan. I never dreamed of being a Missionary, yet here I am in a Mission Land, a pagan land, but one which has received exceptional blessings from God and the way it looks (if Russia does not get in here) many of the Japanese are going to receive the true faith."

US ARMED FORCES RADIO BROADCASTS

"Chaplains with the occupation forces in the Far East also made early use of the Armed Forces Radio Network. Shortly after the arrival of US troops, Chaplain Amos P. Bailey, Methodist, presented the first Christian broadcast from Tokyo since 1941. A weekly schedule, including daily devotions and Sunday services, was beamed throughout Japan and as far away as China and Okinawa."[6] Father Kapaun chose the Beatitudes from Matthew's Gospel as the theme for his talks:

APRIL 18, 1950

O God, give to us this true meekness whereby we will conduct ourselves in the proper manner according to the example of Christ and obtain the land of blessing which was promised to those who are meek. People whose ambitions are confined to the limits of earthly things would be confounded at the beatitude on meekness; likewise they would be equally perplexed at the following beatitude: "Blessed are they who mourn, for they shall be comforted."

The teachings of Christ and the example of living which he gave do not lead to sadness and to grieving. Instead they lead to joy and happiness. People who live according to the teachings of Christ and follow His example are not sad and morose: instead they have true joy and happiness. And mingled in with their joy and happiness they can have true sorrow for their sins and the realization that there is even greater joy and happiness to strive for. Even the saintly person who lives in true joy and happiness can have many sorrows and disappointments. That this is true is evident from the lives of the saints. In order to win the crown of heavenly glory, the saints were expected first to carry a heavy cross in life. This is part of the meaning of the beatitude: "Blessed are they who mourn, for they shall be comforted."

APRIL 19

It has always been a question among people why God permits many innocent people to be treated unjustly. God is aware of all good things and all evil things which take place. Christ had said that not even a sparrow falls to the ground without God knowing about it. He said that even the hairs on our heads are numbered. God is aware of any injustice and of any good. He permits the bad to flourish along with the good. Christ however had assured His followers that God would give complete justice to all men. He may not give this justice in this world in this life, but He will give it in the life beyond the grave. That is why there is a heaven and a hell. That is why many people believe in a purgatory after death. Our Savior referred to the judgment at the end of the world. God will have all nations gathered before Him. The good He will place at his right hand, the wicked at his left hand. To the good God will say: "Come, Blessed of my Father, take possession of the kingdom prepared for you from the foundation of the world." To the wicked he will say: "Depart from me, accursed ones, into the everlasting fire which was prepared for the devil and his angels." With this thought in mind, let us ask God to help us always to be just so that one day the beatitude will be fulfilled for us. "Blessed are they who hunger and thirst for justice for they shall be satisfied."

FATHER KAPAUN'S THIRTY-FOURTH BIRTHDAY APRIL 20, 1950

One of the most impressive scenes in the life of Our Savior is the one on Mount Calvary, the scene of the crucifixion. Jesus was dying on the cross. His enemies were standing at the foot of the cross: some were shaking their fists at Him. Others were blaspheming Him in their speech. Christ was suffering bitter anguish of soul and mind. And intense pain in His body. His life was fast coming to an end. He looked with pitiful eyes upon the people in the crowd, then looking up to heaven He said: "Father, forgive them, for they do not know what they are doing." Out of love for mankind Christ had come into this world and out of love for sinners Christ had died on the cross. One purpose of His life was to obtain forgiveness for sinners. The forgiveness of sinners is called the Mercy of God. "O God, Be Merciful to us who are sinners."

And yet we notice that innocent people suffer tragedies like this. God permits these things, not because He is cruel—for He is all merciful—but because He has some purpose in them. O Merciful God, help us to understand what it means to be merciful: Help us to accept sufferings

and difficulties according to thy Will: Help us to forgive
those who injure and offend us: Make us worthy of the
reward You promised: "Blessed are the merciful for they
shall obtain Mercy.

(RADIO ANNOUNCER: You have been listening to
Morning Meditations, an inspirational period brought to
you six days of the week to refresh and renew your faith in
religion. This is the FAR EAST NETWORK.)

"Even as a military chaplain, Father Kapaun wanted to be
kept informed on the happenings in the Wichita Diocese and
in his home parish. Whenever possible, he was sent a copy of
the diocesan paper, *The Advance Register*, which he read with
great interest and commented upon in his letters. In the spring
of 1950, plans for a new residence for the Sisters were ready to
begin work in Pilsen, with mostly parishioners doing the bulk
of the work. "Even from far-off Japan, Father Kapaun was extremely interested in this new development at his home parish.
In his letters he continually asked questions about the progress
of the new convent, and he was highly pleased when he received good reports.

In spite of his many and varied duties, Father Kapaun found
time every month to participate in a day of recollection in which
a number of Catholic chaplains would gather to spend the day in
prayer and listen to the sermons of a retreat master. Father Kapaun lived by the principle *"Nemo dat quod non habet"*—"Nobody
can give what he does not have." If he wanted to spread some
spirituality among the soldiers who were kept busy with military duties in a far-off land, he himself would have to remain a
very spiritual man, and thus he was extremely faithful to these
special days.

Almost instinctively, Father Kapaun wanted to build up as
great a spiritual reservoir as possible. He had seen the situation

in the Far East go from bad to worse. The United States had suffered a great defeat in China. America spent about $2 billion for civil and military assistance to Chiang Kai-shek, but in 1949, the Chinese Communists were still able to drive the general and his followers off the mainland. By 1950, Chinese Communist volunteers were entering into combat in Korea."[7]

KAPAUN WRITES BISHOP CARROLL

Dear Reverend and dear Bishop:

We have been alerted for trouble during May, the month of Communist exhibitions. Just a short distance from our camp the Communists have their headquarters, flying the red flag with the hammer and sickle. I do not think the Communist officials are planning any demonstrations, but some radical individuals may cause some trouble. We Catholic Chaplains have a monthly "Day of Recollection." Last month we met at Sophia University in Tokyo. All of us profited by it. As a priest, I must refurbish my own spiritual life; only then can I take care of the arduous duties of a chaplain.

LETTER TO MR. AND MRS. LEONARD SCHNEIDER— ALBERT, KANSAS

I think you worry too much, Leonard. Do as I did, join the Army, see the world, and put all cares aside. (More easily said than done.) However, in the Army a fellow might think he has no cares but I guess he has more of them than at home. But I love this knocking around in the Army. Last month I made around 875 miles trying to reach my soldiers and say Mass for them. Some side roads are miserable. My assistant has a hard time keeping my jeep in running order. Last week we had four flat tires.

Thank you for the many prayers. May God reward your great kindness. You are surely wonderful for remembering what very little I did for Timken. In fact, I did nothing whatsoever. All I accomplished was to keep the lawns mowed and the cemetery clean. I had done nothing more than that, except to cause you people a lot of anxiety when I came, and then wonderment about me going into the Army again. But, here I am, happy in my work, and having plenty of it. My outfit is a training unit, and in case of war we will go first. It makes me feel good to think I can go right along with them. In a few days we go up into the mountain to train. However, we do not have any war scare here.

ROBERT WIXOM SEES FATHER KAPAUN AGAIN

"We were on Mt. Fuji on maneuvers June 15th—they said we were saddling up and going back to main camp—didn't tell us what it was—we went back to the camp and knew we were moving out—we checked all our personal things and we loaded up. We worked our way up towards the 38th parallel but we didn't have enough help. I got hit by shrapnel and then machine gun. That's what saved my life—just missed my heart. Take a different view of wars—the guys that start these things are never there—it's the guys in the hole that do the fighting and they have nothing to say. I really didn't know why I was there really until I got back—it's like having someone shoot your brother, you never forget it. [Father Kapaun] was around every day and we got to know his driver and him—he'd do things for guys that wanted to get in touch with parents or something, a guy kinda homesick, Father would come talk to them. Thank God I'm back here."[8]

EVE OF WAR

Early in 1950, Kim Il Sung began to plan a full-scale attack on South Korea with the goal of unifying the country through military force. Before launching such an attack, however, he needed the approval of Joseph Stalin, who, if not his "master," was at least the man supplying the tools of war. He also needed an okay from Chinese Chairman Mao Tse-Tung. After persistent appeals by Kim and a go-ahead from Mao, Stalin gave his reluctant approval for the attack after making sure that sufficient arms and equipment were on hand to provide significant military superiority. He also sent Soviet military advisors to Korea to help plan the campaign. From the most recent evidence, it appears that Kim assured Stalin of a quick military victory, one that would include a Communist-led general uprising against the controversial Syngman Rhee. Moreover, it seems clear that Kim never believed the United States would intervene.

KAPAUN WRITES TO MONSIGNOR SKLENAR

To Monsignor Sklenar:
 It is a long time since I heard from you. I hope you are not sick, or that something has happened. We have moved into a new place. We are painting the buildings and have other work to do until we have it the way we want it. We are about 40 miles from Tokyo. My soldiers are on maneuvers. I am very happy, and very thankful to be an Army Chaplain. About two weeks ago I took tests in Czech language. I did very well—better than I expected. Maybe I will get an opportunity to be an Army Chaplain in Europe sometime.

Oh how plans change…

THE REDS INVADE

In the early morning hours of Sunday, June 25, 1950, a blitzkrieg force of over 150,000 troops of the North Korean People's Army, backed by 150 Soviet-made T-34 tanks, invaded South Korea along the 38th parallel. With no heavy weaponry for a defense and a much smaller ill-equipped army, the Republic of Korea (ROK) Forces did their best to aid roughly two hundred thousand civilians to immediately flee to the southern port city of Pusan in hopes of getting evacuated. US-backed President of South Korea, Syngman Rhee, barely escaped the capital city of Seoul, which was overtaken just three days later. The number of civilians, including North Koreans, fleeing south quickly rose to half a million. Let there be no doubt: this was an attempted genocide of any Koreans that would not submit to Communist doctrine and a blatant attempt to take and annex all of South Korea's territory and unify the peninsula under the authoritarian regime of Kim Il Sung. Without swift action from President Truman and the United Nations, there is no question that all of Korea would have been conquered and millions of lives would have been in peril.

So, in another twist of fate on a global scale, we must look back again to the significance of Japan's surrender in 1945. Japan was not just occupying all of Korea but using it as a staging ground for multiple attacks and invasions of China. China and Russia had both declared war on Japan in WW2. With so much attention being paid to Stalin in Europe, and deservedly so, Russia claimed the Korean peninsula to be theirs. A temporary solution, meant to be resolved at a later date, simply divided Korea at the 38th parallel with the north being Communist controlled, and the south backed by the United States. But US troops were withdrawn and no significant weaponry was left for defense as the US thought the Communist regime would never take such drastic measures with so many US troops still stationed in Japan. It was basically a delusional "gentleman's agreement."

Now President Truman had to decide: let Korea fall into communist hands or defend the fledgling democracy at the cost of American and Allied lives and help them equally as they had Japan in rising from the ashes? If you know anything about the rise of Communism after WW2, you can see why Truman's response was so quick and decisive—the Communists were a growing plague that needed to be stopped. This was precisely why Father Kapaun felt the call to rejoin the army in 1948—the Communists were worse than Hitler. Despite only $110 million in aid promised to South Korea a short while before the invasion, President Truman made perfect use of the recently formed and untested United Nations—he drew a moral line in the sand and called for all nations to defend South Korea for their "collective security." Whether our soldiers who answered the call knew it or not, they may have not known where Korea was on a globe, but they felt the evil fires of WW2 were not all put out and they'll be damned let any Communists threaten others liberty and "the free way of life."

Men from many different backgrounds either joined up or received orders to report for embarkation to Japan—then Korea. By war's end, many of them would share something remarkable—they were all moved, touched, inspired or saved by Chaplain Emil Kapaun.

SERGEANT BILL RICHARDSON
3rd BATTALION, 8th REG, 1st CAV DIVISION

On June 25, 1950, Bill Richardson was home on leave at his mother's house in Philadelphia after spending four years in Europe at the end of World War II. Over the radio, they heard the news that the Reds had invaded South Korea. Soon after, he received the call to start training recruits at Ft. Devens, Massachusetts—the same fort Kapaun had trained at. During his first few days with the company, he realized why he was put in a senior position—the army was hollow, and those that can train men can lead them. After a couple of weeks of training, Richardson and his men were sent to Japan.

JULY 1, 1950—LETTER TO BISHOP CARROLL

Most Reverend and dear Bishop:
We are wondering what the people in the States are think-

ing about this Korean War. This time we are not so unprepared as we were at Pearl Harbor. We have something
to use. Things have been happening very fast in the last
week. It may be all be over very soon, and again this may
be a major conflict. If it is, my men will be right in there
and I will go right in there with them. It would be very
foolish to say that we are not doing anything about this
situation, as surely General MacArthur would not have his
troops unprepared.

The US armed forces in Japan, however, were not nearly so
impressive. Following the end of World War II, America's military had been cut to the bone. In 1945, the United States had
spent $50 billion on its army; in 1950 it spent $5 billion. In 1945,
there were 8,250,000 men on active service; in 1950, there were
less than six hundred thousand. The American people, gripped
by peacetime euphoria and anxious to "get the boys home"
quickly, had not complained.

LIEUTENANT RICHARD E. MACK
5th REGIMENT, 1st CAVALRY DIVISION

About the time Chaplain Kapaun departs for Korea on a troopship (July 14), a career army lieutenant, Richard E. Mack from
Akron, Ohio, arrives in Japan to join the 1st Cavalry Division
in preparing his men for combat in Korea. Though he did not
see action in World War II, his training as a tank destroyer and
an infantry platoon leader would prove quite useful in fighting the disciplined North Korean Army. Mack reflects on the
readiness of the 1st Cavalry Division:

"American divisions were being committed with extremely
low percentages of their authorized strengths; with shortages in
weapons and ammunition, particularly artillery, as well as of field
gear and rations; and equipped with only light tanks. The lack
of readiness was apparent as we prepared to depart Camp Drake

during the first week of August 1950. I can remember being issued an M-1 'single-shot' carbine and two rusty ten-round ammunition clips. I asked if I could have an M-1 rifle—a five hundred-yard-range, hard-hitting weapon—to exchange with a rifleman in my new platoon, since it was known that many riflemen were being armed with only the smaller carbine version, which had a shorter effective range. I didn't get one. There were also no first aid packs; 'I could get one along the line.' There were no compasses available; again, 'Get one along the line.'[9]

It was easy for many historians and reporters to characterize the occupation soldiers of the US Eighth Army in Japan as naïve, ill-trained, drunken skirt-chasers on "guard duty" in 1950—ill-prepared for combat. Perhaps that could be argued in the early days of the Korean War but it quickly became the exception and not the rule. These soldiers were the product of their training and leadership which set the missions and policy of the army in Japan. Leadership qualities are the hallmark of what it means to be an officer in the armed forces and their commanding general, Douglas MacArthur, was one of the most storied leaders in history. So perhaps these young servicemen were not at a satisfactory level for combat, but because of leaders like Chaplain (Captain) Kapaun, that was about to change. In his next letter home to mom and dad he displays hardened honest confidence that they will prevail.

"RUSSIA IS GOING TO GET IT IN THE NECK" KAPAUN WRITES HOME—JULY 3, 1950

Dear Dad and Mom, I do not know what kind of news you have been hearing about this war scare. But things did happen in a hurry, and this time we feel very proud of being prepared for anything. This time Russia is going to get it in the neck. The Japanese were wondering what we would do if Russia ever would start coming this way. They know

now, and they think a great deal of us for calling Russia's
bluff and going to stop her grabbing. As soon as the Russians
started coming into Korea, we were alerted. You should
have seen how quickly we got on our toes. All of Japan
went into action and we were ready for anything. Some of
my soldiers have already gone. Every unit is ready to act. I
give General MacArthur credit for the way he does things.
He not only did a good job in Japan, but he has kept his
army prepared. The soldiers in our outfits are well trained
and they are anxious to give the Russians a good licking.

I hope you are not worrying about me. I am getting
along fine. We are not as excited over here as some of the
people in the States. Everything is peaceful around here. It
hardly seems like war. The fighting is taking place about
600 miles from where we are.

A week later, his unit had considerably narrowed the distance
of six hundred miles. Father Kapaun and "his boys" were on the
way to Korea. It is understandable why Chaplain Kapaun was
so confident—he saw what the army could do in the CBI theater, and the defeat of two major armies as far from the homeland as possible. He had as much sheer confidence in the army
and General MacArthur as he did in his own beliefs and convictions. He practiced what he preached. Kapaun's last reading
on the Armed Forces Network was this Easter Service delivered
on April 22. Perhaps truer words were never spoken. But exactly one year later, on Easter Sunday 1951, suffering tremendous
persecution at the entrance to the Kingdom of Heaven—Father
Kapaun will deliver perhaps the greatest, most profound Easter
sermon ever in the history of war, in the history of faith, in the
history of mankind—and then be called home:

In this present time of year we are in the holy season of
Easter. Just last week was Easter Week. It was on the first

Easter Sunday that our Risen Lord appeared to His apostles and said to them: "Peace be to you." He repeated it again: "Peace be to you. As the Father has sent me, I also send you." Christ had been the bearer of peace. It was through His death on the cross that He obtained forgiveness for men and brought true peace between them and God. Now Christ was sending His apostles also as bearers of this same precious peace.

Before Christ died on the cross, he had His apostles gathered about Him one day, and He said to them: "Peace I leave with you, My peace I give You: Not as the world gives do I give to you. Do not let your heart be troubled or be afraid." The peace which God gives to people is different from the peace known by the world. The world regards peace as freedom from suffering, freedom from worry and care, freedom from want, freedom from fighting. In a way it is sort of a negative thing. But the peace which God gives is a gift which exists even in suffering in want, or even in time of war. The saints who were friends of God had peace of conscience even when they were persecuted, even when they had to suffer many outrages, and some of them even had to part with their lives.

Christ had said: "Blessed are the peacemakers for they shall be called the children of God." People who try to promote peace and love among their fellow men are peace makers in the true sense of the word. And the people who try to bring the peace of God to souls are peacemakers of a higher order.

Christian people who try to practice their faith and remain true to it found themselves persecuted and ostracized by people opposed to the Christian Faith. We can surely expect that in our own lives there will come a time when we must make a choice between being loyal to the true Faith, or, of giving allegiance to something else which is either opposed to or not in alliance with our faith. O God, we ask of Thee to give us the courage to be ever faithful to Thee. Blessed are they who suffer persecution for Justices' sake, for theirs is the Kingdom of Heaven. May the blessing of God, the Father, the Son, and the Holy Spirit, descend upon all of you. Amen.

7

THE PUSAN PERIMETER

Located at the southeastern tip of the Korean peninsula, the city of Pusan was South Korea's busiest port. The North Korean Army was advancing so rapidly many South Korean refugees had no choice but to immediately flee south and prepare a hasty defense or hope to be evacuated. The North Korean People's Army closed in on Pusan rapidly, but they encountered a sort of "natural barrier" that bought enough time for the newly arriving troops and equipment to at least maintain a steadfast defense. This became known as the Pusan Perimeter, with the western barrier formed by the Naktong River that extended roughly a hundred miles north to south. Many of the bridges were immediately rigged with explosives and blown when necessary to keep the advanced Soviet-made T-34 tanks from crossing. The northern line of the perimeter went about fifty miles east to west along very rugged mountains. The story of the Korean War is who controls the ridges and hilltops of so many low-lying mountain ranges. Valleys were a killer if you didn't control the high ground.

With a vast navy and air superiority, the 8th Army was well protected, bringing in tons of supplies daily, forty thousand troops, and ten thousand vehicles in July alone. The troops were rushed to the perimeter but immediately faced a fierce fight from dug-in enemy troops that outnumbered them as much as ten to one and were scattered all over, mostly attacking at night.

General MacArthur flew into Pusan on June 29 when the situation was looking dire. Korean refugees were flooding in along with wounded ROK soldiers. North Korean massacres of civilians were witnessed frequently. MacArthur focused on the enemy strengths and weaknesses that he was hearing about. In perhaps one of MacArthur's greatest battlefield strategies ever, he surmised that the rate of men and equipment and heavy weaponry would stall and eventually halt the North Korean advance. Then he would simply cut the North Korean supply line completely off like a spigot and then squeeze them like a vise. But his plan needed time. He had to assemble as big an armada as the Marine Corps could muster to make a surprise landing on the other coast, three hundred miles farther north at the 38th parallel. MacArthur sent a dispatch to Washington urging the commitment of tens of thousands more soldiers and Marines.

"The Pusan Perimeter, a thin line of weary South Koreans and Americans, was established during the first week of August 1950 to hold off the North Koreans People's Army until enough troops could arrive and organize a counteroffensive. The perimeter's western barrier was formed mostly by the Naktong River which extended about 100 miles north to south, and the Sea of Japan formed the eastern boundary. The northern boundary followed a jagged line of mountains north of the city about 50 miles east to west, and was anchored on the port city of Pusan. Without a seaport with the capacity of Pusan, it is doubtful that the ROK (Republic of Korea) and the Eighth Army could have been supported logistically."[1] Between July

1 and 31, 1950, over 10,500 tons was coming into port daily along with over forty thousand troops and nearly ten thousand vehicles. The North Koreans were closing in fast.

TASK FORCE SMITH

But before enacting such a bold plan, MacArthur needed to establish an American presence quickly and delay the enemy advance. He ordered Lieutenant General Walton H. Walker to dispatch a battalion combat team to Korea immediately. But with no such combat team ready, one had to be cobbled together, and the mission fell to thirty-four-year-old Lieutenant Colonel Brad Smith to get to Pusan and head for Taejon and block the main road as far north as possible. The seventy-five mile trip took five hours over bad roads. When they arrived, General William Dean issued LTC Smith this order:

"When you get to Pusan, head for Taejon. We want to stop the North Koreans as far from Pusan as we can. Block the main road as far north as possible. Contact General Church. If you can't locate him, go to Taejon and beyond if you can. Sorry I can't give you more information. That's all I got. Good luck to you and God bless you and your men."[2]

When the airlifted force of only 406 men landed and saw trainloads of South Korean casualties pouring in from the front, someone exclaimed, "My God. Maybe there's a real war on!" Task Force Smith was sent a couple hundred miles north of the Pusan Perimeter to Osan, South Korea, where the NKPA blitzkrieg was in full force. Without reserves and adequate weaponry, they were about to be mowed over.

IN THIS WORLD THERE ARE TIGERS

In a clumsy but effective press conference, President Truman flat-out refused to use the term "war" to settle matters in Korea. Not wanting to invoke any prospect of officially declaring war to a war-weary nation, he got his way through the United Nations by declaring it a "police action" to repel the North Koreans who he described as "a bunch of bandits." In this way, Truman did not ask, nor receive, an official declaration of war from Congress.

"It didn't take long before nervous American GIs made fun of the term "police action" with grim irony. "If I'm a policeman, where the hell's my badge?" And, "Damn, these crooks over here got big guns!" None of them had been told why they were in Korea, or why the United States was fighting North Korean Communists. None of them cared. They wanted only to get back to Japan. Instead, they were heading for the Naktong River Line, there to make a final stand. They would realize their government had no intention of withdrawing them; if they wanted to live, they would have to fight. They were learning, in the hardest school there was, that it is a soldier's lot to suffer and that his destiny may be to die. They were learning something they had not been told: that in this world there are tigers."[3]

FIRST AMERICAN KILLED

"In the morning hours of 5 July 1950, the antagonism of the world-adversaries came to a head near Osan, South Korea. Soviet-supported North Korean troops met face to face with US soldiers—the first contingent of a United Nations' force. Shortly after 0800, as the surrounding hills trembled with the roar of battle, the first American fell dead. All Task Force Smith's anti-tank weaponry literally would bounce off the thick armor of the T-34 tanks—and they simply rolled on. Smith was further destined for defeat when he was told that overcast skies grounded the effective fighter plane air support so desperately needed. When Smith finally withdrew, nearly 40 percent of his men were killed, wounded or captured, and, of the latter, about 34 later died in North Korean prison camps. The gallant men of Task Force Smith had paid a terrible price, but they would never be forgotten. They did delay the enemy, which allowed the larger forces to ready and organize, and have a safe and secure beachhead to land on."[4]

One of those brave men was Lieutenant William Funchess and two battalions of ill-equipped troops of the 19th Infantry, 24th Division, who were sent to set up defensive positions along a wide front and keep the North Koreans from crossing the Kum River north of Taejon. Funchess led a platoon of fifty men, and they dug into a riverbank to prevent the enemy from crossing the river. Army engineers blew up one of the main bridges as they waited. They wouldn't be waiting long.

Combat medic Sergeant Bailey Gillespie, 27th Infantry, recalls a shocking detail from the early days of the war: "Even though we were medical personnel we had to carry weapons for our own protection. The North Koreans hadn't signed the Geneva Convention and would not abide by its rules. [That night] we lost our first casualties. Some linemen at Andong were caught in a sharp curve and the North Koreans ambushed them and cut their heads off with the ax from their own jeep. That sort of set the standard from that time on how we were going to fight—hard and all out."[5]

CORPORAL THERMAN COSSAIRT, JR.

"I landed in Pusan off an LST [Landing Ship, Tank] on July 7 as a replacement for a 155mm howitzer battery. It was all very different to me because my last unit had been a heavy mortar company. I figured I was only going to be in Korea for two weeks or so, so what the hell! There were railroad flatcars waiting to take us north to Taejon. On the way, as we passed through tunnels, cinders from a coal-burning engine flew into our eyes.

There were young Korean boys standing guard at all the bridges and stations. Someone pointed out they were only armed with wooden rifles. Right then, most of us began to wonder what we were getting into."[6]

"NO, I BELIEVE I'LL WALK"

On the morning of July 16, Lt. William Funchess and his men heard enemy tanks rumbling across the river. The tanks stopped at a destroyed bridge, fanned out, and began firing at William's position with powerful 76mm rounds. A desperate battle ensued and William was not only losing his men but realizing they were taking enemy mortar fire from *behind* their position along the river while enemy tank rounds were hitting them from the front and sides. They were forced to retreat over a rice paddy and had no time to rest before the enemy troops that outflanked them attacked them again, forcing William's company to scatter all over. He ended up in a ditch. What happened next is incredible:

"I heard the distinctive rumbling noise of a tank again. I looked to see if it was ours or theirs. I saw the white star so I knew it was ours. I stayed down until the tank was about 20 feet

Sergeant O.J. Mixon (left) with Lieutenant William Funchess, 19th Infantry, on a phone in their dugout just after army engineers blew up a bridge over the Kum River. A couple of days after this photo was taken, they were overrun by North Korean soldiers on July 16, 1950.

away. I jumped on the edge of the narrow dirt road. I was holding my rifle with the scope in one hand, and frantically waved the rifle to stop the tank. Instead of stopping, the tank spun in my direction and tried to run me over! There was no place for me to go except on top of the tank. I jumped on a track but lost my rifle and I was able to scramble to the top of the tank and began shouting, 'Open up! Let me in!'

Enemy bullets were ricocheting off the tank and I heard someone inside shout, 'That's a GI! Let him in!'

The tank hatch flew open and I went in head first. Those dirty tankers inside were the most beautiful people I had ever seen. The tank commander said there was no place in his tank for an extra person, and I would have to crouch on the floor above the engine and below the 75-mm gun. I said, 'Okay. Let's go!'

We had gone less than a half mile when we were stopped by burning US army vehicles in the road ahead. The tank commander told me there was no way to get through the burning roadblock. He wanted to burn the tank and then try to escape cross-country. I told him I was completely exhausted and couldn't make it cross-country. I suggested he fire everything he had into the roadblock and then attempt to crash through with the tank. He agreed."

The tank fired on a roadblock as they rammed through at full speed. After traveling a few minutes, the tank stopped, and when William got out, he realized they were at a forward headquarters camp with at least a hundred soldiers around them. To William's amazement, none other than General William Dean walked right up to Funchess and the crew and ordered the tank back to the front. When they explained that they had no ammunition left, Dean answered sharply, 'I want that tank to go back and give moral support to the GIs.'

The tank commander asked Funchess if he wanted to go back with them in the tank. [He replied:]

"No, I believe I'll walk."[7]

"MASS MUST BE SAID WITHIN
THE SOUND OF THE CANNON"

"Boston's Roman Catholic Archbishop, Richard J. Cushing, typical of denominational leaders who strongly encouraged their clergy to volunteer, declared: 'Mass must be said within the sound of the cannon. From now on, our priests will have less freedom and more work and can no longer afford to be spiritual millionaires while our men are dying in Korea.' Whether nobly concerned for American soldiers or unwillingly recalled to active duty, however, few chaplains had a real desire to be in another war—especially one which, at least in the beginning, appeared so hopeless. 'When we were getting the pants knocked off us and we got down to that Pusan Perimeter,' said Reiss, 'nobody wanted to go to Korea!'"[8]

During the Korean War, a line of US soldiers file past a group of Korean women and children carrying their possessions southward.

★ ★ ★

"General Dean did his best to slow the Communist advance while other US and UN forces were being readied for shipment to Korea. He sent one unit after another to meet the enemy in their persistent drive south. 'Dean's Delay,' it was called, was nearly suicidal. Every effort was met by seemingly endless streams of the NKPA. One of the first heavy battles raged for 5 days (16-20 July 1950) near Taejon and the Kum River. Among the men involved were those of the 19th Infantry Regiment, 24th Division. Herman G. Felhoelter, Roman Catholic, was one of their chaplains. He had written his mother 4 days earlier:

> Don't worry, Mother. God's will be done. I feel so good to know the power of your prayers accompanying me. I am not comfortable in Korea (that is impossible here) but I am happy in the thought that I can help some souls who need help. Keep your prayers going upward...

Chaplain Felhoelter was just north of Taejon on 16 July, making his way up a hill across the Kum River with roughly 160 men. They were carrying nearly 30 wounded while attempting to escape the enemy force that overpowered them. Felhoelter, who had been in the army from 1944 to 1946 and returned in 1948, was now in the unenviable home of a military congregation—the battlefield. The Korean conflict contained those physical and psychological stresses of every war—deafening noise, rampant confusion, overwhelming fear and fatigue, and indescribable carnage. But there also were the inexplicable acts of self-sacrifice by common men who sought no special recognition or personal honor. By the time Felhoelter's group reached the top of the hill, it was obvious they could not continue carrying the injured and still escape the advancing North Koreans. The chaplain convinced a medical officer to leave with the others while he remained behind with the wounded. Several minutes later from a distance, a sergeant turned and stared through binoculars at the pitiful group they had left behind. He watched in unbelief as enemy soldiers overcame the suffering men and murdered them all—including the chaplain praying over them. The next day would have been Herman Felhoelter's 37th birthday. Posthumously he was awarded the Distinguished Service Cross."[9]

Less than two weeks after American soldiers entered the fight, and just two days away from the arrival of Father Kapaun and the cavalry, the first Army chaplain had already been killed in action.

8

TOMORROW WE ARE GOING INTO COMBAT

"Fear can be described as the shrinking back of the mind from impending danger, or, more precisely, as the agitation of the mind brought by apprehension of impending danger. Finding himself in the Japanese straits of the Pacific Ocean in a large convoy protected by submarines and navy destroyers, was enough to awaken all sorts of thoughts in the mind of Father Kapaun. Only a moron, who cannot realize the existence of danger, is free from fear. The normal reaction of an intelligent person is to feel his mind shrinking back from impending danger, and Father Kapaun was definitely no exception. He was only 34 years of age, in full possession of all his physical, intellectual, and moral strength, and it was only natural for him to anticipate the possibility of an early death with mixed emotions."[1]

In Japan, Father Kapaun was close enough to observe these drastic developments. He was a military chaplain, not of an occupational unit, but of an actual combat unit that had to be ready for any eventuality, and by July 10, 1950, he found himself on

First Cavalry Division soldiers departing Japan on a troopship bound for the southern tip of Korea, July 1950.

one of many transport ships taking American units from Japan to Korea. He writes to Bishop Carroll:

> Tomorrow we are going into combat. I have everything in order, all Mass Stipends, my will, etc. The way the Catholic soldiers are rallying around the priest, is edifying.

To his Aunt Tena, Kapaun writes,

> This letter is being written on an LST [Landing Ship Tank-troop transport boat] in the middle of the ocean, in a large convoy. We have two submarines for protection, the Marines are to come in with us, the Navy will bombard the coast and the Air Corps will bomb the beach so we can make a landing in Korea. This is a big invasion and we are right in the middle of it.
>
> You should see all the ships out here in the ocean loaded with soldiers and equipment. We are expecting plenty of

resistance from the Russians. We are well trained. All our trucks and jeeps are equipped for a beach landing. We have two Navy destroyers also. It hardly seems possible that we are actually going to war. I hope we will be strong enough to put the Russians in their place.

"For most Army chaplains it would mean an all-too-soon end to the relative comfort of garrison duty and the parish-like ministries in occupation zones or the United States. Again the altar would be the hood of a jeep, a jagged stump, or an ammunition crate; the pews would be sand bags or the simple bare ground. The faces in the congregations would be dirty, weary, fear-filled—many of the chaplains' young charges would die in their arms before they could even learn their names. The well-planned services and intricate counselings would give way to whatever hope and comfort could be gleaned from Holy Writ at the spur of the moment. All this because the philosophy chaplains had warned about in citizenship lectures had suddenly become a living enemy on a battlefield, testing the strength of their spiritual muscles."[2]

KAPAUN WRITES HELEN AND EUGENE

Dear Helen and Eugene, I hope you people are well. How do you like your new home? I am just fine and so are my soldiers. We are on an LST now, just one of a large invasion force. It sure looks impressive to see so many ships loaded with soldiers and equipment. The Marines, Navy, Air Corps, Submarines and our soldiers are in this. We just wonder what will happen once we reach our destination. This will be my first beach landing. Our LST will return and take the mail with it. You may not receive this for some time. Here everything seems to be in order and we all are under a tension wondering just what will happen. We hear the news over the radio from the States so you know as much as we do. You will probably hear about us once we reach our destination.

Please do not worry about us, but please remember us in your prayers.

Wishing you God's blessings. As ever in Christ Fr. E. K.

THE 1st CAVALRY DIVISION LANDS IN KOREA

On July 18, 1950, troop ships carrying ten thousand men from the 1st Cavalry Division and two thousand vehicles landed at P'ohang-dong, a fishing village about thirty miles above the port city of Pusan. Because of the sacrificial delaying tactics of Task Force Smith, the North Korean People's Army was prevented from reaching the coast at the southern tip of the peninsula, thus allowing a safe amphibious landing for the division. But ready and waiting for them was an enemy force over eight times their size, just about twenty-five miles inland, and they were well-trained and highly disciplined. The First Cav was undermanned and many hastily trained before being thrown into the breach. Many experienced World War II combat veterans were among the non-commissioned officers, but experienced leaders were lacking. For Chaplain Kapaun, this was nothing like his service in the CBI Theater. This time, he would display leadership that few others could ever muster.

With Chaplain Kapaun on the ship was a young private from Houston named Joe E. Ramirez. Ramirez graduated from Sam Houston High School in January 1950, and at eighteen, he wanted to "see the world," so he joined the army three days later and took basic training at Fort Riley, Kansas, from January to May. By June, he was assigned to Easy Company, 8th Cavalry, in Japan—training as a sniper. When Joe met his chaplain, he told him that he did not want to die in battle forsaken by God.

"I may not be good, Father...but I pray."

Kapaun asked him if he had been baptized. Joe replied that

he had not. Soon after the LSTs landed, Chaplain Kapaun led several soldiers, including Private Joe Ramirez, to an estuary flowing into the Sea of Japan and baptized them in the name of the Father, and of the Son, and of the Holy Spirit. The pouring of the water was done with the chaplain's M1 army-issue helmet, on which he painted a bold white cross front and center.

On the same boat was a sharpshooter and machine gunner named Tibor Rubin. In 1944, Hungarian teenager Rubin was captured by the Nazis and sent to the notorious Mauthausen concentration camp and endured its horrors for more than a year. After being liberated by Patton's army, Rubin was so grateful to the United States that he became obsessed with serving in their army. He found a way to immigrate to America where he arrived penniless and barely spoke English. When war broke out in Korea, he was offered a discharge because he was not officially an American. He refused and was sent to Okinawa for training. Keeping to himself, following orders, and doing his job, it was perhaps fate that would land Tibor a close friendship with the "cowboy priest" from Kansas who treated everyone with respect—Emil Kapaun.

US ARMY

Corporal Tibor Rubin army photo taken in 1950 before he volunteered to fight in Korea. Only two Medals of Honor were awarded for action in the Battle of Unsan: 1st Cavalry members Rubin and Kapaun, who were friends. Rubin is the only Holocaust survivor awarded the Medal of Honor.

US ARMY

Father Kapaun grins while holding up the pipe that was shot out of his mouth by a sniper's bullet as if to say "You missed me." He wrapped the broken stem with medical tape and kept on smoking from it all the way until his demise in POW Camp 5, Pyoktong, North Korea. Picture was taken most likely somewhere between Pusan and Pyongyang during the fall of 1950.

CAPTAIN (DR.) JEROME DOLAN,
1st BATTALION SURGEON, 8th REGIMENT

"I first met Father Kapaun on July 18, 1950, when our LSTs unloaded at Pohang-dong on the east coast of Korea. I believe he was with the other 8th Cavalry Chaplains, Chaplain Carter and Chaplain Mills. There was nothing then that would give you a hint of the greatness within this man. He was slight build and his voice was somewhat high, but he did have a wonderful smile—and he had a pipe. His pipe was Father Kapaun's inseparable companion, even in the thick of battle. A minor casualty occurred when the bullet of a North Korean sniper demolished the stem of his favorite briar. He quit smoking only long enough to whittle another stem from bamboo. In another battle, his pipe was again knocked out of his mouth. A memorable International News photo showed Kapaun holding his broken pipe, patched by medic's tape, grinning cheerfully as if to say, 'you missed me.' Like fish tales, stories of how many times Father Kapaun's beloved pipe was shot out of his mouth grew and grew...a sniper's bullet, a machine gunner spraying him with lead, a mortar round exploding..."[3]

THE 1ST CAVALRY DIVISION ENTERS THE FIGHT

On July 22, detachments of the 8th Cavalry relieved the 21st Infantry Regiment at Yongdong and the horrors of war began in earnest. Superior numbers of North Korean troops attacked along the main highway where US army convoys were vulnerable. Making matters worse, scores of South Korean civilians fleeing to Pusan were used as human shields for the North Korean assault, including hundreds forced to run through Ameri-

EVERETT COLLECTION/
BRIDGEMAN IMAGES

US combat engineers return fire against North Korean snipers after the Battle of Yongdong, July 31, 1950.

can mine fields to clear a path for the enemy. The brutality and sheer number of atrocities being committed by the communists shocked everyone, even combat veterans from World War II. Within hours, the 8th Cav was forced into retreat and the 1st Cav Division started its first cemetery for the interment of casualties.

"From the opening onslaught Kapaun established a reputation for courage and concern for the wellbeing of his men. He showed up wherever the soldiers needed reassurance or religious services. If a lull on the battlefield allowed time for a Mass he said one on a makeshift altar, sometimes just a litter placed atop a pair of ammunition boxes."[4]

RETREAT

American Forces had to withdraw from Taejon and retreat about four miles. Over two weeks of brutal sustained combat had cost the 1st Cavalry and 24th Divisions over 1,000 men just in the last days of July 1950. They had been overrun so often the number of Missing in Action was at least 500, with 1000 wounded and many more suffering heat exhaustion and battle fatigue. Overall, American losses were over 7,800. The amount of enemy soldiers charging them at all hours must have seemed never-ending. The army estimated enemy killed as between 40,000 and as high as 58,000 during the same time period. Just in 1950, it is estimated that about 200,000 Korean civilians had been killed.

"US Forces withdrew from Taejon at midnight and retreated to a position four miles southeast of the city. 17 days of sustained, bitter combat had cost the 24th Division nearly 30 percent of its personnel, of which an unusually high portion had been officers. More than 2,400 of its men had been reported missing in action. Relentless North Korean pressure had driven it back 100 miles from where Task Force Smith first faced the enemy north of Osan.

The 1st Cavalry and 24th Divisions together suffered over 158

KIA, 993 WIA, 471 MIA, and several hundred non-battle casualties. 24th Division lost nearly half its men. It is safe to say that each division lost over 1,000 men during the last 10 days of July 1950. Total American losses, from all causes, were over 7,800. North Korean losses are difficult to assess with the army estimating enemy killed between 35,000 and 58,000 during the same time period. North and South Korean civilians suffered the most with about 200,000 killed just in 1950. By 1953 that number was well over 600,000—about 10% of the total Korean population.

By July 22 the 1st Cavalry Division was in a blocking position across the main Taejon-Taegu corridor, with the 5th Cav traveled as far as Yongdong. Here the regiment got into its first firefight. The most common remark from the rifle company about enemy casualties was, 'We stacked them up like cordwood, but they still kept coming.'"[5]

CHIEF WARRANT OFFICER DOUGLAS HALL
29th REGIMENTAL COMBAT TEAM (RCT)

"This man gave his all to the troops. When we were down and needed an uplift, you could look up and see none other than Father Kapaun. We'd be in the midst of a firefight, they'd be shooting everything up, and he'd come walking down the road like he was in some big city. I said, 'You've got to watch yourself.' And he answered, 'They can't hurt me because I've got God's armor on.' Imagine, he had that much faith! He called us 'his boys,' even though a lot of the guys were older than he was—I was only seventeen at that time. He used to bring us a handful of oranges or a little packet of mail, or just come by to see us. You'd write a letter, he'd mail it—little things that don't mean much but really they do. It gave us a morale boost. It didn't matter what religion you were, he was for everyone. Father was always giving, giving, giving and not worrying about receiving anything back. It's hard to put into words how it affected you to be in his pres-

ence. I think of him all the time. How many people that you
know would lay their life on the line for a half dozen oranges?"[6]

"The bloody battle for Taejon ended on 20 July with North
Korean forces attacking the 24th Division on three sides and in-
vading the city. With General Dean captured, his division was
eventually relieved by the arriving 25th Infantry and 1st Cavalry Divisions. A few days later, the 24th, supplemented with
raw recruits and commanded by General Church, moved to
the southwest to meet a sweeping move along the coast by an
NKA division.

During the fighting south of Taejon and along the southwest
perimeter, Chaplains Carrol G. Chaphe, Methodist, and Edward
S. Dorsey, Roman Catholic, were cut off from their units—a
harrowing experience endured by many chaplains during the
course of the war. It took Chaphe three days and Dorsey four
days to get back to friendly ground. Chaplain Chaphe, a veteran of World War II, was wounded during one battle. 'We were
slapped by one wing of the Red drive on Chinju,' he said from
his hospital bed in Tokyo. 'Our casualties were heavier than the
medics could handle, but they kept working and I gave them a
hand... A light mortar dropped in ten feet from me, and they're
still picking out the metal. When the medics repair this leg I'm
going right back to those boys.'

Also wounded was Chaplain Arthur E. Mills, Advent Christian, with the 8th Regiment of the 1st Cavalry Division. He
had overheard the remark of an officer that a group of wounded
might have to be abandoned on the field as the unit withdrew
from a heavy assault. Mills, who had served in World War II,
quickly responded: 'This is the way we did it in the last war!' He
jumped into a jeep and sped off under enemy fire. Despite the
fact that he too was hit, Chaplain Mills returned with a jeep-
load of men. Besides the Purple Heart, he was awarded the Silver Star—his second for combat bravery."[7]

This left Kapaun as the only able-bodied chaplain in the 8th Regiment. Chaplain Mills states, "Father was with me constantly until the last of July, 1950. He had gone to another battalion to visit the men, and when he heard that I had been seriously wounded he walked several miles to give any assistance he could render. I've never known a braver man, a more devoted Christian leader, a more sympathetic listener or a better friend... I've prayed that he would be spared, but God rewarded him in a greater way... Thank you for giving us your son... He is a hero, a Saint if anyone ever was."[8]

The dangers of going to the aid of a wounded, immobile comrade in enemy territory cannot be overstated. An unarmed noncombatant heeding the call magnifies the bravery more than can be measured. It is quite simply above and beyond the call of duty. Corporal Lacy Barnett, a medic with the 34th Infantry, recalls, "Many of our company aidmen instantly became battle casualties. They were nice guys and had good intentions, but in a combat situation these men were losers. Many aidmen were killed or wounded as soon as their platoon became engaged in a firefight. A rifleman on his left would be hit and he would crawl to the man and render first aid. Before he was finished another man would go down, then another. They'd begin to yell, 'Medic!' Instead of crawling to these men, the excited aidman would jump up and attempt to run to the next wounded man. It was then that he, too, would be hit by rifle fire or a shell burst. The man's desire to act quickly must be admired from a humanitarian standpoint, but from a military point of view, the aidman was now either dead or wounded. Three down instead of two, and no one to treat anyone else. It was a tragic situation which occurred with depressing frequency."[9]

PRIVATE SCHULER WOUNDED

Only two days in the combat zone and the North Koreans hammered the fresh 1st Cavalry troops hard and sent them on the run. On July 24, Father Kapaun's jeep and trailer was destroyed by mortar fire along with his field equipment and Mass kit. While dodging machine gun fire, his assistant, Patrick Schuler, took a bullet to his knee but still managed to escape to the aid station. He was then sent to Japan for surgery and did not return to action until August 29. Father Kapaun delayed sending his monthly report for July until August 14 due to "the urgencies of active combat."

"The destruction of Kapaun's kit for saying Mass and the loss of his records did not dishearten him. He arranged for the army to ship replacements from Japan. After shrapnel hit the second Mass kit and Kapaun decided that it could not be salvaged, Korean priests furnished still another set."[10]

Without a jeep and his assistant, the undeterred chaplain put the Mass kit in a typewriter case and carried it in his field jacket. He procured a bicycle and rode it up and down the mountainous terrain tirelessly to visit the battalions and companies of the 1st Cavalry Division. The bike's tires appeared to have gone flat on several occasions as the chaplain was often seen pushing it.

"During this time, another chaplain who had also served in World War II was not so lucky. Chaplain Byron D. Lee, Nazarene, was with the 35th Reg, 25th Div, as they attempted to stop a communist drive near Sangju on July 25th. As his regiment pulled back from an assault on Hamch'ang, enemy planes strafed the scattering soldiers and Lee was killed. Just about three days into combat and already the second Army chaplain had been killed in action."[11]

JULY 29, 1950—GENERAL WALTON WALKER ISSUES STAND OR DIE ORDER

"We are fighting a battle against time. There will be no retreating, withdrawal, or readjustment of the lines or any other term you chose. There will be no more retreat. There will be no line behind us to which we can retreat. Every unit must counterat-tack to keep the enemy in a state of confusion and off balance. There will be no Dunkirk, there will be no Bataan, a retreat to Pusan would be one of the greatest butcheries in history. We must fight until the end. Capture by these people is worse than death itself. We will fight as a team. If some of us must die, we will die fighting together. Any man who gives ground may be personally responsible for the death of thousands of his com-rades. I want you to put this out to all the men in the division. I want everybody to understand that we are going to hold the line. We are going to win."

EMIL WRITES HIS BROTHER

Dear Eugene and Helen, We had no envelopes so I am en-closing this in the letter to Dad and Mom. Up here in the front lines I have very little chance to write. Some of our soldiers got wounded. A few dead. We killed thousands of the Communists. And after we have to run because they outnumber us so badly. I hope this will be over before long. I am glad that you have a nice place of your own now. Someday with God's help I may see your happy home. Right now my home is a fox hole with heavy artillery shells bursting all around. What a life. Please pray for us.

EXTREME UNCTION

One of the fundamental tasks of a chaplain—especially a Cath-olic one—was administering the Sacrament of Last Rites to the dead and dying. It is also known as "extreme unction" or "Anointing of the Sick," given to those who are gravely ill, espe-cially one in danger of death from bodily illness or from violence already done to the body. In Catholic faith, the effects of the Sacrament are the strengthening and comfort of the soul of the anointed one, the remission of sins and some of their temporal punishments, and the possible restoration of bodily health. The rite begins with a confession or an act of contrition. The dying repeats their baptismal promises or says the Apostles' Creed. The priest anoints the forehead with consecrated oil and says in Latin the words "By this holy anointing may the Lord forgive you whatever wrong you have done." The priest or chaplain recites the Our Father Prayer, and communion is administered. The priest says, "This is the Lamb of God who takes away the sins of the world. Happy are those who are called to his supper." The dying recites, "Lord, I am not worthy to receive you, but only say the word and I shall be healed."

"The body of Christ. Amen." After the dying receives communion, the priest says, "May the Lord Jesus protect you and lead you to eternal life."

CATHOLIC PRAYER FOR THE DEAD

"Eternal rest grant unto him, O Lord, and let perpetual light shine upon him. May he rest in peace. Love always, in the name of Jesus. Amen."

HOMEFRONT

"The Army Chaplaincy was 175 years old on 29 July 1950. Shaken by the gloomy reports from Korea, a crowd of 3,000 gathered in New York City's Central Park to attend a special ceremony for the occasion. Following musical tributes, the main speaker, Bernard M. Baruch, extolled the clergymen in uniform. 'Although few monuments have been dedicated to the corps,' he said, 'its brave men have left their own monument in courage on the battlefield.' Referring to Chaplain Felhoelter's death, he added: 'War brings out all the harshest forms of materialism, yet incidents like this prove that men in war can express the noblest forms of spiritualism.

Despite such laudatory phrases, few of the chaplains thousands of miles away considered themselves heroic. Human as the men they served, their spiritual concerns seemed to grow with the desperateness of the situation. Donald F. Carter, Progressive Brethren, was among the many chaplains in the bleak surroundings of the Pusan Perimeter. He was ministering among the men of the 8th Cavalry Regiment (Infantry), 1st Cavalry Division. "Cooks and clerks were pressed into service as riflemen as the situation became desperate," he remembered. "There was talk that we might be pushed into the sea... Through fear and uncertainty many men talked to me about spiritual things."[12]

REUTERS RUNS STORY OF CHAPLAIN MILLS AND KAPAUN

"Front Line, Korea, July 31. 1950 (Reuters) Chaplain Arthur E. Mills of Santa Ana, Calif., who has been hit four times in a week by Communist bullets and shrapnel while rescuing American wounded under enemy fire was evacuated from the front line here today.

'I was merely doing my job,' he told a reporter, adjusting his spectacles with feeble fingers as he lay in the stretcher. Chaplain Mills, who is married and has an eight-year-old daughter, is not seriously wounded. Before he was put on the hospital train he left his last message with another chaplain:

'The boys need all the New Testaments up there that you can get. They want them. They had their eyes opened a little.'

Major General Hobart Gay, commander of the First Cavalry Division, recommended Chaplain Mills for the Silver Star for rescuing three wounded men north of Yongdong. Mills, an 8th Reg chaplain alongside Kapaun, went back to rescue more wounded when he was struck by bullets and shrapnel and evacuated to an army hospital in Japan.

"I assembled 18 wounded to carry out," he said, "then a mortar shell landed right in the middle of us." He was struck in both legs and an arm by shrapnel. Chaplain Mills, a Northern Baptist, reported: 'Father Emil Kapaun of Kansas is still back there doing a great job. He will look after my boys.'"

"It must have been a great comfort to the parents at home in the United States when their soldiers wrote that their chaplain was right with them in the thick of it. Their chaplain was wearing the same kind of uniform, except that his military insignia was a cross. During the heat of the day, his uniform showed the dirt and sweat as well as theirs. He had to fight off the multitude of mosquitoes and jump out of the way whenever an explosion of shells came too close. He saw his soldiers being killed and severely wounded; he saw some of them crack up, actually going insane. No matter what happened, whether they advanced or were driven back, the chaplain was always there. He had the holy oils always ready to anoint the wounded. His Mass kit was with him, and whenever possible, the back of the jeep served as a temporary altar on which he said Mass for his men. If ever there was a true front-line chaplain, Father Kapaun was one of the best."[13]

9

THE BATTLE OF TAEGU
AUGUST 5–20, 1950

Captain (Doctor) Jerome Dolan was the 1st Battalion surgeon for the 8th Regiment, 1st Cavalry Division. Ideally there would be six battalions in each regiment comprised of about six thousand troops. The 8th Regiment started with four battalions, and after five days of sustained combat, they had less than two with only one battalion aid station taking in the wounded—all while under small arms and mortar fire. The mortar fire was so deadly that Dolan had his medics build a wall of ammunition boxes filled with dirt to protect the patients from shrapnel. Next to them was an artillery battery of howitzers shelling the enemy virtually nonstop. The 8th Regiment had two Protestant chaplains and Father Kapaun, who rotated daily. They visited the companies on the line, but if they had casualties, a chaplain was always on watch in the battalion aid station, and often that chaplain was Father Kapaun. Captain Dolan recalls one remarkable episode:

"Before dusk on the 26th, we began to receive small arms and mortar fire from our rear and from our left flank as well as from the front. We had wounded in the Battalion Aid Station at the time. Father and at least one chaplain's assistant were there. We had the wounded ready for transport but couldn't contact the battalion commander and we were praying for a break in the action to evacuate the wounded when suddenly my truck and jeeps exploded and we were in a dense cloud of burning oil and debris. I found out later that one of our own American tanks had blown our vehicles to give us a smoke screen because the road to our rear was taken and that was the only way out was under the bridge.

As Colonel Kane was getting the battalion reorganized beyond the railroad, one of my medics came to tell me that his platoon leader had been wounded in the leg and had ordered his men to leave him because he would burden them and hurt their chance of getting out. I promptly told the Colonel and he proceeded to command a recon team of two squads to go back and see if they could get the wounded lieutenant. When I turned around, Father Kapaun and his assistant were gone with a litter. When the recon team returned, Father Kapaun and the chaplain's assistant were with them, and they not only had brought out the platoon leader but another wounded man whose buddy had been killed so that no one realized he was missing up to that time. Whether Father Kapaun intended it or not, his courage in that action created a wonderful esprit de corps in that battalion. Despite several days in combat we had taken relatively light casualties and we had good officers, but it took that baptism of fire to show these green troops who had never seen combat before that they could survive this war if they took care of one another. After Yong-dong-ni the rallying cry of the battalion was: 'No matter what mess you get into, 1st Battalion will get you out!' And it was Father Kapaun who led the way while the rest of us were a little slower to react."[1]

Dolan was so moved by the selfless and bold act that he recommended Kapaun for the Bronze Star. Just a few days after braving enemy fire to rescue two wounded men behind enemy lines, Kapaun still hovered around the battalion aid stations, under fire, being useful wherever needed, celebrating Mass, and still thoughtful enough to remember Dr. Dolan's wedding anniversary.

What Chaplain Kapaun and "his boys" were up against was truly astounding. Had they known by how much they were outnumbered, they might have just given up. Five NKPA divisions were massing around the city of Taegu, preparing to cross the Naktong River and wipe out the 1st Cavalry, who were now replacing the decimated 24th Division and the ROK II Corps. It was nearly a suicide mission for the early troops to engage such a fierce and powerful Communist army, but the delay they caused was vital to allow General MacArthur to keep building additional forces in Pusan with countries like Australia, Canada, New Zealand, and the United Kingdom contributing naval ships and later ground troops in support of the UN action. Naval power and American air supremacy over the Pusan Perimeter contributed greatly to blunting the North Korean advance. Lieutenant General Walton Walker was so confident in the 8th Army's ability to hold the Pusan Perimeter that he established Taegu as the 8th Army's headquarters. The days ahead were destined to be brutal and bloody.

Chaplain Kapaun bore witness to nightly attacks by the North Koreans and come daybreak had to face a grim reality—many

American GIs keep watch on a bridge over the Naktong River, August 6, 1950.

of "his boys" were getting killed. In country only two weeks and Kapaun writes this stark letter to his friends, Mr. and Mrs. Fred Schugart in Timken, Kansas:

Received your kind letter of July 26. My hand is not steady as we have gone through a whole lot. We found this paper in a Korean house. I pity the people. They had to run, taking what they could on their backs. The Reds were too strong for us. They kept pushing us back, as we tried to hold off for more help. We have some help now. Maybe we can beat them. I have been on the front lines for eight days. We were machine-gunned, hit by mortars and tanks. Three times we escaped with our lives. The night before last was the first I slept under a roof. The hard floor felt good. I hope that by the time you get this letter the fighting will be over.

Many thanks for your prayers and for the vigil lights. God has been good to me. Others have not been so fortunate. There are many horrors in war. A fellow can stand only so much.

The next day, again, there is more grim news from the front as he writes to his aunt and uncle, John and Tena Maier in Lincolnville, Kansas:

Many thanks for your kind letter. I wrote an answer but the Reds overran us and I could not get it in the mail. We are right in the front lines of fighting. This is the worst and hardest war I have been in yet. Three times now we were overpowered and had to run. They outnumber us about 15-1, coming at us from all sides. But we will win this thing yet.

My, how nice it would be to sleep in a bed. These fox

US ARMY

With his jeep and trailer destroyed by enemy fire, Chaplain Kapaun fixes a bike to make the rounds to "his boys."

holes are anything but comfortable but they feel good when the enemy shells start bursting around us.

During another night of combat, Kapaun was crawling to the front lines to aid a wounded soldier when a rifle bullet struck the stem of his pipe and shattered it. It's unknown if he violated the oldest sniper trick in the book: at night, if you light up a cigarette or pipe on the battlefield, the orange glow will be easily seen and provide a perfect target for snipers. Kapaun is said to have picked up the stub of his pipe and continued puffing.

CAPTAIN WILLIAM "MOOSE" MCCLAIN
EASY COMPANY, 8th REGIMENT

"Even after the rear tire of his two-wheeler went flat, Kapaun still pushed it along a dusty road. He was looking for a pump and grape jelly. He wanted the jelly to put in the tire to stop the leak." McClain, who later would become a POW with Father Kapaun, recalls the chaplain's bravery: "He seemed to appear from nowhere during a combat operation and stay long enough to perform his duties and then disappear. He was never bothered by enemy mortar and small arms fire coming into the vicinity of where he was helping others. He would conduct religious services whenever possible. He expressed no fear of the enemy and stories of his brave deeds of dragging soldiers to safety, tending to their wounds and suffering circulated among the officers and men. How many lives were saved because of him? Only God knows for sure. His exposure to the terrible combat operations was for him, I believe, a dress rehearsal, for what followed."[2]

FATHER KAPAUN AS WRITER, HEALER, CHAPLAIN AND CHARACTER

A military chaplain is an unarmed noncombatant. Time and time again Kapaun served the role of a combat medic and was awarded the CIB (Combat Infantry Badge) that is only awarded to soldiers performing duties who come under fire in active ground combat. A very rare award for chaplains. And even the plainspoken language used in Father Kapaun's letters, repeated in slightly different ways to a variety of family and friends, gives a profound view of the horrors of war and how to deal with them. Kapaun is utterly and wholeheartedly driven to be on the front lines, eager to immediately provide comfort and aid to those maimed by such shocking and indiscriminate violence. Like a confession or as a therapeutic treatment for prediagnosed PTSD, he writes prolifically at every precious lull in the fighting. Father Kapaun seems keenly aware he is a witness to significant historical events drenched in total chaos and uncertainty. This is a man learned in at least five languages, a theologian, and a priest who had written hundreds of pages of class notes and papers, a master's thesis in education, and hundreds of homilies. The writing skills in his "foxhole letters" are so compelling because we can see how intellectually honest he is at reflecting the truth of his combat experience and situation nearly in real time. He does not hold back or censor his experiences. By contrast, battles in World War II were overwrought with embedded, seasoned and even famous writers, eager to advance their careers and reputations. Names like Bill Mauldin, Ernest Hemingway, J.D. Salinger, Gore Vidal, James Jones, Norman Mailer, and many others. Combined as one diary, Father Kapaun's letters alone provide a meaningful and brutally honest depiction of war as profound, stark and succinct as any of the great wartime writers. But he goes deeper than that. Like a twentieth century living embodiment of Homer's *Odyssey* and *Iliad*, Chaplain Kapaun is a classical archetype fulfilling the "hero's journey."

WAR IS HELL

Dear Elsie and all my Friends:
I ransacked a Korean house and found this paper and ink… The Reds got everything I had with me. Three times I escaped with my life and that was all. I went through machinegun fire, bullets whistling all around; an 80 mm tank shell missed my head about four feet, it blew off my steel helmet. The prayers of loved ones helped me escape. I have seen soldiers with both legs blown off; one had the top of his head completely blown off. He did not know what hit him. This fighting is nerve-wracking. Many of my soldiers crack up—they go insane and scream like mad men. It seems like a dream. I don't know if I will live through the day or night. We are close to heaven but really we are more like in hell.

"On August 12, Father Kapaun reported to his bishop in Wichita. His opening sentence was an excuse for the poor kind of paper. In this day and age when it is so often taken as a characteristic of masculinity to be impolite, it is refreshing to notice a man like Father Kapaun, even in the heat of combat, apologizing out of his natural politeness for not observing the best form for writing to his bishop, who publishes it in the local paper anyway:

My dear Bishop Carroll:
Please excuse the crudeness of this letter. Yesterday I found this paper and ink in one of the abandoned houses of the Koreans.

    I received your two letters written in July. Many thanks for your kindness and remembrance in prayers. It must be the prayers of others which have saved me so far. Three times we have been trapped by the Reds and have had to flee for our lives. I lost everything I had except what I carried on my person. I lost my jeep and trailer with all my equipment. My assistant was shot and is now in the hospital. The Protestant Chaplain who was working besides me, was hit by a mortar shell and lost part of his leg. I was the only one who escaped unscathed. I got another Mass Kit so I can say Mass when conditions permit. Lost all my records so I will have to guess about what to report. In July I said Mass every Sunday except one (when I had no Mass Kit), attendance about 200. I prepared soldiers in Confession and Holy Communion, I guess between 300 and 400 times. Most of my Catholic soldiers are well prepared. I baptized two boys before battle and prepared about six or eight for their First Confession and Holy Communion. I carry the Holy Oils and the Blessed Sacrament with me at all times. For nearly two weeks we were in battle, with no rest. Many of my soldiers suffered heat exhaustion and sun stroke in this awful heat and climbing mountains. We are on the front lines but the Reds have not tried to advance for several days. That gives us a little much-needed rest. We killed thousands.

Father Kapaun on church rectory porch, early 1940s.
Photo Credit: Catholic Diocese of Wichita; colorization by Jecinci

Iconic photo taken on October 7, 1950, by Colonel Raymond Skeehan as Kapaun celebrated Mass in a field three miles south of Munsan, South Korea. The 1st Cavalry was just a few miles from the North Korean border and starting to cross the 38th parallel the same day. This is believed to be the last photo taken of Father Kapaun before his capture on November 2.

**Photo Credit:
US Army Colonel
Raymond Skeehan/
Courtesy Father Kapaun Guild**

Father Kapaun assists a distraught soldier off the battlefield during the Battle of Tabu-Dong, South Korea, in early September, 1950.
Photo Credit: US Army

Top: Close-up photo of Chaplain Kapaun's Medal of Honor.
Photo Credit: Author photo

Bottom: "On March 2, 2021, the Defense POW/MIA Accounting Agency identified the remains of Chaplain Emil Kapaun, who had been unaccounted for since the Korean War."
Photo Credit: Department of Defense

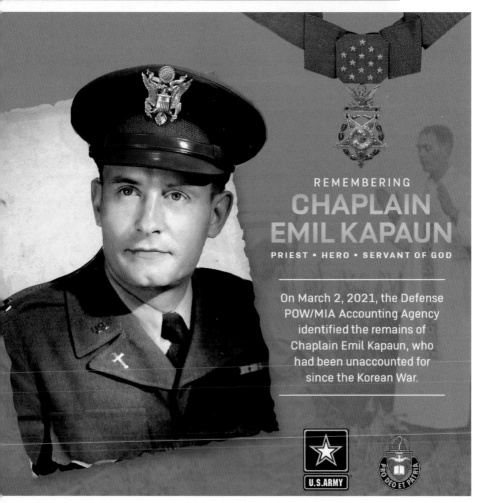

REMEMBERING
CHAPLAIN EMIL KAPAUN
PRIEST • HERO • SERVANT OF GOD

On March 2, 2021, the Defense POW/MIA Accounting Agency identified the remains of Chaplain Emil Kapaun, who had been unaccounted for since the Korean War.

Top: Portrait photo of Colonel (Doctor) Raymond Skeehan taken summer of 1950 in South Korea as the 1st Cavalry Division was pushing north. The color quality of this photo means it is possible this camera was used to shoot the famous photo of Kapaun celebrating Mass at his jeep on October 7, 1950.
Photo Credit: US Army

Bottom Left: The chaplain's jeep on permanent display outside the US Army Chaplain Center and School at Fort Jackson, South Carolina. The number on the hood denotes the date of Father Kapaun's death: 5-23-1951.
Photo Credit: Author photo

Bottom Right: Herb and Joyce Miller attend Father Kapaun's funeral service on September 29, 2021, in Wichita, Kansas. On November 2, 1950, Father Kapaun saved Herb Miller's life on the battlefield of Unsan, North Korea.
Photo Credit: Courtesy Catholic Diocese of Wichita

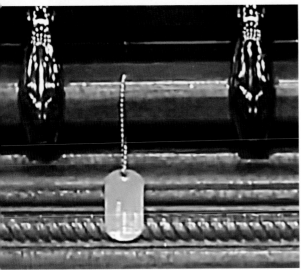

Top: Kapaun's casket carried by army escort, Hartman Arena, Wichita.
Photo Credit: Courtesy Catholic Diocese of Wichita

Bottom: Close-up of Chaplain Emil Kapaun's dog tag. Though his original dog tags were confiscated, the Department of Defense made new ones in 1954 to keep track of all remains still awaiting identification.
Photo Credit: Courtesy Catholic Diocese of Wichita

Official army portrait of Captain Kapaun. Shoulder patch is for service in the CBI Theater (China-Burma-India).

Top Far Left: This crucifix carved by Major Gerald Fink is a huge part of the Kapaun story. It was carved in a POW camp by a Jewish Marine Corps fighter pilot in honor of Father Kapaun—a man he had never met.
Photo Credit: Author photo

Top Left: Full-size photo of "Christ in Barbed Wire."
Photo Credit: Author photo

Bottom: This crucifix was carved with homemade tools in POW Camp 2, North Korea, and had to be smuggled out at the war's end in the fall of 1953. It was dubbed "Christ in Barbed Wire."
Photo Credit: Author photo

Top: Display cabinets of Chaplain Kapaun items at Kapaun Mt. Carmel High School.
Photo Credit: Author photo

Bottom: Battlefield ciborium used by Captain Kapaun in the conduct of field services. The ciborium was stolen by Chinese camp commander Ding Chan and given to his daughter to play with. The ciborium was returned to POW Captain Nardella, who'd refused repatriation unless it was returned. Its retention by the Chinese would have caused the Chinese to lose face.
Photo Credit: Father Kapaun Guild/ Kapaun Mt. Carmel High School

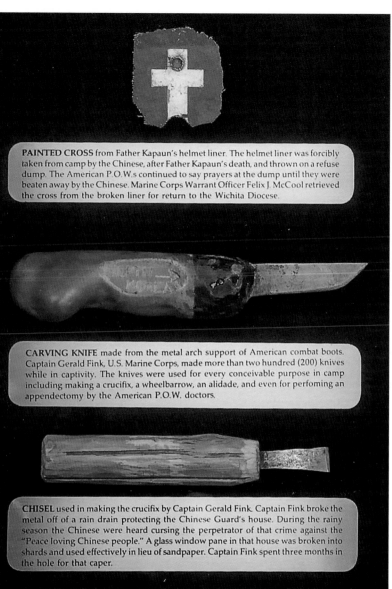

These are the homemade tools fashioned by Major Fink to carve the crucifix in the POW camp. They were smuggled out at the end of the war.
**Photo Credit:
Photo by Devon L. Suits/
Department of Defense**

PAINTED CROSS from Father Kapaun's helmet liner. The helmet liner was forcibly taken from camp by the Chinese, after Father Kapaun's death, and thrown on a refuse dump. The American P.O.W.s continued to say prayers at the dump until they were beaten away by the Chinese. Marine Corps Warrant Officer Felix J. McCool retrieved the cross from the broken liner for return to the Wichita Diocese.

CARVING KNIFE made from the metal arch support of American combat boots. Captain Gerald Fink, U.S. Marine Corps, made more than two hundred (200) knives while in captivity. The knives were used for every conceivable purpose in camp including making a crucifix, a wheelbarrow, an alidade, and even for perfoming an appendectomy by the American P.O.W. doctors.

CHISEL used in making the crucifix by Captain Gerald Fink. Captain Fink broke the metal off of a rain drain protecting the Chinese Guard's house. During the rainy season the Chinese were heard cursing the perpetrator of that crime against the "Peace loving Chinese people." A glass window pane in that house was broken into shards and used effectively in lieu of sandpaper. Captain Fink spent three months in the hole for that caper.

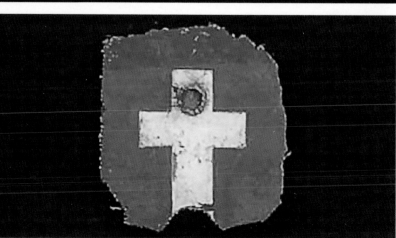

The chaplain insignia cut out of Father Kapaun's helmet liner by Felix McCool and smuggled out of the POW camp in the fall of 1953. On display at Kapaun Mt. Carmel High School, Wichita, Kansas.
**Photo Credit:
Photo by Devon L.Suits/
Department of Defense**

Top: Kapaun Mt. Carmel High School student backpacks left outside a classroom under a display of Kapaun pics and items. Kapaun received a master's degree in education from Catholic University.
Photo Credit: Author photo

Bottom: Chaplain (Colonel) Rajmund Kopec, a senior chaplain assigned to US Army Forces Command, says a prayer over Chaplain (Captain) Emil J. Kapaun's casket on the tarmac of the Wichita Dwight D. Eisenhower National Airport, Kansas, September 25, 2021.
Photo Credit: Photo by Devon L. Suits/ Department of Defense

Top: Kapaun's remains being escorted from the DPAA/DoD facility in Hawaii to be placed in a casket for return home to Kansas.
Photo Credit:
Department of Defense

Bottom: Locals and followers of Father Kapaun gather in Pilsen, Kansas, to await a private service two days before his official funeral service in Wichita. An abundance of baby blue T-shirts were made proclaiming Father Emil "Home at Last."
Photo Credit:
Photo by Devon L. Suits/
Department of Defense

Top Left: Adjacent to the Pilsen church parking lot is a memorial statue depicting Chaplain Kapaun assisting a wounded soldier. Visitors are encouraged to grasp the extended hand of Father Kapaun for inspiration and support.
Photo Credit: Author photo

Top Right: The casket holding Father Kapaun's remains is carried into St. John Nepomucene Catholic Church, Pilsen, on September 25, 2021, where the parish had an opportunity to honor its native son.
**Photo Credit: Karen Mikols Bonar/
The Leaven**

Middle: St. John Nepomucene Church in Pilsen, Kansas, completed in 1915, a year before Emil Kapaun's birth.
Photo Credit: Author photo

Bottom: View of Pilsen church from where the former Kapaun home once stood.
Photo Credit: Author photo

Insignia of US Army Chaplains Corps, established 1775, on the wall of the Chaplain Center and School at Fort Jackson, Columbia, South Carolina. It is Latin for "For God And Country."
Photo Credit: Author photo

Nephew of Emil Kapaun, Ray Kapaun, accepts the posthumous Medal of Honor on behalf of the Kapaun family from President Barack Obama on April 11, 2013.
Photo Credit: Photo by Pete Souza/ The White House

The director of the US Army Chaplain Corps Museum at Fort Jackson, South Carolina, Marcia Davis McManus, smiles in their records room after examining the Medal of Honor that was awarded to the now-famous chaplain— Emil J. Kapaun.
Photo Credit: Author photo

Top: Father Kapaun's flag-draped casket lies in state at the altar of his beloved St. John Nepomucene Catholic Church, after he was declared MIA for seventy years. Private Pilsen ceremony, September 25, 2021.
Photo Credit: Photo by Devon L. Suits/ Department of Defense

Bottom: Chaplain (Captain) Emil J. Kapaun is welcomed home with honors at the Wichita Dwight D. Eisenhower National Airport, Kansas, September 25, 2021. In March, the Defense POW/MIA Accounting Agency fully identified Kapaun's remains.
Photo Credit: Photo by Devon L. Suits/ Department of Defense

A 1st Infantry Division honor guard readies Chaplain Kapaun's casket to be loaded onto a horse-drawn caisson, Wichita, September 29, 2021.

Photo Credit: Photo by Devon L. Suits/ Department of Defense

Funeral service for Father Kapaun at Hartman Arena, Wichita, Kansas, September 29, 2021.

Photo Credit: Courtesy Catholic Diocese of Wichita

Members of the 3rd Battalion, 8th Cavalry Regiment from Fort Hood, Texas, escort Father Kapaun's flag-draped coffin atop horse-drawn caisson. The casket was entombed at the Cathedral of the Immaculate Conception, downtown Wichita.

Photo Credit: Photo by Master Sgt. Miriam Espinoza/ Department of Defense

Top: The tomb built for Father Kapaun weighs 5400 pounds and rests in the Cathedral of the Immaculate Conception, Wichita, Kansas.
Photo Credit: Scott Carter/Father Kapaun Guild

Bottom Left: Father Kapaun's marble crypt rests in an alcove on the side of the nave of the Cathedral of the Immaculate Conception, Wichita, Kansas.
Photo Credit: Scott Carter/Father Kapaun Guild

Bottom Right: Honorary Cavalry Stetson made for the Father Kapaun Guild. Baby blue hat band symbolizes the ribbon for the Medal of Hono[r]
Photo Credit: Author photo

They outnumber us about 15-1 (we were told). Now since we have received more help, they outnumber us about 3-1. If that is the case, we should give them a good licking. War is terrible! I feel sorry for the Korean people who have to leave their homes. As the Reds approach, nearly everything is destroyed—homes, lives and food. I hope these people can return in time to harvest their rice so they have some food for winter.

We have no mail censorship and this letter does not contain any vital information except the ratio of outnumbering. Maybe this has been printed in the newspapers already. Our mail reaches us fairly well. I am glad to be with the soldiers in time of need. So far, I have been right on the front lines giving absolution and Extreme Unction to the dying. I had no chance to change clothes and my uniform got all bloody. I've got a clean one now and I hope it will not be stained with blood.

True to his ways, the emphasis in his letter was a report of his spiritual activities, and he only mentioned the actual combat as a background. He wrote that during the month of July, he had tried to say Holy Mass every Sunday and as often as possible during the week. However, one Sunday it could not be done because he did not have his Mass kit.

Considering how little time there was for rest and the constant nervous strain under which the men had to live, it is amazing that he wrote at all, but he reported to his bishop in Wichita twice during the month of August. He even mentioned the number of soldiers attending the Sunday and weekday Masses. This is all the more amazing since the religious exercises had to be held under the greatest possible handicap. But Father Kapaun's training showed itself in his thoroughness in reporting things to the best of his ability."[3]

THE KID FROM KANSAS

Chaplain Kapaun, knowing the enemy's penchant to commit atrocities on civilians and captured soldiers, even gave a sincere sermon that as Christians, we betray our heritage if we take revenge on wounded enemies or prisoners. In a brutal war of attrition, attempted genocide, and a complete dismissal of the Geneva Convention, morals or decency by the Communist forces—Father Kapaun stood high on the moral ground and practiced what he preached.

"After we developed a reasonable defense line on the Naktong River in early August, we actually had some dull, peaceful days," reports Captain Dolan. "Then, either the American Legion or some beer company were sending beer and Coca Cola over once a week. But then the beer suddenly stopped and the rumor was that the WCTU (Woman's Christian Temperance Union) had pressured President Truman to protect these American soldiers from the demon rum. Morale fell, but here came Father Kapaun again, the kid from Kansas, and he came with his pockets bulging with apples. It wasn't the same as beer but it was a welcome change from the dirty-mouth taste of C-rations mixed with too many cigarettes. And Father always carried two canteens of water so that you could wash things down if you had not had a chance to fill your canteen. And we had a problem with that because our water points were blown early on and all of us had diarrhea from drinking water taken from rice paddies and dosed with chlorine tablets. But Father found a way to build morale.

What I remember especially is the simple eloquence of his sermons. We didn't call them homilies then. A recurring theme was the need to forgive our enemies. The 'Pacific Stars and Stripes' had published a picture of men from the 5th Cavalry Regiment who had been captured, tortured and executed, but after that atrocity, some of our troops were ready to retaliate in kind. I remember Father's sermon at that time, that as Christians and as Americans we would betray our heritage if we took revenge on the wounded or on prisoners. I don't know if Father deserves the credit, but the prisoners I saw were well treated. This took some doing on occasions. Initially, when a prisoner was taken by the I & R [Intelligence and Reconnaissance] Platoon, he would first be interrogated with a ROK interpreter at battalion headquarters and then sent to the rear with the interpreter. More than once, they would go down the road a bit, you'd hear a shot, and the interpreter would come back saying 'He tried to get away.' After that a GI took the prisoner back. I saw some of our American soldiers protect prisoners from ROKs who wanted to take revenge on the North Korean prisoners. This occurred mainly later because we had integrated so many green ROK troops into our unit, people who had not had any previous combat training."[4]

LETTER TO BROTHER EUGENE AND HELEN

Dear Eugene, Helen and Angela, Gee, I sure did get a surprise. What a nice long letter you wrote, Eugene. Thank you very much for the letter and for the pictures. I see you folks have a nice home. Sure am glad for you. That is much better than paying rent, and you got it in the right time for I imagine everything is going up again.

So you are having a lot of rain. Sounds unusual for Kansas. I guess there will be a good corn crop. Yesterday we had a rain too so this morning I am trying to dry out my stuff that got soaked. This fox hole gets messy when it rains and a fellow gets soaked regardless of what he does. Right now I am soaked with sweat as the hot sun is beating down on the wet ground. My fox hole is here in a soy bean patch. I wish I had my camera. Some of these fellows sure look funny this morning. What a life!! Well, I am glad it is not cold and snowing!!

I think I wrote you I lost everything I had with me. Most of my stuff I left in Japan. My Plymouth is there. I even lost my assistant as he got shot in the leg with a Red 25 caliber machine gun—5 holes. Chaplain Mills and I were working together in the same unit. The first time we got trapped by the Reds he and I got separated. I thought he got killed and he thought I got killed. So we were sure glad when we met again. Running over these mountains and trying to hide from an enemy who was not taking any prisoners was anything but peaceful and calm. We had quite a time. All I had with me was a towel that I grabbed by one of the trucks to keep my hand from bleeding so fast. All I got out of the deal were some minor cuts and bruises. Over here a cut gets infected very easily but I got rid of the infection all right.

My boys and I are having a great time. I have been on the front lines with them all along. Some got killed and others got injured. I had a freak accident—got hit in the elbow by a 50 caliber slug. I was rescuing the body of a pilot who cracked up his F-51 fighter plane on the side of a mountain. He was thrown clear of the wreckage which was burning as we rescued the body. The ammunition was going off in the fire and one of the slugs hit me. It must not have had much momentum for I still have my elbow without injury.

The Reds are taking an awful beating. In one day we are told we killed some 10,000. Boy, we sure did work hard. But next day they got us. And we had to run. They come from all sides and before we know it they have us in a pocket.

Gee, it sure looks good to see our airplanes come over. They are using rocket bombs. I have watched the jet planes fighting on the front. The Reds are scared of them. These planes travel around 600 miles per hour. You should see them dive toward the target, release the rocket bomb and straighten out again, those fly boys must have a lot of fun.

Well this is war. I hope you are safe from this one. We expect it to be over before long.

Please write again. As ever in Christ Fr. E

Sentence by sentence, you never know what Father Kapaun is going to report on next. Treacherous bloody battles or self-deprecating humor about jumping in a ditch filled with water to avoid machine gun bullets. In this letter, several major events are just listed off like it's just another day at the office: his assistant was shot in the knee and is in the hospital, he thought his fellow chaplain had been killed and vice versa, he is staving off infection, he calmly states they killed 10,000 enemy soldiers in one day, and all while having "quite a time."

But another couple of lines stand out. Kapaun mentions a "freak accident" where his elbow was struck by the ricochet of a .50 caliber bullet coming from a crashed fighter plane, on fire, while the ammo was "cooking off." No big deal as he recovers the body of an F-51 Mustang fighter pilot near enemy lines taking only a "boo boo" to his elbow! Although this may have been "just another day on the battlefield," it is noteworthy for a couple of reasons. One is that it again displays Kapaun's undaunted courage and bravery to try and aid or recover the body of a casualty without any hesitation despite the tremendous danger of ammo cooking off and flying every direction from a burning fighter plane which has three .50 caliber machine guns in each wing. This is the epitome of the US military's creed to "leave no man behind."

Remarkable too is just how similar this attempted rescue of a pilot is to the recovery a few months later in the Chosin Reservoir of USMC Corsair pilot Jesse Brown. Jesse was shot down in enemy territory, and his wingman, Captain Thomas Hudner, crash-landed his own Corsair to try and save Jesse's life. While unsuccessful at saving his life, he was able to coordinate a helicopter rescue for himself and escape the enemy soldiers closing in. Sadly, Jesse Brown's body was never recovered. For his actions, Captain Hudner was awarded the Medal of Honor by President Truman.

While we will never know all the details of Kapaun's seemingly routine recovery only mentioned once in a letter home, research reveals that the F-51 Mustang pilot shot down before the date of Kapaun's letter of August 16 most likely was Captain Robert Newland Howell, Jr., of the 67th Fighter Bomber Squadron, 6002nd Tactical Support Wing. Shot down on August 5, 1950. He was from Kirksville, Missouri and because of the efforts of Father Kapaun and his fellow soldiers in the 1st Cavalry, Captain Howell was able to be returned home for burial.

THE REDS ARE NOT TAKING PRISONERS

As more and more American soldiers are getting overrun and captured, a very disturbing trend emerges and every American in uniform in Korea is coming to understand what kind of men they faced. On August 15, the mortar platoon of H Company, 5th Cavalry was suddenly overtaken without a fight. All thirty-four men were found executed the next day when the North Koreans retreated. Two days later, North Korean soldiers shot dead forty-five American prisoners in a trench with their hands tied. These atrocities were just beginning.

HILL 303 MASSACRE

"On the night of August 14, North Korean forces crossed the Naktong near Waegwan, in the 1st Cavalry Division sector, and out flanked an American infantry company defending Hill

303. The North Koreans easily overran US mortar positions on the reverse slope. Surrounded by enemy troops, the rest of the company withdrew to the hillcrest, where it held out for two days before fighting its way to safety.[5]

"The image of twenty-six dead American soldiers, lying bound and barefoot, shoulder to shoulder in the sun, left an indelible mark on PFC Floyd Akins of the 5th Cav:

"Several days later, out on patrol, my squad found twenty-six American GIs. They were lying in a ditch and they had their hands tied behind their backs. They'd all been shot in the back of the head. What made it so bad for me was finding my old company commander from back at Camp Drake, Japan. Right then and there my heart made a change. I told a lieutenant standing next to me I was now ready to fight the North Koreans to the death if that's what it took. Lieutenant Barr, that was his name, said, 'OK, you blood-thirsty GI, we're going to give them hell if we capture them now. We'll give them some of their own medicine.' Since that day I don't think I've ever been the same."[6]

"WE HAVE TO BE ARMED"
LETTER TO FATHER JOSEPH GORACY

Dear Fr. Joseph I received a letter from my parents today saying you had a Mass for me on Monday, so I want to write you and thank you.

This is a fox hole letter. Little did I dream that someday I would be in Korea in a fox hole. I am right in a soy bean patch with rows of sugar cane about us. This sugar cane is now about 10 or 11 feet high. And it is hot!! Flies by the thousands, and at night mosquitoes by the millions. What a life!! Yet I am right on the front lines. Have been hearing hundreds of Confessions. Gave Extreme Unction many times to the dying. It sure is a pity to see the terribly wounded bleeding to death. One of my soldiers had both legs and his arm blown off. What a pitiful sight. I used to get sick at the sight of blood and wounds. Recently I was messed up with blood myself. I grabbed a towel to stop my hand from bleeding. That was the only thing I saved as the Reds nearly got us that time. Three times now I have had very narrow escapes. I honestly believe that it was the prayers of others which have kept me unscathed so far. Chaplain Mills (Protestant) here with me was not so fortunate. He got hit by a mortar shell and it wounded his leg and arm—the doctor said it will take him at least 4 months to recover in a hospital.

My mother has written me about the new convent for the Sisters. It must be very nice. Surely you were fortunate to build it when you did as I suppose now materials and labor has gone up because of this war. The big guns are going off as I write this letter and I jump every time one shoots. The airplanes (fighters) are flying around here. Day before yesterday I saw the B 24s bomb the place. They were so high we could not see them but the bombs sure did lift up the mountains where the Reds were digging in.

If the boys ever needed a Catholic priest they sure need one in battle. I have been able to be at the side of the dying so far without being seriously wounded myself. I am very grateful for that. Both Catholics and non-Catholics have great respect for the Chaplain. Incidentally in this war we have to be armed. The Reds are not taking prisoners. So we resolved to fight them to the finish because we would not have a chance if we chose to surrender in any particular hopeless situation. Please give my regards to the good Sisters at St. Johns this year and to Albina.
As ever in Christ. Fr. E. K.

Kapaun clearly sees the Reds are not taking prisoners and he states unequivocally, "We have to be armed." Chaplains in any war simply did not talk like this save for the famous line from

Richard E. Wallack, USMC, prepares to fire a bazooka with a .50-caliber machine gun crew next to him during fighting along the Pusan Perimeter, August 1950.

World War II: "Praise the Lord and pass the ammunition." Imagine factoring in this information if the time ever came when you must choose between fighting to certain death or surrender with certain torment, torture, and execution. Given what all these UN Forces saw with their own eyes or learned from others repeatedly every day—no one wearing an army uniform fighting for South Korea could reasonably expect to live more than a few hours upon capture.

POWS "MOST PROBABLY DEAD"
LETTER TO BISHOP CARROLL

Most Reverend and dear Bishop:
We have been on the front lines all through August, with very little rest and constant nervous strain. In our regiment we have 40 killed and 43 missing in action (most probably dead, too, because Reds are reported to have killed most of

the prisoners taken). This is confidential. My report for August: 12 Sunday Masses, 246 attended; 15 weekday Masses, 118; 13 Rosary devotions, 56; Holy Communions, 176, Last Sacraments, 2. The Advance Register does not reach me anymore, but it is surprising the way letters come in for the soldiers, who are always anxious to hear from home.

"WE HAD TO LAUGH ABOUT THE MARINES"

Dear Dad and Mom, Thank you for the paper and envelopes. It is hard to get paper and envelopes here. I had no chance to write last week. We were busy moving around. We have been in the front lines all the time but the Reds did not bother us much. Some of the prisoners said they were trying to attack the other units. I am sending you the pictures which Eugene sent because I am afraid they will get ruined. When it rains, everything gets wet. I am sending you a paper Korean flag which we found in a school house. I guess the children made it. I am writing this letter in a rice paddy. Airplanes are flying around and our big guns are firing. They make a fellow jump every time they go off.

I have been getting a lot of mail. Don't know if I can answer it all. You people must be all excited over this war. It seems odd to see the new soldiers coming in here, fresh from the States. They left the USA only ten days ago. Their clothes are nice and clean, whereas we fellows are all dirty and many have not shaved because they had nothing to shave with and no place to shave and little time. We lost so much stuff because we were fighting hard, then had to fight our way out of a trap. But so far the Reds were not good enough to get us, and now with much more help from the USA, England, the Philippines, Australia, etc., we surely should whip them. We had to laugh about the Marines. They came over here with a lot of publicity and we were glad to know

Chaplain Kapaun sits in an open field writing a letter home, using his knee for a desk.
His uniform is dirty and worn. On his helmet is the prominent white cross indicating
very clearly his spiritual mission in Korea. But as he looks toward the camera, his facial
expression is unusually severe and dire. His customary smile has momentarily escaped.
Here is a man facing the very grim business of war, and he realizes this well.

they were here. They went in with a big push and it looked
like they were set on giving the Reds a good licking, but the
Reds did the same to them as they did to us—got them in a
trap. The Marines found out this is a tough outfit to fight.
Don't worry about me. Am praying for you, too.

1st CAVALRY DIVISION WAR DIARY

"The operations of the 8th Cavalry Regiment during the month
of September can be broken down into two distinct phases.
Phase I consisted of the defense of the 'Bowling Alley' sector, as it was popularly termed, just north of the city of Taegu
from the beginning of the month until 21 September. During
this period of defense there was a series of hard-fought battles
for the Walled City, a prominent terrain feature situated on the

A soldier comforts another after deadly action along the Pusan Perimeter, Haktong-ni area, South Korea, August 28, 1950.

right boundary of the Regiment which provided its occupants with an advantageous command over the surrounding territory. Phase II consisted of a breakthrough by the United Nations Forces at Tabu-Dong and the pursuit of the withdrawing enemy forces to Ansong during the remainder of the month.

During Phase I the Regiment assumed the mission of defending the area in the vicinity of Tabu-Dong. The enemy exerted a tremendous effort to break through the 8th Cav lines and access Taegu. Time after time friendly units were forced to withdraw from positions made untenable by the enemy's mass attacks and infiltration tactics. The Regimental Commander at times deemed the situation to be so dire that the necessity arose to use all available troops to strengthen the front lines and throw back the enemy.

Love Company occupied Hill 570, relieving elements of the 19th Infantry Regiment. The regiment ordered Love Company to move forward in the vicinity of Hill 400 to protect the left flank of the 1st Bn, 8th Cav. Meanwhile, Item and King companies had occupied the high ground overlooking the road junction at Tabu-dong. The enemy was able to attack slowly and consolidate his positions by fanatical 'banzai' charges."

"WHEN I DIE I HOPE TO GOD
THEY BURY ME ON THE FLATS"

A marine, Private First Class Doug Koch, overhears some grim sentiment: "We ambled past a Graves Registration tent. Here there were rows upon rows of stretchers; on each, covered by a poncho, lay a dead man. Most of them belonged to Army units that had been fighting in this area. The Graves Registration people were trying to identify each body. We were a pretty quiet bunch of guys. We walked higher into the hills. Finally, one guy said, 'Goddamn, you die and they can't even bury you down on the flats, they gotta bury you on the side of hill. When I die I hope to God they bury me on the flats.'"[7]

10

THE BATTLE OF TABU DONG
SEPTEMBER 1–18

In the two months it took to break out of the Pusan Perimeter, the 1st Cavalry, 19th Infantry, and other units faced sustained tooth-and-nail combat on a continual basis as they fought to push the North Koreans back to where they came from. With rugged hills, valleys and ridges all over, it was hard to tell if the enemy had outflanked the forward units during the night. In the area around Tabu Dong, Lieutenant Ernest Terrell found himself in enemy territory, made his way back to friendly territory after daybreak, and met Kapaun as he sat in his jeep holding a rifle. Recognizing Kapaun as a chaplain, he asked him why he was carrying a weapon. Kapaun replied, "The Lord helps those who help themselves." The chaplain clearly had made up his mind to defend himself if necessary. "If it's a question of a North Korean sending me to heaven or me sending him someplace, I'm not prepared to go to heaven right now." Despite his talk, however, no one ever reports seeing the chaplain actually fire the weapon.

LIEUTENANT WALT MAYO
99th FIELD ARTILLERY, 8th REGIMENT

"I first met Father Kapaun about the 2nd of September when we were fighting outside of Taegin (Taejon). I was an Artillery Observer. We were attacking hill Number 401 and were having a difficult time. I was up in a forward position trying to get artillery on the hill when I turned around and there, sitting right behind us exposed to a sniper's bullet, was a chaplain 'carrying' a carbine. I said 'hello' and warned him of the snipers but he did not get excited. He merely moved a few feet down into the gully and asked where he could find some of the wounded. He spent the remainder of the afternoon and evening taking the wounded back, constantly under fire. From then on I saw him pretty often, as I went to Mass on one side of a hill with the top under fire and the enemy only about 400 yards away. He was always burying the dead enemy soldiers and helping graves registration with ours when things were quiet. Always with his pipe or cigar in his mouth, he was an inspiration to everyone, being so calm and cheerful in a difficult situation. Wherever and whenever there was action, he was always there to help the wounded and give solace and the last rites for the dying. It was the same all the way up from Taegen to Seoul to Kaeseng to Pyongyang to Anju and then to Unsan."[1]

CHAPLAIN KAPAUN AWARDED BRONZE STAR

By command of Major General Hobart R. Gay, Chaplain and Captain Emil J. Kapaun-Chaplain Corps, US Army, 8th Cavalry Regiment, 1st Cavalry Division, is hereby awarded the Bronze Star for his display of heroism in action against the enemy near Kumchon, Korea, on 2 August 1950. Chaplain Kapaun received information of a wounded man in an exposed position in territory controlled by the enemy. With total disregard for personal safety, Chaplain

Kapaun and his companion, under intense enemy machine gun and small arms fire, successfully evacuated the soldier thereby saving his life. This heroic action on the part of Chaplain Kapaun reflects great credit upon himself and the United States military.

SEPTEMBER 4, 1950—1st CAVALRY WAR DIARY

"The 3rd Bn's position on Hill 486 was attacked and the enemy succeeded in gaining a foothold on the Northern slope of the Hill, but the enemy regrouped his forces and made another attempt to gain back the ground and a see saw battle developed for this ground. The enemy gained an O.P. on their high terrain enabling them to direct intense mortar and artillery fire which made the area untenable [and they were forced to withdraw].

Meanwhile Co 'D' 8th Engr Bn. and Co 'E' 8th Cav were steadily making progress toward the center of the Walled City under intense small arms and mortar fire. A driving rain limited observation and therefore retarded the use of supporting weapons. (Supply was a major problem and with the ammunition supply low, orders were issued to make every shot count. One man, Pfc Melvin L. Brown, Co D, 8th Engr Bn., expended all his ammunition and then went out and gathered all available grenades to use on the enemy. When the grenades were gone, he pulled out his entrenching shovel and continued killing the enemy by splitting their skulls as they climbed over a small wall. For this action Pfc Brown has been awarded the Congressional Medal of Honor.)"

CHAPLAIN KAPAUN RECOVERS A DISTRAUGHT SOLDIER FROM THE BATTLEFIELD

In the picture, Captain Jerome Dolan of the Medical Corps is holding the right arm of the battle-weary soldier, name unknown. The man being helped had been on the firing lines for weeks with-

One of the most iconic images ever taken of battlefield stress, war, and a chaplain's and doctor's compassion. Chaplain Kapaun on right assists a grieving soldier with both fists balled up over his eyes after seeing his crew wiped out on the battlefield. On the left is Dr. Jerome Dolan helping the soldier with his left hand while holding a .45 sidearm in his right hand. Battle of Tabu-Dong, early September 1950.

out any relief, very little sleep, little food, and always surrounded by a fanatic enemy. Even then he did not want to leave, but had to be pulled out of the line. After a few days' rest he said he wanted to go back. Father Kapaun is supporting the GI's left arm.

"Your readers might be interested in some of the incidents surrounding that picture and something about those portrayed… The North Koreans had thrown a banzai charge through the valley at Tabu-dong, between the 8th Cavalry's 2nd Battalion and 1st Battalion, of which I was battalion surgeon. They were a force of 4500 and we were about 100, including Headquarters Co. and my aid-station crew, and we were isolated from our line companies. At the time that photo was made, the North Koreans had command of a rise 350 yards from us and also had captured the road to our rear, effectively cutting our escape route. For nine days we fought the elements and the Koreans and finally beat both to bring our wounded out to safety. Incidentally, by the grace of God, all ten of our wounded made it.

The GI on the extreme left, I don't recognize, nor do I remember the name of the kid who had fought through hell from July 20th till that day, with little sleep, too little food, and that cold C rations, no chance to bathe, without a day away from the firing line, always against an enemy that outnumbered him by at least ten to one. This boy had finally reached his limit, but we had to practically drag him out of action. After a few days rest when we reached friendly lines, he was ready to go back again to 'his team.'

Supporting the kid by the left arm, the GI in the field jacket is Father (Capt.) Emil J. Kapaun, of Marion, Kansas, our battalion Catholic chaplain and one of the finest men it has been my privilege to meet.[2]

TIBOR RUBIN AND ITEM COMPANY

"Item Company suffered heavy casualties in the defense of the Pusan perimeter: on one day alone eighteen men were either killed or seriously injured. The promised replacements never arrived, even as the unit's numbers dwindled. One typical morning in September the riflemen faced an all-out assault of twice their number. As they held their ground behind sandbags and trenches, a mortar shell sent Tibor reeling. An officer hovered by his side as he became conscious. The officer, a captain, spoke in a low voice, reciting some kind of poem. Tibor couldn't make out the words; the blare of the shell still rang in his ears, but the voice was calm and soothing. As Tibor came to his senses, he realized Father Kapaun was reading him the last rites. Although he didn't think he had been mortally wounded his leg was numb and wouldn't move. Still, he didn't want to interrupt the priest, who was just doing his job.

Tibor had admired Father Kapaun since their first meeting during a firefight. They'd traded quips ever since that day, and now it seemed like Father Kapaun was doing the right thing by ministering to Tibor like he was one of his own. Tibor listened a few more seconds, just in case he really was dying. Then he picked up his head and glanced down at his prone and numb body. Other than his right leg, which was a bloody mess from the knee to the ankle, he was unharmed. But Father Kapaun, his eyes at half-mast, continued to pray over him.

'Okay,' Tibor said when he couldn't keep still any longer. 'You don't have to say nothing else. I'm gonna make it.'

Father Kapaun opened his eyes, tapped him on the shoulder, and smiled."[3]

Tibor was evacuated to a field hospital and was told he should go to a hospital in Japan. Even wounded, Tibor talked them into letting him stay and he rejoined his unit.

CAPTAIN JOSEPH O'CONNOR

"My first recollection of Father Kapaun as a fearless individual, that is, fearless of man-made obstacles, occurred in September of 1950. He came to me when I was in charge of setting up headquarters and asked if he could say Mass for the men in that area at that time. I said 'Father, things are pretty hot here at present and I don't think you should be up here.' We had been getting interdicting artillery fire in and around that position for a few hours previously.

Father said, 'Then I think we need a Mass, Captain, and if you can spare the men for a few minutes, I'll say it.' I finally told him that I'd go along and allow as many Catholics as possible to attend, and picked out a spot in an abandoned Korean

PHOTO BY US ARMY COLONEL RAYMOND SKEEHAN / FATHER KAPAUN GUILD

One of only two photos taken of Chaplain Kapaun celebrating Mass from the hood of his jeep. He is facing the altar, wearing a white chasuble with a large ornate red cross.

house yard and he proceeded to offer Mass. I attended. During the Mass the North Koreans opened up on us with artillery. Rounds were hitting the top of the hill and 150 yards to the rear of us. We didn't know if we were under actual observation or not, but assumed as much, all of us were highly nervous and ready to seek cover, but Father continued the Mass. The look on his face—a look I can't describe, a look of saintliness or maybe one of unassuming dignity—one of a man so engrossed in the Holy Sacrifice that he was oblivious of what was happening—dispelled our fears. Not a man moved.

Had we been under direct observation, and I believe we were, we had what is known in the service as a bracket of us, and it was only a small matter for the enemy to make the proper range adjustment to eliminate us. A heavy barrage of fire hit about 400 yards to our left and then ceased. I think that this barrage was intended for us and through some miraculous power was deflected. After Mass, Father Kapaun thanked me and asked if I could find him a ride to the next battalion. He had lost his jeep in enemy fire. He hated to impose on me. I gladly managed to find a jeep and sent him happily out of that area."[4]

SERGEANT BILL RICHARDSON

"I hoped to hell he got more fire support. We were all hanging by a thread. Dead North Korean soldiers were stacking up in front of our foxholes. But they kept coming. Wave after wave. I could hear Walsh screaming at the men to stay in their holes. I was frantically changing the magazine in my carbine as two of the North Koreans were within ten feet of me. Walsh and Hall saw them too and opened fire, cutting the North Korean soldiers down. I saw another North Korean to my right and fired. He staggered back and dropped to the ground. I stayed low in my foxhole and kept firing straight ahead. Hall and Walsh kept firing to the rear, hitting the North Koreans attempting to move through our position. We had them in a cross fire, and in minutes our position was littered with North Korean bodies. Sliding a fresh magazine into my carbine, I poked my head up waiting for the next wave. But it never came.

'Stay alert. Some of them may be alive. If you see any movement, shoot them.'

We waited a few minutes and then finally climbed out.

'Check around your holes for live Koreans.'

The bodies of about a half dozen North Korean soldiers lay crumpled in between our foxholes. I slowly picked my way, my rifle at the ready. My nerves were on fire. I'd never been this close and was ready for even a slight movement. Two were badly wounded and kept muttering in Korean. I saw Hall kick their weapons away and then drag them to the rear of our positions. Eventually our medics would take care of them. We dragged the rest of the bodies away from our position and piled them to one side. I didn't look at their faces. I didn't care.

As daylight peeked its head over the hills, a tall, scrubby-looking infantryman carrying a carbine approached me from out of the mist. As he got closer, I saw the small white cross painted on his helmet. He stuck out his hand as he approached.

'Chaplain Kapaun,' he said, giving me a firm handshake. 'Where are you from?'

His uniform was dirty and he, like the rest of us, needed a shave. It was clear he'd spent the night close to the fighting and not safely in the rear. There was a peacefulness about him, though, that put me at ease. A quiet confidence. He seemed to care where I was from, and I watched him as he spoke to the rest of the section. Each time, he asked where the soldier was from and gave him a firm handshake. It was not long before he had us all smiling.

When Kapaun finished making his rounds, he sat down near my foxhole and took out his pipe. It was missing most of its stem.

'What happened to your pipe?' I asked, as he filled it.

'A sniper,' he said. 'Shot it out of my mouth a few days ago.'

We both had a laugh. I noticed the carbine lying across his lap.

'I thought chaplains couldn't carry weapons.'

He smiled and nodded. 'If they are going to shoot at me I'm going to be ready to shoot back.'

With that, he stood up and, cradling his wounded pipe, disappeared over the ridge to visit Miller's men."[5]

1st CAVALRY WAR DIARY

Enemy artillery shelled two of the field artillery battalions protecting Chaplain Kapaun and the 8th Regiment, forcing them to disperse because of the intensity and accuracy of the enemy fire. It was estimated that one round came in every two seconds. Still, 1st Cavalry Division artillery returned fire with 185 missions using 4,073 rounds of HE (high explosive), WP (white Phosphorous), and illuminating shells, resulting in an estimated five hundred enemy killed. Piles of spent shell casings, waist-deep, littered the battery positions over a hundred yards wide and forty feet deep. Estimated enemy losses for September 7 were 720 KIA and 7 POWs.[6]

LIEUTENANT RICHARD MACK

"Among the peculiarities of the terrain north of Taegu in the
Pusan Perimeter were razor-edge ridges, mostly bald; they sloped
steeply on both sides and made control of units attacking simultaneously on both sides of the ridge extremely difficult. On
about September 13, a regimental chaplain, Fr. Emil Kapaun,
visited our company and said Mass for our troops. He was a
fabulous individual, often seen riding a bicycle along rice-field
dikes to his 'parish.' As often as not, his uniform was as tattered
and dirty as those of the 'grunts' he so respected. The respect
was reciprocal."

In observing the men and leadership of the 8th Cavalry Regiment, Mack writes, "There are two types of people who seem
to fail consistently: those who seldom follow the rules, and those
who always do. There is an absolute requirement that on the
battlefield, the leader must follow. He must know what the rules
are but be flexible enough to follow the best possible course of
action to achieve the mission."[7]

11

NO BULLET GOT ME YET

General Douglas MacArthur was given the green light to do whatever it took to defeat the North Koreans. While the United States scrambled to replenish trained troops and marines for battle, MacArthur knew the best way to defeat such a powerful blitzkrieg on a narrow peninsula was to conduct a large surprise amphibious landing behind enemy lines and abruptly cut off their supply routes near the original border between the two Koreas. The 8th Army with the 1st Cavalry Division at the tip of the spear could break out of the Pusan Perimeter and then advance north and close the vise. But in the summer of 1950, there were not enough troops to attempt such an operation, and the UN forces were doing all they could just to survive. Summer temperatures could reach 110 degrees. Coupled with an incessantly rainy season, the humidity was frequently in the 90 percent range. Carrying weapons and ammo and a heavy pack often led to heat stroke and exhaustion considering just how many hills dot the Korean landscape. When they took one hill, they need only look north at the next one that needed to be taken. A Korean War motto quickly emerged: "Not this hill—the next one!"

SEPTEMBER 13—WAR DIARY OF THE
1st CAVALRY DIVISION

"At times the attacks appeared almost hopeless. 2nd Battalion (Bn), 5th Cav reported having only 100 men remaining in the Battalion (normally 700). General Walker, Eighth Army Commander, visited the 5th Cav and the 8th Cavalry units and amid a few sporadic rounds of artillery, remarked that the days of defense were numbered as the delays allowed the UN forces to take the offensive. Walker stated that an amphibious operation would be made on the west coast within the next few days and that the North Koreans probably knew this already. He mentioned briefly the history of the Regiment and said that General MacArthur had stated that the 1st Cav Div was the most ferocious outfit he had ever seen; that General Chase, the 1st Cav Division's former Commanding General, was the most ferocious commander he had ever known. Gen Walker expressed the hope that when the Regiment moved forward they would have only one thought in mind and that was to kill. 'No prisoners are needed now,' he said, stating further that he 'hoped the present members of the 7th Cavalry would be the equals of the killers of the 7th Cavalry in history who served in the Regiment when Gen Custer commanded it.' He said if the men did that, then they 'would have done what God placed them in the world for.'"

General George Custer may have had some military successes during the Indian wars of the 1800s, but the Battle of Little Big Horn was not one of them. Custer's last stand became synonymous with arrogant blundering into territory when vastly outnumbered. So it is with sad irony that the 3rd Battalion of the 8th Cavalry would be in the fight for their lives just a month and a half later. Overwhelmed and out of ammo, they would suffer a similar fate as Custer's men, and it would not be God's plan, but the blundering of arrogant generals.

OPERATION CHROMITE
MARINES LAND AT INCHON

The successful landing of over forty thousand troops and marines at Inchon Harbor on September 15, 1950, was a turning point in the Korean War. Around 260 ships were involved with the transports preceded by sixty warships, six cruisers, and six aircraft carriers. MacArthur had now turned the battles into a tactical offensive, and the South Korean capital of Seoul was soon liberated. UN ground forces trapped and destroyed what units of the NKPA were left stranded from resupply. Talk immediately began of going home by Christmas.

US NAVY

Operation Chromite, September 15, 1950. General MacArthur successfully lands over forty thousand marines at Inchon, South Korea, near the 38th parallel. First Lieutenant Baldomero Lopez leads the 3rd Platoon, Company A, 1st Battalion, 5th Marines over the seawall. Lieutenant Lopez was killed in action within a few minutes while assaulting a North Korean bunker and was posthumously awarded the Medal of Honor.

The well planned and executed operation was probably General MacArthur's finest hour and one of the most memorable operations in American military history. The day after the marines landed at Inchon, Chaplain Kapaun and the 8th Regiment of the 1st Cavalry along with ROK forces and other units that formed the 8th Army under General Walton Walker's command broke out from the Pusan perimeter and sent the North Korean Army into full retreat, headed north. During the NKPA's retreat, they massacred trapped civilians, killed and mutilated their POWs, and poisoned water sources, adding to the danger and anxiety of the advancing UN forces. At least thirty soldiers lost their lives drinking poisoned water. North Korean Army dead were roughly thirty-five thousand, while UN losses were at 5,500 American dead and sixteen thousand wounded. Another 2,500 were either MIA or taken as POWs.

"Phase II saw the enemy's resistance begin to weaken. This was brought about mainly by the landing of United Nations Forces at Inchon and Yongdok on 15th September. The 8th Cav was then given the mission to push north and join forces with the 7th Cav on our left and secure the town of Tabu-Dong. From that point the Regiment was to proceed north, cross the Naktong River and pursue the enemy as far as our supply lines would permit.

Love company still had difficulty locating enemy automatic weapons fire which was holding up their progress. Item company was able to observe Love company's progress and assisted where possible in firing on enemy emplacements. Enemy cook was observed feeding his troops from a large rice bowl by dipping a ladle of rice into each bowl which was held up by the enemy soldier from his fox hole without exposing his body. A 57mm recoilless rifle crew eliminated the cook on his return to the kitchen area."[1]

"The Inch'on landing, breaking the rear positions of the NKA, brought a long-desired relief for Walker's Army and allowed them to make their first successful assaults from the south. Chaplain Donald Carter [who was with Chaplain Kapaun], with lead elements of the 1st Cavalry Division, remembered the sudden stillness as the enemy pulled back: "...men looked at each other with wonder. The enemy was just gone! Then the company was ordered to assemble and the weary soldiers began to tumble into the defile where we were waiting. Such shouting and exultation and laughter followed with men beating each other in the back, hugging and dancing in joy and release from tension. The chaplain was included in this spontaneous demonstration..."[2]

BREAK OUT OF THE PUSAN PERIMETER

With the Marines landing at Inchon and retaking Seoul, the North Korean army was effectively cut off from their northern supply chain and wholly without naval or air support. F4U Corsairs and F-51 Mustang fighter planes armed to the teeth gave the enemy the "whole nine yards" on a daily basis, including the dropping of napalm bombs. But as the 1st Cavalry advanced with a renewed confidence and determination, they faced a grim reality with every town they overtook from the desperate Inmun Gun (North Korean) soldiers—they were killing all civilians and captured American soldiers before retreating. As a warning to UN Forces, American prisoners were seen hanging from structures and even bound with their hands behind their backs around tree trunks with their severed head in the lap. Scores of American and ROK soldiers were discovered lying in ditches with wrists bound by wire, their bodies mutilated by bullets, beatings, and stabbings. Resentment and hatred quickly rose through the ranks against the thousands of North Koreans being taken prisoner and marched south to UN POW camps. So while American soldiers did violate the code of military conduct, it was nowhere near on the scale of the atrocities committed by Communist forces. The 1st Cav already witnessed many atrocities during three months of fighting around the Pusan Perimeter—now it was growing exponentially. Everyone grew to understand that being captured was a fate worse than death.

SEPTEMBER 25—FATHER KAPAUN WRITES LETTER TO FRIENDS IN PILSEN, KANSAS

To Albert, Pauline and Family, Sanjon, Korea (Klenda family of Pilsen)

Dear Albert, Pauline and Family:

We are moving now, but have a few hours at this dilapidated town so I got some Korean paper and am writing this to you. My, how war does ruin things! You should see these towns (I ran out of ink so must proceed with pencil). The heavy artillery and the bombs blow everything to pieces. Bridges are blown up, roads are mined. The enemy went through the houses and took what they wanted. They upset what was left so that everything is one big mess. We have the Reds on the run. All along the road and fields and on the mountains and hills we find their unburied dead. They had to run so fast they left guns and ammunition. Our soldiers are quite happy now since we are moving forward. We had an awful time for a while when we had to back up. But it looks different now.

Please excuse this paper. I picked it up in a wrecked house. I am sure you will enjoy the Korean characters. I found a bottle of Korean ink so will try it out. In war a fellow uses anything he can. We have soldiers who were in the last war in Germany, others were in the Pacific. They told me this war in Korea is the toughest.

I thank you for all the prayers, etc. My boys need them worse than I do, for some way or another I have not been hit, although we were in some tough spots with bullets whistling past our heads. A fellow's nerves take an awful strain and a fellow surely can pray when these big shells explode around the area. It is no fun.

Kapaun learned from captured enemy officers that their North Korean leaders had treated them as poorly as their South Korean foes. He writes to his brother Eugene, "They said that the Communists did not care how many Koreans got killed or how hopeless a drive would be & they would order the soldiers to drive on even though all of them got killed." He also reiterates his narrow escapes from injury or death from enemy fire: "The Reds started shelling us with mortar and artillery... I was caught up on a ridge & had no fox hole. Boy, that seemed to be the last for I know what those shells can do to a fellow."

"Korean civilians walking down the highway turned to the troops and raised their arms with a lust 'manzai!' The men who were dozing immediately rushed for their weapons. (They were mistaking the word 'manzai' which means 'welcome' for 'banzai' which is 'charge!') No patrols this day. Most units awaited road clearance to move north. Orders were given to proceed to Ansong. Hot meals were served this morning. Troops were inspected and vehicles were lined up for the impending move which was scheduled for 1000 hours. Colonel Johnson reserved one half hour in the morning for a memorial service in honor of the members of the battalion who had died in combat, officiated by Chaplains Kapaun and Carter, and the battalion commander, each offering a prayer.

At 1300 King company mounted tanks while the rest of the units boarded trucks and began the long dash to Ansong. The trip was long, winding, and precarious. Men were cautioned to be particularly attentive to any harassing fires on the east, and if they were fired upon, to stop and return the fire. Otherwise, they were to ignore any action from the east or minor sniper fire on the west. It was necessary to cross a series of mountain passes late that night but hairpin turns too difficult for the tanks to negotiate and weak collapsing bridges, caused them to turn back and proceed on a different route. The convoy drove all

night long by villages where civilians lined the streets to greet
and cheer along the UN troops in pursuit of the enemy.

After more than fifteen hours of riding the column stopped
two miles east of Ansong after receiving heavy sniper fire. The
first troops of the battalion (King) arrived at Ansong at 1230
and began to flush the city by screening the hills to the north,
killing and capturing many enemy. Lack of defense shows they
were caught off guard. Ansong was an enemy Corps headquarters, and they were just eating lunch when they were surprised.

During the month of September, enemy losses were estimated
at 12,315 KIA (Killed in Action) and nearly 4000 POWs. For
the first time since the fighting started, the enemy began to surrender in large numbers. At least 31 machine guns and 120 artillery pieces were also captured. At the end of the month, the
assigned strength of the 1st Cav Division totaled 13,413 but the
authorized strength was 18,914."[3]

"THE MOST DRAMATIC RECITATION OF THE LORD'S PRAYER I HAVE EVER HEARD"

On September 29, General MacArthur flew in to Seoul to tour
the devastated capital with President Syngman Rhee. Similar
to what MacArthur saw in Manila in 1945 was the bodies of
more than 20,000 civilians murdered for supporting the Rhee
regime. Many more American soldiers were also found, bound
in wire and executed. What they witnessed was a resounding
reminder of what a final Communist victory would have looked
like had they succeeded in taking the entire Korean Peninsula.

At the National Assembly Hall, General MacArthur addressed
the large crowd:

"Mr. President: By the grace of a merciful Providence our
forces have liberated this ancient capital city of Korea." He went
on to speak of the UN's 'righteous wrath,' referred to a 'spiritual revulsion against Communism,' and concluded by leading
the assembly in a recitation of the Lord's Prayer. One eyewit-

ness said it was the most dramatic recitation of the Lord's Prayer they had ever heard.

Our Father who art in Heaven, Hallowed be Thy Name. In the distance, artillery fire could be heard and occasional rifle fire.

Thy Kingdom come. Boom! An artillery blast hits so close to the hall that it shakes the building and breaks out windows. Soldiers put their helmets on. Of course, MacArthur didn't even pause.

Thy will be done On Earth as it is in Heaven. Amen.

The echoes of "amen" died away, and then MacArthur turned to Syngman Rhee standing beside him and said, "Mr. President, my officers and I will now resume our military duties and leave you and your government to the discharge of civil responsibilities."

The two shook hands with tears streaming down their faces. Rhee then told MacArthur, "We love you as the savior of our race. How can I ever explain to you my own undying gratitude and that of the Korean people?"

GENERAL MACARTHUR IGNORES WARNINGS OF CHINESE INTERVENTION IN KOREA

Korean war historians for decades have generally assumed that the reason China entered the war was because UN Forces commenced to pour over the 38th parallel into North Korea in October of 1950. However, new letters have emerged from Chairman Mao at the time, stating basically the impetus for the Chinese offensive was decided when Truman made the case for the UN intervention in Korea in July 1950. Mobilizing hundreds of thousands of troops for combat cannot happen overnight—it would take months to prepare and be very hard to conceal. So the months in which the NKPA was getting soundly defeated, Mao was using great diplomatic prowess to ensure further backing from Stalin and Russia, especially air power. He couldn't possibly predict an annihilation of the 8th Army and control of the entire peninsula, but he could assume a taking back of North Korea and thus keep "Wall Street" off their direct border. He also predicted that the west would not go nuclear again, something even Stalin believed. Chinese diplomats sent a message on October 3, 1950, through the Indian government that China would confront any US troops entering into North Korea. Despite intelligence showing four hundred thousand Chinese troops massing on the border of North Korea, Washington dismissed the show of force as a bluff and a "defensive" movement. When about 250,000 Chinese "volunteers" began entering North Korea between October 19 and 22, Washington and Truman failed to detect them.

KAPAUN WRITES TO BROTHER EUGENE

Ansong, Korea—2 Oct 1950

Dear Eugene and Helen, Congratulations on your wedding anniversary coming soon. I have no decent present to send you, but get yourselves something you need.

We had a tough time lately and were trapped. I still wonder how we got out alive. No food for 2 days no water supply for 1 day. Luckily it rained at night and I caught a drink in my slicker. How are you folks? Hope well. I am fine but tired and sore feet. Could not write as we were cut off and got no mail for 10 days. Now we are running ahead fast. The Reds sure did get it in the neck. I hope the war will be over soon.

May God bless you, As ever in Christ Fr. Emil

FATHER KAPAUN LETTER TO BISHOP OF WICHITA, MARK CARROLL

Thank you very much for your kind letter sent last month. It took some time to reach us as we had been trapped by the Reds and could not get any mail or anything else. This was the fourth time we were trapped, and the first time I had no fox hole to run to. With these high-powered shells exploding on all sides, one trembles and prays that none will land nearby. When a man is hit he screams for help or the others near him scream for him if unconscious. The whole experience is nerve-racking. We have broken over the Red lines and have advanced over a hundred miles. We just wonder if the war is nearly over. During this awful conflict I was impressed with the way most of the soldiers were prepared spiritually. I hope that all of them who lost their lives have found a merciful Judge.

I wish to thank you and all the good people who have been sending prayers heavenward for us in Korea. Something saved us besides our efforts, for many of us are convinced we are living only on borrowed time.

May our good Blessed Mother protect all during this month of the Holy Rosary.

"DAYS OF TENDERNESS AND LOVE"

Father Kapaun's letter to his bishop can only be read in its entirety to be absorbed and understood for what it is—a sublime experience of beauty and love in the midst of war:

Most Reverend and dear bishop:
As we have a couple of hours of waiting until our convoy takes to the road again, I want to write you about my latest experience at Ansung (City) Korea. We came into Ansung last Wednesday afternoon and completely surprised the town. The Communists were not expecting us at all. Our jeeps drove up to the City Hall and the Communists started jumping out the windows in hasty flight. We caught most of them. At the Police Station the Reds were just eating their noon meal. They jumped up, left their rice on the platters, and ran, but we got many of them, too. Some of them were wounded, some killed, as they tried to escape.

Joe Stalin's picture and the Korean Communist leader's picture were side by side over the main entrances to the public buildings. Also, they had many posters around depicting the barbarous United States and the atrocities we commit. One of our wounded Red prisoners told our interpreter that they expected us to cut off their noses and ears when we captured them. The Russian Reds had told them that is what we do.

As soon as we had the town in hand and the shooting ceased, I started to look around. I saw a building with a red cross on it, a hospital. I went there and was met at the door by two nurses and a doctor. None of them could speak English and I could not speak Korean. I pointed to the white cross on my steel helmet and tried to tell them I was a Catholic Chaplain. I made the sign of the cross and they showed me their blessed medals and rosaries. I took out my confession stole, which I carry with the Blessed Sacrament and with the holy oils, and they kissed it reverently. They knew I was a priest, pointed to the north, and tried to tell me where the Catholic Church was. The nurses told our Korean interpreter that they would show us the Catholic Church. Together we made our way through narrow lanes between mud houses until finally we reached the Church compound. It was littered with all kinds of debris. We went into the Church. The altars were intact, but all paintings, statues, and crosses were destroyed. I told my interpreter to tell the people I was a Catholic priest—they gave me the famous oriental bow of the head (a bow which nearly touches the ground).

At 9:00 on Thursday the people assembled in their church which was now a very clean and respectable building. The Reds did not destroy it, intending to use it for their own purposes. They would not permit the people to go to church. They said they do not believe in God and would not let any of their people worship God. These people lost their two Korean priests and three Korean Sisters on July 5. I asked where they were. The people did not know. All they knew was that the priests fled to the mountains. Where the Sisters went I do not know. The people celebrated that Mass on Thursday with great awe. It was the first time they saw an American Chaplain and the first Mass in their church since the godless Reds took over this community. Two Korean boys served and their Latin was perfect. As I said the prayers at the foot of the altar I could not help but think I could not speak the language of these people nor could they speak mine, but at the altar we had a common language. I imagine the people felt the same way. Some of my soldiers were at Mass and went to Holy Communion. The people could see very easily the difference between the United States soldiers and the godless Reds who closed their church. They told me through the interpreter that they had a choir. I arranged to have Father Maguire of Division Artillery to say the Sunday Mass as I had to go up into the hills to say Mass for my soldiers. Father Maguire said the Mass and later told me that this was the most impressive Mass he ever had in his whole Army experience. The church was packed with Catholic Koreans and American soldiers. The choir sang beautifully. After Mass the soldiers gave a donation to the community of some 60,000 won (Korean) (about $30.00 in American money). The ironic part about the Sunday Mass was that the Military Police had set up their prison compound next to the Church. While Mass was being celebrated and the choir was singing, there were some 300 Communist Red prisoners in the prison compound. They were the ones who said they would not let anyone believe in God, yet now, right in the building next to them, a free people was worshipping God in a free way, and the Reds were in prison.

However, they should be grateful to be in the prison of a decent people, for we know what these same Reds did to our soldier prisoners.

The Catholic people at Ansung told me: "Now we have a Father again." I told them that I would not be here very long as we would be moving ahead to a different place. And today we are moving. That is the life of a Chaplain. It has its rough days when a person is face to face with death, and it has its days of tenderness and love as we found at Ansung City, Korea.

...(I ran out of ink so must close this with pencil.) May God bless you and the whole Diocese."

The everlasting politeness and relentless faith of Father Kapaun was again showing through.

THE ROAD TO SARIWON

Captain John P. Gannon recounts a profound incident after the 1st Cav crossed into North Korea: "Father Kapaun, in my opinion, is one of the finest men who ever lived. If he had fear of anything in combat, it was only fear for the lives and well-being of our soldiers and none for himself. The last time I saw him and spoke to him was October 9, 1950, just above the 38th parallel on the road to Sariwon. We were attacking through the Kaesong defense line when we were hit from three sides and stopped—partly surrounded. Having received two hits myself, I was returning to our aid station and escorting a North Korean whom I had taken the time to capture. (We needed information badly and he had it.) We had to take cover and move fast into the ditch along the road because the Koreans were firing at anything that moved. A cloud of dust coming from our rear revealed a jeep coming fast. It stopped and out jumped Father Kapaun and his friend, Protestant chaplain Donald Carter. I said, 'Hello, Father. It's pretty hot here, so take to the ditch and keep low.' Father smiled, thanked me and said, 'I'll be all right.' He was smoking a pipe. We left and I moved to the road as a hill gave us cover at this point. For some reason I turned and looked back to see how Father was doing and a mortar shell landed exactly on the spot where the chaplains had been walking. Out of the dust and debris I saw legs and arms moving as the two of them, miraculously unhurt, high-tailed it for the ditch. I was relieved! That blast had only broken Father's pipe. He taped it together and I heard from my former platoon sergeant, Bill Killion, that Father used that pipe up to the time he died. Father Kapaun was admired as a fine example of everything that is good, clean and charitable."[4]

"NO BULLET GOT ME YET" LETTER TO MOM AND DAD

Kaeson (on border with South Korea)

The news is the same. We are still well and alive and hoping the war will be over before long. The Reds are moving back and are getting a good licking. We are right on the 38th parallel north and a little west of Seoul. You can probably locate it on a map. The envelopes and paper you sent came in handy. Did Dad celebrate his birthday? I guess you had a big celebration on September 28, when Bishop blessed the Sisters' Convent. I see Bishop Carroll put my letter in the paper and even the Record Review had it. I better be careful or the sheriff will be looking for me. That would be about as bad as what happened recently to my assistant. He got a notice from the draft board to appear at the physical examination room to be drafted and he is in the Army now over two years.

Well, we soldiers are thankful for all your prayers and Masses. Father Goracy wrote that many people came to the Mass for me, even the whole choir, so they had a High

Mass. Somebody must be praying hard for us. No bullet got me yet although my pipe got wrecked and the day before yesterday a machine gunner sprayed us with bullets but we jumped into the ditch too quickly.

May God bless you and keep you in good health.

In this letter, Kapaun may have been referring to October 9 when his pipe got wrecked (again!) when he dove into the ditch to avoid the mortar round explosion. He mentions being missed by a machine gunner but not a mortar round. Through his entire time in combat, Kapaun survived near misses from hundreds if not thousands of bullets, banzai charges, countless artillery and mortar barrages, tank shells, and even friendly fire. He truly wore "God's armor."

"GOD HAS CHOSEN ME TO BE HERE AM0NG THE DYING AND THE DEAD"

This letter was written about two weeks before Kapaun was taken prisoner but remained on his person the entire time as he had no army postal carrier to give it to. No other letters came from him after that until news of his death in 1953. Yet again another profound letter and relic that not only revealed such utterly beautiful prophecy but also stands as a symbol of perseverance, faith and miraculous survival—having to be kept hidden from camp guards over a year and a half before being ultimately smuggled out by the last surviving POWs who were released in fall 1953.

American Red Cross—Kaesong, Korea—October 12, 1950

Dear Fr. [Goracy]
It really was a wonderful treat to receive your nice letter, Father, and the word that you have had a High Mass for me. Father, I have nothing with which to thank you, ex-

cept to say that I appreciate it with all my heart. Somehow or another, God has chosen me to be here among the dying and the dead to be of what help I can to them. To do it, all of us here have to face death, and we see it on all sides of us. We wonder when our turn is next; and to hear that you people back home are doing so much for us makes us feel—well I don't know how to describe it.

Yesterday I received a clipping with pictures of the new Sister's Convent in Pilsen. Father, you are to be congratulated. And your account of purchasing the Elk church for Marion—good for you. I hope everything works out well. I had to smile at your invitations to be with you in Pilsen at Christmas this year. If the North Koreans do not give up, and if I do not get shot up, I suppose we will celebrate Christmas right here in Korea. We are right on the 38th parallel now, directly north and perhaps a little west of Seoul. If you have a map you can pin-locate us. Anyway we are all praying and working hard that this war will end (and soon, we hope).

Thanks again, Father, for everything. May God bless you and your whole parish. Please give my regards to the good Sisters—they do not know me, nor I them.
As ever in Christ, Fr. E. K.

With Kapaun's poignant statement about God choosing him to be among the dying and the dead to be of what help he could be to them and, "To do it, all of us here have to face death, and we see it on all sides of us," little did Father Goracy know the full extent to which Father Kapaun was as humane and respectful to the dead of his Communist enemies as he was to his own side. On more than one occasion after a battle had ended, Kapaun asked for help in burying dead North Korean soldiers after their own had been taken care of.

"WE DO HAVE A FEW LAUGHS
IN SPITE OF THE EVILS OF WAR"

Kaesong, Korea—October 13, 1950

Dear Helen and Eugene, It has been a long time since I heard from you or wrote to you so while we are waiting to move along the road again I am going to write this letter on an old map which I found. How are you by this time? I am well and getting along fine. Hope you are the same. You wrote me that you had a lot of cold and wet weather in September. It is getting cold here in Korea too. In fact we have a light frost at night. This outdoor life is quite the thing—that is, for people who like it. I prefer to live in a house once in a while. Three days ago I took some millet and hay and slept on it rather than on the hard cold floor of the shack we found. My, that sure did sleep good in spite of all the 155 mm guns going off during the night. On Monday and Tuesday this week we had another slaughter. Several of our soldiers got killed and many wounded. My pipe got wrecked again as a Red machine gunner sprayed us with lead and we had to hit the ditch. It is funny how a fellow can jump so fast into a ditch. This time it did not have water in it. The last couple of times the ditch had water in it and you can imagine how we looked. We do have a few laughs in spite of the evils of war.

It looks like the war will end soon. We pushed the Reds over 150 miles now. We are right on the 38th parallel right north and a little west of Seoul. Maybe you can locate us on a map. I surely hope that all is well with you. I sent your pictures home so they would not get ruined out here in the dust and mud.

God bless you and help you, As ever in Christ Fr. E. K.

Father Kapaun's last letter sent to his brother is quite a unique document. Since he was always scrounging for paper to write on, he apparently had this military map of the Inchon area where thousands of marines had landed just a month before. The back was blank, so he perfectly filled the space with his elegant cursive handwriting in pencil. His words again epitomize the very humble, curious, and kind soul of just *who* Father Kapaun was during extremely dangerous and traumatic experiences. He always maintained a rock-steady sense of humor. Every single sentence reveals something about his character, the character of his fellow soldiers, the enemy, or just a clean joking around that must have been his way (and others too) of coping with constant trepidation and fear of a violent injury or death during war. In this letter, Father Kapaun inadvertently left a blood smear on the page.

"ONLY A HUMBLE PRIEST IS A GOOD ONE"
LAST LETTER TO FRIEND FRED TUZICKA

American Red Cross—Kaesong, Korea—October 14, 1950

Your kind & long letter reached me yesterday up here on the front lines. We are north of Seoul, on the 38th parallel. We wonder just what is going to happen and hope that this war will end soon. Many thanks for your kind letter as I know you are very busy & do not have much time to write. It is different with me. I have no difficult Dogma to study or any classwork to do. Nothing to do but to take care of my boys. Sometimes we are very busy, and other times we sit and wait. We are sitting right now in our jeep waiting to start moving to a different place. So I am making use of the time by writing some letters. I have no ink, so please excuse this crude letter. It sure is grand to hear that you are getting so close to your goal. You mentioned that you were so unworthy. If you ask me I think those are the kind that our Lord likes, and they are the ones who make good priests. Only a humble priest is a good one. The proud man should not be a priest. Yes, Fred, since we last talked together many things have happened. God has been very good to me. He chose me for some reason or another to be with soldiers in this war. The work is always gratifying, but to see so much destruction of lives & property is heart-breaking. Both my soldiers & I are thankful that we did not have to fight this war in the US. There sure would be a lot of suffering if we did.

Many thanks to you and to your whole family for the many remembrances in prayer. You are very fortunate to have such a blessed family. Please give them my greetings when you write. I think of you folks often too but do not have the chance to write. God bless you Fred in your preparation for the Priesthood. Please give my greetings to the Fathers at Conception.

As ever in Christ, Fr. Emil Kapaun

KAPAUN'S LAST PACKAGE SENT HOME TO BISHOP CARROLL

"On October 16, Father Kapaun sent Bishop Carroll a packet which contained the following note: "Enclosed are some items of interest which we picked up in the communist-infested country. Perhaps some school might like to have these as items of curiosity. God had been very good to us and we are still alive."

The items in the packet were as follows:

- A large painting on rough canvas of the Commander in Chief of North Korea.
- A sketch of Lenin surrounded by Stalin, Trotsky, and other Russian revolutionaries.
- A full-length picture of Stalin standing before a harbor.
- Several pieces of Korean paper money.

Communist propaganda Chaplain Kapaun found in Seoul, Korea, and mailed to Kansas before his capture.

- Some posters and arm bands with the characteristic red star in the middle.
- A pledge to be taken by the North Korean Communist soldiers, which is translated as follows: "I am a good soldier of the Korean People's Republic. When I enter the people's army I will act with all confidence and will accomplish my duty as the government orders. I will fight for our Korean People's Republic till I die. I will fight for our people and Korea's freedom. I will also keep the secrets of my people's army, absolutely. If I break this most important regulation, I will be willing to accept any kind of punishment from the people's court."

The packet and the note of October 16, 1950, were actually the last communications anybody received from Chaplain Emil Kapaun. The young priest who was so faithful in writing letters would soon find it impossible to communicate with them any longer. As a prisoner of war of the Chinese Communists, this opportunity would be denied to him. There are certain international regulations on paper about the treatment of prisoners of war, and one of them provides that a prisoner of war should be allowed to send short messages to his nearest relatives. The sad reality is that they set aside these international agreements and had no regard for fair treatment. Happily for us, the officers and soldiers who were in contact with Father Kapaun during this time were so impressed by this man of God from Kansas that we have ample material for reconstructing what happened to Father Kapaun in the next few months."[5]

FATHER KAPAUN'S LAST CHAPLAIN REPORT TO THE MILITARY ORDINARIATE

"Even in the confusion and horror of war, Kapaun was faced with the task of answering the routine questions for the Military Ordinariate. In October 1950, he could have easily omitted the September reports to New York, but patiently he answered the tedious questions:

'Where is Holy Mass celebrated?'

'In the following way: Sundays—on table indoors and on hood of jeep outdoors. Weekdays:—On table indoors and on hood of jeep outdoors.'

'Where is the Blessed Sacrament reserved?'

'On my person.'

'Is a light constantly burning before it?'

'No.'

This clearly shows what kind of man Chaplain Kapaun was. He could easily have balked and said he was too busy to answer any routine questions and that he was doing the very best he could under the pressure of the circumstances, but as long as routine questions were a part of his duty, he did not neglect them but answered them nonchalantly."[6] The report concludes:

Summary: About 10 Extreme Unctions.
1 Catechetical Instruction.
General Remarks: Was awarded the Bronze Star Medal.

12

THE CAPTURE OF PYONGYANG

"I don't know how Truman and MacArthur feel about each other, but one left the Waldorf just as the other one entered. That was three days ago, and the revolving door is still spinning."—A Bob Hope joke from this time.

THE WAKE ISLAND CONFERENCE

To say the Wake Island meeting between President Truman and General MacArthur on October 15, 1950, was one of the most pivotal meetings in human history would be an understatement. Truman had full confidence that MacArthur would have the war concluded by Christmas. MacArthur, overconfident following the successful Inchon landing, believed he could wrap up the war by then as well. But the problem was defining what a successful conclusion looked like and who exactly would be signing a surrender of North Korea's territory over to a unified Korea with no North or South boundaries. The only way to achieve that would be to physically occupy, with UN

Forces, ROK Forces and the 8th Army, all territory right up to
the border of China and Russia—totaling about nine hundred
miles. At the time of their meeting, MacArthur had already
been sending the 1st Cavalry Division, ROK Forces and other
units over the 38th parallel for a week. In addition, the Marines
were headed into North Korea along the east coast of the peninsula. While both the president and the general believed capturing Pyongyang would "end the war," they were both utterly
naïve to believe China and Russia would do nothing and allow
a Communist neighbor to be wiped away.

Say what you will about General MacArthur's pompous and
egotistical traits that led to some brash failures in WW2—he
did achieve the momentous victory over Japan celebrated the
world over and tamed the remaining population into a peaceful
and ultimately prosperous democracy. Koreans will never forget being occupied by Japan from 1910 until 1945. But China
and Russia were at war with Japan in WW2 as well and with
the US distracted by the threat of the Soviet Union in Europe,
the defense of South Korea had waned severely by the time of
the North Korean invasion in June 1950. Anticipating an incur-
sion of Chinese troops into North Korea in the coming weeks,
MacArthur told Truman that as long as he had significant air
and naval superiority over China, he could bomb them into
submission and still win the Korean War with the entire peninsula being unified. Even if that meant declaring war on China.
MacArthur then went much further in his strategy to win, saying, if necessary, they would have to bomb significant portions
of China and that even nuclear bombs should be at his disposal
to end the Communist threat.

The meeting ended with no clear answer given to MacArthur
publicly about China entering the war. They both foolishly believed, despite growing intelligence to the contrary, that China
would stay out. But within just two weeks of their meeting, on
October 30, 1950, MacArthur lambasted President Truman say-

ing in effect he did not trust the Commander in Chief to have the American or Korean people's national security interests at heart—basically you either stop Communism now or it will be a threat forever. It is with sad irony that literally the next day, Halloween 1950, that the first major clash between Chinese and American troops occurred deep in North Korea at Unsan—the canary in the coal mine foretelling just how much they underestimated the will of Mao Tse-tung and Joseph Stalin to launch a second offensive into Korea with numbers five times greater than the original offensive. Chaplain Kapaun and the members of the 5th and 8th Regiments, along with ROK units, had no idea the extent of the trap they were waltzing right into.

THE FIRST CAVALRY CROSSES THE 38th PARALLEL

"We were told to saddle up for the ride into North Korea. When we neared the border, a World War II combat veteran announced, 'Remember this day, you guys. We're makin' history.' The spontaneous reply, delivered in unison: 'Buuuulllshit!'"[1]

PRIVATE PATRICK SCHULER

"Going north, our convoy ran into resistance about 8:00 one morning. Father Kapaun left in the jeep and when he hadn't returned six hours later, I drove up front to look for him. There he was, quite calm, under machine gun fire.

'I broke my pipe,' was all he said. 'A sniper opened up on me and I had to crawl to reach a wounded man… I broke my pipe.'

'He'd sit there, just as calm. What a man!'"[2]

KAPAUN SAVES LIFE OF AN ENEMY SOLDIER

Captain Dolan recalls: "After we broke through the thin North Korean lines, our biggest problem was taking the thousands of prisoners that wanted to give up. Again, on this occasion, Father's courage was manifest. When my jeep arrived on one scene, there was an enemy soldier in some underbrush and he had something in his hand. It looked like a 'potato masher' grenade, one that was easy to activate and throw just by striking it. Some of the GI's wanted to shoot him, but Father gestured to the enemy soldier with his canteen in an international language. Ultimately—it didn't happen very quickly—the guy dropped his grenade to the side and crawled out. He was thirsty and hungry, as they all were."[3]

By October 17, the 3rd Battalion advanced to Sariwon, North Korea, with the 27th British Brigade. They were taking North Korean prisoners at a rate of at least twenty per hour and handing them off to Division Intelligence teams, which would interrogate them before shipping them to UN POW camps down in the southern tip of the Korean peninsula where tens of thousands of prisoners were starting to accumulate.

OCTOBER 20, 1950

As the 1st Cavalry entered Pyongyang, the North Korean capital, they were met with very little resistance. Skittish residents with no interest in fighting hid in their homes to see what the green army men would do. Around town and on the wall of the city hall building hung enormous portraits of Stalin and Kim Il Sung. 1st Cavalry troopers immediately set out to tear such portraits down and collect souvenirs while others grabbed paint and brushes and painted the distinctive yellow-and-black Cavalry logo all over town. Lieutenant Phil Peterson and Lieutenant Walt Mayo, both friends with Chaplain Kapaun, were forward observers (FOs) for the 99th Field Artillery Battalion working with the 3rd Battalion of the 8th Regiment. They procured a bottle of poor quality Russian champagne from the Russian Embassy and gagged it down despite its nasty taste as a symbol of victory. After so much intense fighting, they could finally

Using a Sherman tank for cover, soldiers from the 1st Cavalry Division advance on the North Korean capital of Pyongyang, October 20, 1950.

unwind. Father Kapaun was given some liberated whiskey but saved it, not wanting to partake just yet.

Fitting with his arrogant style, MacArthur himself landed at the Pyongyang airfield for a surprise visit and morale boost for the 1st Cavalry. When he got off the plane, he joked, "Any celebrities here to greet me?" and "Where is Kim Buck Tooth?" in a mocking nod to North Korean leader Kim Il Sung. The moment turned solemn, however, when he asked anyone in the cavalry who had been with the unit from the beginning to step forward. Of the two hundred assembled, only *four* men came forward, and each one had been wounded at some point. Right then and there he had to realize that hundreds of his beloved 1st Cavalry were killed in action in just three months for him to even stand on that ground. MacArthur shook some hands and then got back on the plane. He never spent even one night in Korea during the entire time he commanded.

Still, MacArthur's visit and departure was a sign that the war was indeed over and euphoria was in the air. The 1st Cav started turning in ammunition; they were getting three hot meals a day; a USO show was in the works and artillery ammunition was being off-loaded. But the real confirmation came when boxes of traditional yellow cavalry neckerchiefs arrived and the order given that they be worn all through the week until they would be in Tokyo for a planned victory parade for the First Cavalry Division.

"WE'RE ALL GOING HOME"

On October 25, Major General Laurence (Dutch) Keiser, commander of the famed 2nd Infantry Division, announced to his officers: "We're all going home and we're going home soon—before Christmas. We have our orders." When an officer asked where they were going, Keiser said he couldn't tell them, but it would be a place they would like. The speculation began: Tokyo? Hawaii? Stateside? The preparation for a troop movement back to their base in Japan had barely begun when they were ordered to prepare to move.

CAPTAIN JOSEPH O'CONNOR

"Another point was Father's attitude towards those men who died in the earlier stages of the war. After we had occupied Pyongyang, North Korea, and had thought the war was over, Father was attached to our battalion for rations, etc. Normally, when he was in our outfit he would be around taking care of the spiritual and moral needs of the men. During this period he was conspicuous by his absence and quite frequently was late for, or missed his meals. I was naturally curious and asked him what was going on. He said he had a lot of administrative work to do. I asked him if I could get one or two of the men to help him. He refused, saying that this was something he had to do personally.

Shortly after, I found him in a dilapidated and abandoned Korean hut adjacent to the large building the battalion occupied. He had an old ammo crate for a desk and an ammunition box for a seat. He had approximately five to six hundred cards of men who were killed or who had died while in combat. Also,

on each card he had the address of the next of kin and a nota-
tion as to whether or not he had administered the last rites to
the individuals. He was writing a personal letter to each of the
next of kin.

This, to the best of my knowledge, is definitely not required
of an army chaplain. Father Kapaun and the Protestant Chaplain, Captain Carter, were taking it upon themselves to do this
so as to better ease the minds of friends and relatives of the deceased. The building Father used had holes in it and was extremely cold. I asked him why he didn't request office space
from me in battalion headquarters. He thought I was too busy
and he didn't want to interfere with my work. That is the type
of man that he was. He would ask for nothing and give everything, even his life."[4]

DR. JEROME DOLAN

"The last time I saw Father Emil Kapaun was in late October
1950. We had been with one of the first units to cross the 38th
parallel and to capture the North Korean capital, Pyongyang. It
was a quiet time and Father and I each had rooms in what must
have been a military academy. By modern standards it was not
very elite but after the ground, it was marvelous. I went by to
see Father in his room and I found him writing letters to the
families of the KIAs and MIAs. I offered to help write some letters but he said, 'This is the Chaplain's job.' He must have found
some ink and paper and envelopes somewhere because we had
been using brown paper or other paper we had received from
home to write our own letters with pencil because we had no
source of paper, envelopes or ink. But Father was the world's
champion 'scrounger.' If you needed something, he would find
it. And apparently he did the same thing in the prison camps.
He did allow me, however, to address the envelopes so I felt that
the last time that we were together I was of some help to him."[5]

BOB HOPE PERFORMS IN PYONGYANG

Bob Hope performed a USO show with popular singer and actress Marilyn Maxwell at Pyongyang Airfield for two hours while the sound of artillery boomed in the background. Eight thousand soldiers attended, including William Funchess. One of Hope's writers was Larry Gelbart, who later went on to produce the *M*A*S*H* TV show. This is a partial transcript from that night, when Bob Hope interviews Sergeant First Class Harvey Hyslop of the 24th Division:

HOPE: Ladies and gentlemen, no brighter pages have been written in our history books than the new additions made in Korea by our fighting ground forces. Against overwhelming odds and, for a time, against superior weapons, the doughty GIs moved up from a potential Dunkirk to a point where the enemy was in full rout. In the thick of it, side by side with the First Cavalry, was the 24th Division of our Army. I'd like to introduce now a man who's been up front with the 24th since the first week of the trouble—Sergeant First Class Harvey Hyslop!

(applause)

HOPE: At one time you almost had to retreat to Pusan, didn't you?

HARVEY: Pusan? We almost had to retreat to the Royal Hawaiian Hotel in Honolulu. Incidentally, Bob, they don't call it retreat…it's called "strategic withdrawal."

HOPE: I see. But tell me…just what's the difference between a retreat and a strategic withdrawal?

HARVEY: About twenty more steps to the minute.

HOPE: Those first days around Osan were rough, weren't they, Harv?

HARVEY: That's the understatement of the whole campaign. My company went into action with 123 men and came out with 47. We couldn't seem to stop the North Koreans.

HOPE: I know, Harv. You were really outnumbered, eh?

HARVEY: Outnumbered and definitely up against superior weapons. We'd bounce those 2.36 bazooka rockets and 75 millimeter shells off those T-34 tanks and they just kept right on coming.

HOPE: Tell me, Harv, were those Russian-made tanks?

HARVEY: Frankly, Bob, none of us stopped to look.

HOPE: We've all got to take our hats off to the 24th Division.

HARVEY: Well, thanks, Bob. And while you're at it, I'm going to take mine off to the First Cavalry that's been in action since July 25th, the rocketing ROKs, and the great support we've been given by the First Marine Division, the Air Force, and the Navy.[6]

OCTOBER 27, 1950—FATHER KAPAUN CELEBRATES MASS

Word of the Bob Hope show spread like wildfire. But despite Father Kapaun's many references to jokes they made and the sarcastic "fun" the boys were having in between the deadly battles, he felt now was not the time to let loose under the thinly veiled promise that the war was over and they would be returning home. Making his usual low-key invitation for anyone to attend his Mass and prayer session, he attracted about twenty men to attend, including Bill Richardson who was not Catholic. In a makeshift chapel in one of the hospital rooms, he covered a table with purple cloth with a chalice centered in the middle. Still with him was his cracked black leather Missal with gold lettering on the cover which contained his prayers for Mass. Richardson recalls the gold letters reduced to pieces of gold specks from the wear. They huddled on rickety benches and bowed their heads.

"Heavenly Father, thank you for protecting these men as they did your work."

For the rest of his life, Bill Richardson thought about his precious time with Father Kapaun all the time. He summed that day up by simply saying:

"I was not a religious person, but I felt like one that day."

13

THE BATTLE OF UNSAN

At the end of only one week that the 1st Cavalry and 24th Division occupied Pyongyang, the signs were there loudly signaling an end to any confidence or hope of "winning" the Korean War that had only began five months prior. The arrogance or ignorance of disregarding strong intelligence about massive movements of literally hundreds of thousands of Chinese troops days away from a full-scale second offensive against UN Forces in North Korea cannot be underscored enough. While thousands of American troops celebrated what they believed to be the end of the Korean War, only Chaplain Kapaun and maybe a handful of others were reticent to accept this as fact. So while Bob Hope, one of the biggest names in entertainment the world has ever seen, laughs it up with eight thousand soldiers attending his show at the Pyongyang Airfield, Father Kapaun holds a solemn Mass for about two dozen soldiers, praying for a resolution to the uncertainty of war with China that only a very few felt was inevitable. While many saw hope and going home in Bob Hope's show, that was drained

First Cavalry members greet airborne troops around an M24 Chaffee light tank near Sukchon, North Korea, about a hundred miles north of Pyongyang on October 24, 1950. Though unidentified, these troops and tanks could have been with Chaplain Kapaun and the 3rd Battalion, as just a week later, two Chaffee tanks were destroyed in the Battle of Unsan, November 1–2.

away less than twenty-four hours later when elements of the 1st Cavalry were ordered north to help secure the entire border of North Korea at the Yalu River. It was a trap of epic proportions.

"When the 8th Cavalry reached Unsan, the chaplains of the 8th Regiment agreed to rotate among the battalions; near the 1st of November, Chaplain Carter, living with the 3rd Battalion held in reserve, exchanged places with his friend, Kapaun, in the 1st Battalion. Carter wanted the priest to 'enjoy a day or so' away from the tension where the heaviest attack was expected."[1]

On October 31, the 3rd Battalion established its command post and assembly area ringed with a perimeter of trenches and machine gun crew positions in an open area bordered by mountains to the north and low-level rivers to the south and west. The low, flat cornfield, within observation and shooting distance from the mountain ridges, was a dangerous place to set up defensive positions. The only road in was the regiment's main supply route (MSR) chock full of the many vehicles and support sections that follow a regiment. They normally would have been set up much farther south but because of the lack of mobility, the supply train for the 8th Regiment was allowed to move closer as no attacks were expected. The convoy had support vehicles like administrative offices, kitchens, ammunition supplies, motor vehicle maintenance crews, etc., all of which were not used in direct combat operations. Armor support for the 3rd Battalion consisted of three Sherman tanks spread apart in the perimeter and two General Chaffee light tanks protecting the rear. Back farther in the rear, mortar crews were dug into pits and well behind them various artillery batteries were dug in and supplied with copious amounts of rounds. The total strength of the 8th Regiment that day was about 2,500 men.

As the various companies dug in, they noticed several columns of black smoke rising into the sky from three sides. Command was oblivious to the fact that the Chinese army, fearful of daytime fighter plane attacks, burned piles of cut trees and brush to conceal their movements behind walls of towering smoke. Without realizing it, the entirety of the 3rd Battalion was already surrounded by tens of thousands of Chinese troops that only attacked at night.

At the new command post the former 3rd Battalion CO, Lieutenant Colonel Harold Johnson met with Major Robert Ormond to voice his concern about their position before going back south to command the 5th Regiment. He flat out told Major Ormond they should be up on the high ground as they were too vulnerable in the valley and would have scant defense if hit head-on. But the observation was shrugged off as it was not a direct order. Colonel Johnson left the meeting shaking his head in disbelief.

Bill Richardson and his men were given the mission of securing the ninety-feet long concrete bridge at Camel's Head Bend, which was about a mile south and not visible from the 3rd Battalion Command Post. Two rivers converged near the bridge but were almost dry, leaving numerous places for enemy vehicles or troops to cross. As Colonel Johnson passed over the bridge to return south to the 5th Regiment's CP, he stopped to warn Richardson that pesky road blocks were popping up over fifteen miles to the south and the enemy may use the riverbed to withdraw right up into Unsan.

Confident in his men and their ability to defeat the North Koreans thus far, Richardson thanked the colonel and said: "Sir, if they come up this riverbed, they've had it."

Colonel Johnson smiled and simply replied:

"Be careful."

THE HALLOWEEN PARTY

In the afternoon of October 31, Major John Millikin, commander of the 5th Cavalry Regiment (now located to the southwest of the 8th Cavs rear flank) observed through his binoculars an entire hillside that appeared to be alive with ants as waves of enemy soldiers approached their lines. Artillery strikes were called in and continuous shelling of the enemy occurred, but it was impossible to gauge if it was doing any good. Fearing a "double envelopment" of the 8th Cavalry, Major General Hobart Gay took this report and requested I Corps call for the 8th Cav to be withdrawn six miles south of Unsan to a much more defendable position across the Kuryong River to Ipsok. The request was denied.

BANZAI!

At about 10:30 pm, all of 3rd Battalion's attention was grabbed by the eerie foreign sounds of bugles, perhaps flutes and Asian bagpipes intended to rival the sound of nails dragged on a chalkboard and amplified with public address speakers. The noises came from seemingly all directions clearly meant to strike fear into their enemy. From out of the hills, thousands of Chinese soldiers sprinted toward the sparsely manned American positions and simply overwhelmed them to the point the Americans didn't know whether to shoot forwards or behind. The Chinese simply sacrificed many of their troops on the outset in exchange for wounding or killing far fewer American GIs. Bodies were strewn all over the place. Despite the chaos, Major Millikin lined up a convoy of about ten deuce-and-a-half trucks, with a Chaffee tank in the front and rear, to get the wounded loaded and carried down south to the closest aid stations. Father Kapaun helped load some wounded and Sergeant Ben Boyd asked if he would stay with the trucks when they departed. Kapaun refused, saying he must go back to the CP and protect the rising number of wounded there—even if it meant having to surrender.

The convoy didn't make it very far before the lead tank was destroyed and the ten-truck convoy halted. Like shooting fish in a barrel, the Chinese forces decimated the convoy from the high ground on both sides of the valley road, leaving very few survivors. Once again, Kapaun had dodged a bullet in the service of others. Had he been killed in the convoy, the many wounded still stuck in the CP would never had a chance.

PRIVATE PATRICK SCHULER

"Father and I had our pup tent in a cornfield near the Third Battalion aid stations and Command Post. Father had said four Masses on All Saints' Day. We went to bed early but got up on the alert to move out, about 11:00 that night. We loaded the jeep and trailer and moved forward to join up with the First and Second Battalions. They were trying to get out by turning onto another road. The road behind us wasn't safe. But we ran into a Communist roadblock ahead and had to turn the vehicles around. Father and I picked up a lot of wounded, put them on the jeep and trailer, and came back to the Third Battalion CP. The medics took care of the wounded on the road. 'Stay with the jeep and say your prayers,' Father Kapaun told me. 'I'll be back.' A few minutes later, the Chinese attacked us right there. I set fire to the jeep and ran looking for Father. I shouted his

name but could not find him. Then I went back across the river
with two others. I figured that Father would leave too."[2]

PRIVATE PETER V. BUSATTI

"I never knew my chaplain until the night of November 1,
1950. All hell broke loose on this night, mortars were falling
in on us, machine gun fire broke out from all sides, men were
running and screaming at us from all directions. It was a mas-
sacre too difficult to describe in detail. Almost all of the group
I was with were killed or captured. I moved across the valley
to where I heard the most firing, figuring at least I would have
someone to fight with. I finally found myself within yards of
the GI stronghold, awaiting the proper opportunity to make a
run for it. As I was lying in a large fox hole getting ready to go,
someone came flying to my fox hole. This was my first meeting with Father Kapaun. He asked me my name and how I felt.
I told him my leg was stiff and my back hurt; an old shrapnel
wound in my back had reopened. He ripped open my shirt and
put some liquid on it. I asked him if he was a Catholic Chaplain and he said 'Yes.' He said an Act of Contrition with me and
blessed me. He told me I was about 50 yards from the GI Perimeter, and that I had better get out of there fast. A few minutes
later I made a run for it and jumped over the sandbags which
encircled the area.

Lt. Mayo, whom I consider the best combat officer I've seen,
stood in the middle of the perimeter and was shouting orders
to all the men in this defense set-up. I believe this was the last
organized resistance of the battle. Mayo placed me in a position just right of the perimeter. During the fighting, someone
shouted, 'there goes the chaplain.' We looked over and saw a
few Commies running down the road with the chaplain. Lt.
Mayo shouted, 'Shoot them!' A few men directed their fire
on the captors and the chaplain got away. This didn't stop him

though—he was still administering last rites and taking care of the wounded all around the area.

Lt. Mayo picked me and four others to go get some North Koreans who were in a ditch preparing to set up a machine gun. All I can remember is that all four of us were screaming 'Banzai' and getting the [enemy]. Larry Nolan and I got back into the perimeter; the other two were killed. Just about this time my mind sort of snapped and I don't remember what happened until the next day when I found myself in a large covered hole full of wounded men. Some GIs told me later that the chaplain had pushed me into this hole."[3]

LIEUTENANT WALT MAYO

"On the morning of November 1st, 5 miles southeast of Unsan, the Third Battalion 8th Cavalry was in a small valley approximately fifty miles from the Yalu River. Father Kapaun said Mass that morning as he had on most previous mornings since we had come up from Pyongyang four days before. That night the Chinese hit us and hit us hard. They were right in amongst us. Half hour later, at 1:00 am on the 2nd, I went over to a dugout by the side of the road where Battalion Headquarters were situated. It was covered with logs and dirt and was large enough to hold about 40 men. Everything was mixed up. Chinese everywhere! But in that dug-out, Father had gathered about 30 men and was tending them. We guarded the entrance and gathered more men and fought Chinese until morning when they started to drop mortars right into the entrance which was about wide enough to drive a truck down. By that time we had gathered about 20 more wounded and put them down there.

All the while, Father was carrying them down into comparative safety. He refused to leave them when we had to leave at dawn to fall back into the field behind and establish a perimeter defense. He showed up later at about 10:00 A.M. and was crawling out into the open and dragging our wounded back into the perimeter all day long. He would sit up on a parapet scanning the field in full view of the snipers who were knocking the men off fast. His pipe was shot out of his mouth but he put adhesive tape on it and continued to smoke. He must have dragged about fifteen or twenty men out of that field into our trenches. When night was approaching, he told us he was going back to the dug-out which was about 150 yards from our outposts. He said he had to be with those 50 wounded. And back he went."[4]

The first major battle between Chinese and American forces was a horrendous frenzy of death with bullets and grenades exploding literally everywhere—and that was in between tank rounds and mortar and artillery shells exploding shrapnel like confetti at a parade. The Chinese were also firing White Phosphorus (known as WP or "Willy Pete") mortar rounds—the chemical cloud created by the explosion is so toxic it can burn through metal. If inhaled, it will literally burn your throat and lungs. The machine guns on both sides used orange and red tracer rounds to stream bullets towards the targets. *Newsweek* magazine later referred to this battle as "The Halloween Party." While Chaplain Kapaun was stationed at the command post to protect the wounded, he wouldn't hesitate to dash out over the perimeter and help retrieve his wounded men. And while he was doing this, Chinese soldiers are rushing through the same perimeter, Burp Guns and rifles blazing, and then if they can still run, continue through and disappear into the night. Injured men from other companies started making their way to the dugout as well just to wait out the onslaught. Amazingly, the 3rd Battalion was able to hold off the enemy as daylight approached and the Chinese disappeared back over the ridgelines. They had the advantage of time and superior positions. They would be back and the 3rd Battalion knew it. Come daylight, the destruction was plain to see—most of the vehicles had been destroyed or inoperable—the only way out was by foot. Hundreds of dead bodies littered the ground.

NOVEMBER 2, 1950
ALL SOULS' DAY

The next day, Bill Richardson was standing in a trench putting a machine gun in place when Chaplain Kapaun came along and asked how he was doing.

'You know, Sergeant,' the chaplain said, sporting his broken pipe, 'it's All Souls' Day.'

'I hope the hell someone's looking after our souls because we sure need it,' I said back.

Kapaun smiled at me. 'Well, He is, He is.'

The word among the men now quickly spread that the enemy was so numerous because they were endless Chinese conscripts—not North Koreans. Knowing Chinese tactics, the remnants of the 3rd Battalion, along with stragglers from other units, set up defenses all day, dreading the strange bugle blowers that would return that night. By nightfall, they had about 170 men able to fight, over 50 wounded unable to be evacuated, and nearly 100 dead.

PRIVATE TIBOR RUBIN

"The battalion's dugout was now a hundred and fifty yards outside the new line of defense. Forty or fifty wounded were inside, too badly hurt to fight. Father Kapaun and Captain Anderson, the battalion surgeon, had stayed with them, to do what they could to tend the worst cases. The dugout was in a precarious position, but the first light of morning revealed that five riflemen were still defending it. Buffered by piles of corpses, they had hunkered down behind cover so as not to draw sniper fire.

Air Force fighters appeared overhead, racing toward the Chinese positions, loudly challenging the enemy to show himself. Suddenly a window opened for the Third to regroup. Exhausted but now hopeful, the small band furiously dug a network of trenches to the command post and the vehicles that they had abandoned the night before. One hundred and fifty wounded were dragged into the perimeter, along with rations and precious ammo. Major Ormond was found, badly injured but alive.

The airplanes were holding the Chinese at a distance when Tibor heard the sound of a helicopter. He turned and looked up. The chopper, a medical unit come to pick up the worst cases, approached from the south and began to descend. Just as the rotors began to slice the air over Tibor's head, it drew fire. When it got within fifty feet, bullets ripped into the bird's midsection. Belching oil, the damaged bird lurched precariously then pulled back and veered off. Soon it was gone. Air support came in for another pass. One small plane dropped a package of morphine and bandages inside the perimeter. The radio on a tank picked up news that help was on the way. The men's spirits rallied.

Although the besieged Third was unaware of it, their rescue had already been attempted. Two companies from the Fifth Cavalry had approached the Third from the south, only to encounter armed resistance at a place called Turtle Head Bend. The Chinese, who had been hidden on a hill that overlooked the road, hit them hard from above. Three hundred and fifty UN troops had been killed or wounded. The remainder of the two companies sent word to headquarters that the road between Turtle Head Bend and Unsan was simply impassable.

Midday, the division commander, General Gay, authorized the remaining elements of the First Cavalry Division to withdraw. His instructions were directed at all three battalions. Two of them had already dispersed: their few survivors were struggling to return to friendly lines. Only the Third now remained trapped. Toward the end of the day, as the light began to fail, the general made what he later called the hardest decision of his military career: to call off the rescue mission."[5]

With no cavalry coming to the rescue and no ability to evacuate safely on foot, the 3rd Battalion braced for the inevitable second assault on their position that came again in the middle of the night.

LIEUTENANT WALT MAYO

"Chaplain Kapaun constantly made the rounds of the entire perimeter under direct enemy observation and automatic weapons fire from distances no further than fifty yards. All the while, white phosphorous mortar rounds landed in heavy volume over the entire perimeter. He assisted in rendering medical aid to the wounded and talking to each individual soldier. On one occasion, having heard of the existence of two badly wounded men outside the perimeter… Chaplain Kapaun advanced outside our lines in quest of the wounded drawing intense fire on himself. He gave last rites of the Church to one of the men who had died and carried the other man back to the safety of the command post dugout… Although he might have sought protection in the dugout, he continued his voluntary mission of mercy. From the early morning hours until dusk, Chaplain Kapaun allowed himself no rest; he was constantly on the move. But for these continuous acts of bravery…many of these men would otherwise have died, and the will to fight might have quickly collapsed."[6]

SERGEANT HERB MILLER WOUNDED

From Pulaski, New York, Herb "Pappy" Miller saw combat serving with the 42nd Division in World War II. He rejoined the army in 1947 and with just six months to go on his three-year enlistment he was ordered to join the 8th Regiment of the 1st Cavalry Division when they landed in Korea just 5 months prior. At only twenty-four years of age he had seen about ev-

Army portrait of Sergeant Herb "Pappy" Miller before entering the Korean War. Having served in combat with the 42nd Division in World War II, he already has a chest full of commendations, and he is about to get many more.

erything an enemy force could muster, thus earning the nickname "Pappy."

The core fighting at Unsan was basically over in two nights. At about 11 pm November 1st, the Chinese again blew their crazy horns and swarmed 3rd Battalion's perimeter like a plague of locusts. The fighting was as intense as it gets, leading many a Korean War veteran to shake their head afterwards and say, "We stacked them up like cordwood, but they still kept on coming." Then, long before dawn, the Chinese troops would fall back into the hills, giving the impression that 3rd Battalion had held their ground despite being outnumbered 10 to 1. For those that could still move, the day of November 2nd was spent digging in deeper, gathering ammo and tending the wounded. By nightfall, the Chinese had gained even more fresh troops, and before midnight, they came in shooting from all directions.

Herb Miller was in the center of the perimeter, watching tracer rounds come in from multiple directions. He couldn't distinguish Americans from the Chinese soldiers that were crisscrossing the perimeter as if they owned the place. Grenades were being tossed into positions that were once held by friends but now were taken by the enemy. There was nowhere to fall back to for Miller and about 35 men huddled in a ditch nearby. In fact, nowhere in that perimeter was going to be safe that night and he finally realized that at around 3 am. Miller managed to order the men to get running, but as he was clearing the ditch himself, a Chinese grenade blew up right under his feet. The blast ripped his leg apart and he lost use of his muscles. With many broken bones in his foot and shrapnel in his hands and other leg, he could no longer move and had to play dead.

LIEUTENANT WALT MAYO

"That night the Chinese attacked us in force and it was hand to hand fighting at times. We knew that they must have gotten into the dug-out. That was the night of the 2nd. I found out that the Chinese had thrown two grenades down into the dug-out and killed some of the wounded. But then a wounded Chinese officer that we had captured and put into the dug-out with the Americans went out and stopped the Chinese from killing anyone else and brought them down into the dug-out. They took Father along with about 25 wounded who could walk. Father had cared for this Chinese officer and sent him out to stop the grenading."[7]

SERGEANT JAMES R. PETERGALL

"We had orders to withdraw. Any wounded who thought they could make it could leave with us. I was told that Father Kapaun and Dr. Anderson were going to stay behind with the other wounded. When we left, the area was under artillery fire. The Reds were dropping white phosphorus on us. That's the last I saw of Father Kapaun."[8]

"On Nov 2 or 3, 1950, Father Kapaun's unit was entirely surrounded by the enemy. Father Kapaun constantly administered the last rites under enemy fire. When the unit finally decided to attempt a breakout, Father Kapaun elected to stay behind with the wounded. After this, Father Kapaun was the only officer left on his feet, and the men asked him to arrange a surrender with the enemy. Believing that they were North Koreans Father Kapaun did not do so. After the position became untenable, owing to the enemy throwing hand grenades into their midst, however, Father Kapaun went out under a white flag and arranged the surrender."[9]

Sergeant Robert Morrison: "It was Father Kapaun that surrendered the wounded from the medical bunker in 3rd Battalion. There is no doubt that they would have been killed by the Chinese where they lay had he not done that. You probably are far too young to realize that at that time, the military had a creed to never surrender, so none of the NCOs or captains would dare surrender the wounded. The Chinese did not treat their wounded unless it was very minor. I had witnessed Chinese soldiers set to digging their own graves, even though wounded, and then shot and simply pushed in and covered up. That was an eye opener for me, when I was first captured, to see that happen."[10]

"LET ME HELP YOU UP"

With the battle now over, the Chinese soldiers methodically checked American and Chinese bodies to find any still alive. If still alive, they were shot in the head to finish them off. This sickening war crime included shooting even their own wounded. If they were able to stand, some were permitted to dig their own graves before being dispatched with a bullet, as caring for them was not worth the time or effort. Herb Miller had pulled a couple of dead bodies on top of him to hide but was now concerned that because it was so cold, his breath might give him away. This was about 2 pm on the afternoon of November 3. Father Kapaun had already surrendered the CP and all able-bodied prisoners were being lined up to be marched out. They were just across the road from Miller when suddenly, he was discovered by a Chinese soldier and pulled out of the ditch. Seeing his mangled leg, the soldier didn't hesitate to put a rifle to Herb's head. Herb closed his eyes waiting for the shot. Father Kapaun had seen enough and quickly crossed the road and abruptly pushed the rifle off Herb's head and ignored the enemy soldiers who now stood, mouths agape, just stunned at this incredibly brave act of courage and love. They could have shot both of them right then and there and no one would have been surprised. But they didn't do anything. They could only watch as the 8th Reg chaplain simply said 'Let me help you up' to a man he had never met. Kapaun put Miller into a fireman's carry and got back in the prisoner's line. He didn't think twice about his decision. He was going to protect and help Miller even at the cost of his own life if necessary. For this singular action alone, Chaplain Kapaun was eligible for the Medal of Honor.

Just a truly bizarre battlefield scene occurred the afternoon of November 3, 1950. The Americans still able to fight were scattered about in hiding places while the Chinese were on sporadic patrols. When the Chinese left the command post, they marched Major Ormond, Doctor Anderson, Father Kapaun, Herb Miller and about a dozen others that could walk on the start of their death march. Afterwards, several American soldiers crawled through the ditches to reach the CP. When they pushed the pile of dead Chinese bodies blocking the entrance aside they were amazed to find more wounded inside that had not been executed—a miracle that no doubt Chaplain Kapaun had a hand in, influencing their new captors who spent plenty of time executing other wounded outside the CP—including their own wounded. With many Chinese soldiers scattered throughout the hills it's unclear if these remaining wounded were able to be rescued as the fighting Americans remaining were needed to support last ditch efforts of resistance.

1st CAVALRY DIVISION UNIT
HISTORICAL REPORT—NOVEMBER 1950

"Thus at 1600 hours 5 Nov the 3rd Bn 8th Cavalry had made its last resistance as an organized unit. It had fought off over 2,000 [later amended to be 10,000] Chinese and beaten them back. Cut off 20 miles from friendly lines, surrounded, outnumbered, no food and little ammo they fought as the Cavalry of old fought. The Army can be proud of these men like Father Kapaun, Captain Anderson, and Major Ormond. In the annals of modern warfare, there have been few units who have inked in their blood the gallant story of their last battle."[11]

"THE LOST BATTALION"

Nothing can describe the 3rd Battalion, 8th Regiment of the 1st Cavalry Division more accurately than the sad moniker "The Lost Battalion." The Battle of Unsan, often compared to Custer's Last Stand at Little Big Horn, suffered six hundred killed from three battalions of the 8th Cavalry Regiment. Later, almost three hundred died of their wounds. Many say the dead were "the lucky ones" compared with what was about to follow for the POWs. Major Veale Moriarty, the battalion executive officer, managed to rally over a hundred 8th Cavalry troops outside of the perimeter and attempt a rescue of those still trapped. But by November 6, they too became surrounded and captured. By day's end, the 3rd Battalion no long existed as an organized unit.

"Chaplain Kapaun was the first of several Army chaplains who suffered in captivity. A mere 2 days after his capture, another chaplain fell into the hands of the Chinese. Kenneth C. Hyslop, Northern Baptist, was with the men of the 19th Regiment, 24th Infantry Division, who were attempting to stop the Communist drive south of Unsan near Anju. The 6-year veteran of Army service received the Bronze Star earlier for remaining with wounded who were cut off and eventually leading them back to friendly lines. Hyslop was captured on 4 November. Primarily because of internal injuries as a result of mistreatment by his captors, he died of starvation (in Chaplain Kapaun's arms) 38 days later on 12 December."

Within a month of the Chinese entering the war, two more chaplains also became POWs: Wayne H. Burdue and Lawrence F. Brunnert. Two other chaplains were killed: Samuel R. Simpson and James W. Conner. The fate of the four captured chaplains was unknown until the release of surviving POWs in 1953. Sadly, none survived."[12]

THE SIGNIFICANCE OF THE BATTLE OF UNSAN

Simply put, the Chinese victories at Unsan and Anju were overt "canaries in a coal mine" brought on by one of the most significant intelligence failures in US military history. Had such warnings been heeded then, the disastrous losses and setbacks to come days later in the massive Chinese offensive around the Chosin Reservoir may have been averted and the Chinese blunted in securing the entire northern portion of the Korean peninsula. These failures also caused nearly 5,000 troops to be taken prisoner by December 1950, and fully *half* of them died that winter in record-breaking freezing temperatures. These early victories emboldened the Chinese to go all out and swarm the UN and ROK forces with superior numbers and nationalist resolve.

THE BATTLE OF ANJU—LIEUTENANT WILLIAM FUNCHESS AND LIEUTENANT MIKE DOWE

Lieutenant William H. Funchess was captured by the Chinese on November 4, 1950, eight to nine miles from the town of Anju, North Korea, about fifty miles north of Pyongyang. A bullet had gone through his foot but he was determined to walk after witnessing what the Chinese did to those prisoners who could not march. He recalls:

"It wasn't long before the enemy had regrouped and they were coming at us by the hundreds. We fired everything we had at them but only slowed them down. There were just too many of them. Finally out of ammunition, our company commander Lewis 'Rocky' Rockwerk ordered us to withdraw and we were forced to travel cross-country in an effort to rejoin other units of the 19th Infantry Regiment. Three squads of my platoon had withdrawn a few minutes earlier, leaving me with a dozen men. We provided cover fire for them and then attempted to withdraw under heavy enemy fire, joining the four survivors of Mike Dowe's platoon across the road. The terrain was rough and we were traveling along the base of a mountain to our left and a narrow valley to our right. There was a lot of smoke and visibility was poor. Mortar rounds were exploding and the sound was deafening. Suddenly I spotted a group of soldiers to our front and across the valley. It was so smoky I couldn't tell if they were US or enemy soldiers. At that time I turned and asked my men if they could distinguish who they were. Some-one answered from the rear, 'It's too smoky to tell, Lieutenant.'

I replied, 'Well, just keep quiet and we'll get out of here.'

That must have put an idea in one man's mind as he suddenly shouted in a loud voice, 'Hey, don't shoot, we're GIs.'

In just an instant I heard the sound of a machine gun bolt slamming forward and knew what that meant. I immediately turned left and started up the face of the mountain. I only got six or eight feet up the slope before an extended burst of bullets sprayed the area. Suddenly, I felt a sharp pain in my right foot and realized I had been hit. I stumbled, and Lt. Mike Dowe and a GI grabbed me. The GI took my carbine and then the two of them began pulling me up the mountain. At that time I be-came extremely thirsty but knew there was no time for a drink of water. I turned my head to look behind and saw only dead and wounded GIs on the ground. The Communist machine gun crew had done its job. A few surviving GIs were climbing the mountain about 40 yards to our rear.

The surviving GI slung my carbine over his shoulder and then he and Lt. Dowe got on each side of me and began helping me up the mountain. I was holding on to both of them as we struggled up the steep slope. Suddenly the GI was hit by small arms fire and he fell backwards. My carbine went with him as he fell down the mountain side. We took a few more steps and rested for a minute beside some trees. At that time Lt. Dowe assured me he was going to help me walk and would not leave me to fend for myself. He was true to his word as he tugged, pulled and pushed me toward the top of the mountain.

Mike and I were going through a stand of saplings when, all of a sudden, a Communist soldier appeared no more than a dozen or fifteen steps away. He immediately let go with a volley of rounds from his 'burp' gun and I saw bark flying from the trees in front. Luckily, neither of us was hit. I saw a dumbfounded expression on the Communist soldier's face as he was, no doubt, wondering why we didn't fall. By the time we could get a few rounds off with Lt. Dowe's carbine, the soldier had disappeared. We didn't bother checking to see if we had killed him."[13]

"WE ARE MAD AT WALL STREET"

Funchess and Dowe then found themselves surrounded by at least forty Chinese soldiers and were forced to surrender.

"It was the most helpless feeling I ever experienced. The soldiers stood in a semicircle around us, each with his weapon trained on Lt. Dowe or me. They were still yelling and I saw anger on their faces. At that time I realized our captors wore uniforms that were not familiar to us. I suspected they were probably Chinese although I had been assured by my superiors earlier in the day that no Chinese forces were in North Korea. My suspicions were later confirmed as those were, indeed, Chinese troops. They turned out to be seasoned soldiers who had been engaged in China's recently-fought civil war.

Suddenly a small enemy soldier, scarcely five feet tall, burst through the crowd. He wore the same cotton padded uniform as the others except he had on fur-lined leather boots. He walked within inches of me, stopped, reached up and pulled my right arm down and started shaking my hand. Then he spoke in perfect English:

"We are not mad at you. We are mad at Wall Street."[14]

14

FATHER KAPAUN'S VALLEY

The amount of time these brave POWs spent on not one, but three death marches in the winter of 1950–51 is heartbreaking. After three weeks forced to march over sixty miles to Pyoktong, they had only just arrived when it was heavily bombed by the US Air Force, causing them to endure another forced march about twelve miles to the village of Sombokal. The number of POWs grew quickly to a couple thousand. The Chinese guards had no compassion for stragglers falling behind for whatever reason. Once out of view from the main group, a shot would ring out and their body was left in the ditch. Private Joe Ramirez overhead two of his fellow prisoners talking after a straggler was killed for not keeping up:

"They're shooting those boys." The sobering reply was: "Yes, and they'll shoot you too if you don't keep up."

The steady stream of American prisoners of war, the first the Chinese ever had to contend with, were marched north with little thought to their welfare or destination and not without great danger. Those unable to continue the march, unless other prisoners were willing or even able to come to their aid, were in most cases shot by the guards and left by the roadside. In at least one instance, 8th Cavalry prisoners, being moved during daylight immediately after the battle, were mistakenly attacked by an American aircraft sent to Unsan to destroy abandoned vehicles and equipment.

Eventually, prisoners of the 8th Cavalry were joined by other American prisoners being moved north ahead of the advancing Americans. Soon, abandoned huts in villages served as way stations for the move north. Thousands more would soon travel along this "underground railroad" for prisoners. Around the Unsan area, groups of wounded prisoners were temporarily held in the abandoned shacks and barns of local farmers. Most groups were left unattended for several days under the care of North Korean Home Guards; some were lucky and received care from local farmers despite the guards. Regardless of any care the prisoners received, the wounded continued to die for lack of medical care, adequate shelter from the increasing cold, and brutal treatment (or outright murder) by the guards. As more Chinese soldiers became available, the wounded also began the move north."[1]

Officers were hampered in their efforts to help organize carrying the wounded as they were told they had no authority over the enlisted. But instead of issuing an order, Kapaun motivated the others by loudly proclaiming, "Let's pick 'em up!" when their rests were over and they were forced to keep moving. He led by example.

And he continued to carry Herb Miller or see that his stretcher was carried. "I kept telling Father Kapaun to put me down, you can't carry me like this. He said 'If I put you down, they'll shoot ya.'" Miller was so badly wounded in the leg that for at least 30 miles, he alternated between leaning on Kapaun and being carried by him. A true hero. Upon arrival at the

Pyoktong prison camp, Miller was sent to the enlisted compound and Kapaun was sent to the officer's side.

SERGEANT BILL RICHARDSON

"The guards shoved us into a cluster of huts. We were jammed into the room so tightly that my legs rested on another soldier. The only good thing about sleep this way was that we were warmer. I heard O'Keefe's Boston accent reciting the Twenty-third Psalm in the darkness.

Yea, though I walk through the valley of the shadow of death, I will fear no evil: For thou art with me.

As he said this prayer, a quiet came over the group. Afterward, I took off my boots for the first time in days. It was so cramped that I couldn't reach my feet. So I massaged the feet of the guy across from me and he rubbed my feet. We both put our boots back on, but a few guys left them off. We were all dead tired and had no trouble falling asleep. I woke to a bunch of guys raising hell.

'Where the fuck are my boots?'

'Get up! Get up!' the soldier yelled, so that he could look for his boots.

But we knew what had happened. When we went outside the hut, a few of the guards were wearing the boots. The North Koreans gave some of the men open sandals to wear instead. The cold was not only taking a toll on us, but also on the guards. A cold front from the plains of Manchuria came roaring down and slamming into the very mountains we were struggling through. We were facing the coldest winter in fifty years."[2]

TIBOR RUBIN MEETS FATHER KAPAUN AGAIN

"As the Chinese moved them farther north and more POWs joined the march, Tibor recognized other familiar faces from the Third Battalion: Father Kapaun, Dr. Anderson, several officers, and fifty or so confused and frightened enlisted men. Their numbers seemed to grow by the hour. Tibor stopped counting at four hundred.

There was no medicine for the wounded. The twenty or so who couldn't walk had to be dragged on improvised litters made of burlap bags and tree limbs. As the temperature dropped, discipline began to lapse. Four boys hauling a wounded man became tired, set him down, and walked away. When Dr. Anderson ordered them to go back and retrieve him, they refused. The doctor and three other volunteers lifted the man up and continued. Father Kapaun was doing the work of two men, bracing a corporal whose knee had been shattered by a grenade. Tibor did what he could to help men who appeared to be failing; the problem was that there were just too many of them.

They were still high in the mountains when men started to fall by the side of the road; too many for Tibor to help. He called to the others, the ones who appeared self-sufficient, but most of them refused to break ranks, even when a man went down in front of them. Every few minutes another poor soul dropped to the ground. As the line slinked on, a guard fell back and a shot rang out. With each new report Tibor felt a wave of pity and shame. The incline turned steeper, the breeze stiffer. Approaching a bend in the road, Tibor saw two Koreans bear down on a soldier who had dropped to his knees. Before the GI could lift his arms to protect himself, guards slammed his head with rifle butts, until he was flat on the ground, his young face swollen and bloody. Then Father Kapaun arrived at his side. Looking up from the now still figure—his shoulders marked by gaping wounds—the priest sadly remarked that they were too late. Then Tibor noted a flicker in the downed man's eyes. The priest sprinted down the line and soon returned with a crude litter. Two GIs, inspired by Kapaun's grit, lifted the prostrate man and rejoined the formation. Although he was barely conscious, the soldier had been lucky. Still, Tibor's dreams were haunted by the savage beating he had endured."[3]

LIEUTENANT WILLIAM FUNCHESS

With only a crutch to aid him, Lieutenant Funchess spent two weeks stumbling over increasingly steep and icy terrain before he and some fifty other prisoners were stopped on a hillside just as they arrived at Pyoktong. And so too did the US bombers. They firebombed the town as the prisoners cheered. That night, the prisoners were moved to a valley (Sombokal) where they would stay from November until the end of January.

"As darkness fell, we were assembled and told to move out… We went cross-country for a while before reaching a dirt road. After getting on the road, we walked uphill for an hour or so and then it was downhill for a couple of hours. Finally, we reached an isolated snow-covered valley about six or seven miles northwest of Pyoktong. It was sparsely settled, and I saw a small group of mud huts with thatched roofs and another group of shacks several hundred yards away. They took me to a room and pushed me inside. The room contained a number of GIs and I was the last one to arrive. A guard threw in a bundle of dried corn stalks as bedding. The stalks were about three-fourths of an inch in diameter and were too hard to sleep on. Closer inspection revealed some of the stalks still had a 'nubbin' ear of corn attached. We ate the dried corn immediately and threw the corn stalks out the door. This was to be our home for the next eight or nine weeks. We called it 'The Valley' for lack of a better name…"[4]

FATHER KAPAUN MEETS MIKE DOWE

"My first meeting with Father… I'd heard stories about him from the other people when we were in the schoolhouse, about this fabulous priest and the doctor. And I was carrying a stretcher and this guy's in the back…and I said, 'Who are you?' And he said, 'My name's Kapaun.'

I said, 'Oh, Father, I've heard of you,' and he said, 'Well, don't tell my bishop!'

He was quite a guy. And he helped, I mean really helped. Driving people to carry wounded so they wouldn't be left behind and slaughtered. And somehow, although some people died in the march—we had a couple of air raids and a couple of people were hurt in those—but we made it up to what was to have been our prison camp, Pyoktong and then on to the valley at Sombokal."[5]

"DON'T LET THE BASTARDS GET YOU DOWN"

"Kapaun discovered that if he seemed relaxed, everyone felt better. So he grinned and introduced himself to newcomers, 'My name is Kapaun, glad to have you share our paradise.' The oppressive conditions in The Valley did not disturb Kapaun's demeanor. He and Mayo often exchanged a grin and a couple of catch phrases: The Chaplain spoke the Latin words, *Ni illegitimi carborundum esse*, and Mayo replied with a rough English translation, 'Don't let the bastards get you down.'"[6]

FIRST POW CAMP BOMBED UPON ARRIVAL AT PYOKTONG, NORTH KOREA

Clearly the North Koreans and the Chinese were not prepared for such a vast influx of prisoners. This fact, along with a disgusting lack of compassion for human life, was the core reason why the coming winter was bound for disaster. Most of the 24th Division and 1st Cavalry Division soldiers who were captured first were taken on a death march to Pyoktong, North Korea, which lies on the Yalu River. The border of China is across the river. Kapaun and Rubin arrived there with about six hundred POWs, and just as they arrived, it was unfortunately firebombed by American B-24s, which wrecked many of its buildings. The North Koreans had to scramble for a solution, which ended up costing many more POWs their lives as the days and nights grew much colder. After the bombing, they were forced on another death march about twelve miles southeast to the small village of Sombokal, where they remained through January 1951.

When the POWs were forced to march back to Pyoktong on January 21, 1951, the POW camp had been hastily rebuilt to house a large population and became known as "Camp 5" after negotiations began in July 1951. The conditions in the camps were ridiculously harsh and brutal, resulting in virtually unparalleled deaths for prisoners of modern war. It is almost a misnomer to even call them POW camps as the Communists never abided by, nor intended to abide by, the rules of the Geneva Convention and instead used the death marches and the camps to serve as concentration camps—reluctantly taking prisoners and purposely eliminating them by not allowing treatment for wounds, causing starvation and allowing the inclement weather to inflict them with preventable diseases, frostbite, exposure, as well as subjecting them to brainwashing and physical torture, and even resorting to out and out murder.

ROBERT MORRISON

"We were billeted in the center of town, formed into 25 man groups, with each group crammed into a room 8 by 10 feet, that included the owner's furniture as well. There was no barb wire as yet, but each room had only a door of paper, and no windows. A guard with an automatic weapon was posted outside each room with orders to shoot into the room if anyone touched the door. The very next afternoon (November 20th) the US Air Force bombed the town and fortunately we were on the outskirts in houses."[7]

When the air raid was over, the Chinese guards drove the POWs out of their huts and forced them into the hillside to shiver the rest of the night as the town burned. The next morning, they were on a second death march to Sombokal.

AMNESTY AND PROPAGANDA RELEASE

On November 20, Robert Morrison and twenty-six other walking wounded were given a "propaganda release" and sent south to the UN lines. Father Kapaun was there to see them off, wishing them all to "go with God." While that certainly sounds like something Father Kapaun would say, there is a lot more to the story of what happened that day. Amnesty was also offered to Tibor Rubin and he turned it down flat. This bold move would cost Rubin two and a half years living in squalor, mistreatment, starvation, and the possibility of death on any day. You would think he would have had enough surviving a Nazi concentration camp but then you don't know Tibor Rubin. He was not afraid. He knew he could save others' lives in that camp. He had a defiance and confidence not seen in most individuals or soldiers. He took it as a challenge, first to the Nazis and now to the Communists. Without witnesses, no one would have known such bravery existed.

Robert Morrison wrote about this day too in letters to the military and others stating the strength and greatness he witnessed from his chaplain. Another POW released that day was First Sergeant Samuel Cleckner, who states he slept in the same room with Father Kapaun at Pyoktong until the day of his release, which he states was November 20. He states this date emphatically as of course he made it to South Korea the next day and was sent stateside. Through a chaplain at Ft. Benning, the following letter was forwarded to Father Kapaun's parents in August 1954:

Letter from Military Ordinariate to Enos Kapaun:

"I am sending you an enclosed copy of a letter, which I received today from Father Richard A. Malloy, Chaplain at Fort Benning, Georgia regarding the capture of Father Kapaun. It doesn't add much to the information which we already have but during this period of waiting, every detail seems precious. With every good wish, I am Sincerely yours, James H. Griffiths, Auxiliary Bishop, Chancellor"

Information given by Sergeant Samuel Cleckner in 1951:

"Sergeant Cleckner was with Father Kapaun until the 20th of November, at which time Sgt. Cleckner was released.

When the sergeant left on Nov. 20th, he said that Father was in good shape mentally and physically, although he had lost quite a bit of weight, but was doing an excellent job of keeping up the spirits and morale of the men. I questioned him as to whether the enemy knew that Father was a Catholic priest and his answer was 'yes.' At one time, when all the captive officers were called for interrogation, they said that they did not want Father Kapaun as he was not a 'military officer,' probably meaning a combatant. The sergeant said that upon his return, he recommended Father for the Distinguished Service Cross. I trust that this information may add a little bit to what you already have.
—Richard A. Malloy, C.S.P."

These two brief communications seem rather mundane, but upon closer scrutiny, they are highly relevant and important details offering further insight into Chaplain Kapaun's actions reflecting his valor and bravery "above and beyond" even what has already been recorded and told from the US Army's point of view. When Cleckner returned to the States, he immediately recommended Kapaun be awarded the Distinguished Service Cross (DSC), the army's second highest decoration for soldiers who display extraordinary heroism in combat. Cleckner's testimony had to have been corroborated by others, because Kapaun was awarded the DSC in absentia in 1952 without anyone knowing at home that he had already passed away.

THEY ARE MOVED TO SOMBOKAL

As a result of the bombing of their first camp, a hasty new death march ensued late November 1950. Though a shorter distance than last time, it would still prove deadly for more POWs. The temperature was dropping each day and food and water were scarce. Just over fifty miles to the east of them, the Chinese were pouring more troops over the border and battles surrounding the Chosin Reservoir were getting underway on an epic scale. Many new POWs would be joining them over the next month, mostly Marines.

Sombokal was in a narrow valley ravine flanked by two mountains and a dirt road with a rocky ditch running through the camp. The upper and lower compounds were made up of poorly constructed barracks with unheated rooms. Housing about three thousand men with only the clothes on their backs, they were about to face one of the coldest winters on record with temperatures plunging as much as thirty degrees below zero. The death rate for these POWs was rising exponentially—it was a frozen hell.

DEATH OF CHAPLAIN KENNETH HYSLOP

"Even before the prisoners had completed their freezing journey from Pyoktong to The Valley, Kapaun's character was being tested again. Chaplain Kenneth C. Hyslop, a Northern Baptist minister, grew weak and fell behind the line of march. Unable to eat because the Communists had kicked in his ribs when they captured him, Hyslop was dying. Kapaun heard about the plight of his stricken colleague and found him in the dark. He comforted Hyslop throughout the night, remaining at his side as the chaplain slipped into a coma. When death ended Hyslop's ordeal, Kapaun made sure that his Christian colleague received a decent burial."[8]

LIEUTENANT WALT MAYO

"I saw Father when we were at Pyoktong, after being bombed and on the way to a small valley 10 miles southwest. It was the evening of the 20th of November and I never was so glad to see anyone in my life. He was carrying a stretcher and he carried it for the ten miles. We were carrying about 40 of our men on improvised litters up and down mountains. We would take turns carrying, but Father carried all the way. We arrived at this small valley the next morning and all the officers were put into a small Korean farmhouse at the top of the valley. The Chinese and Koreans would not let us go out to see the men but Father would get out and sneak down to see the sick and wounded first and then to see the men and say prayers. When they died he would get on the burial detail and dig the grave out of the rocky, frozen ground. He did that continuously. We were pretty hard up for food and were starving, so Father would go on ration run to get our cracked corn, millet and soy beans. Before he went, he would say prayers to St. Dismas, the Good Thief. They helped, because Father would steal, or get away with, sometimes two one-hundred-pound sacks of grain plus pockets full of salt which was very scarce. Pretty soon all of us were praying earnestly to St. Dismas, but Father succeeded much better than the rest of us. Some of the officers would trade their watches, which they managed to save, to the Koreans for tobacco. They would give Father a lot of the tobacco but the next day he would be smoking dried garlic leaves, oak leaves, etc. He had given it all away to the sick and wounded on his visits. The Chinese and Koreans always were after him and tried to catch him down the valley. They said he was an agitator and that the men did not want to see him and requested the Chinese to stop his coming. They no more stopped him from going down there than did the men request the Chinese to stop him. Every night we held prayers and he prayed not only for deliverance of us from the hands of the enemy, but also prayed

for the Communists to be delivered from their atheistic materialism. On January 21, 1951, we were moved back to Pyoktong."[9]

Sombokal was so cold and so crowded that the men had no
choice but sleep on their sides like sardines in a can. With no
coats or blankets it was best to lie down head to toe with your
bare feet in the armpits of the soldier next to you. Switching
from one side to another meant waking up everyone in your
room. Every night someone either accidentally or intention-
ally rolled away from their sleep buddy and would be dead
from exposure by daylight. The lice infestation was so bad you
could pick them off all day and still not come close to being rid
of them. Some men actually died from the blood loss caused
by such parasites. The blood loss was made worse by the now
horrendous diet the men faced: cracked corn no different than
common bird seed or chicken feed. They were lucky if they received even ten ounces a day.

CAPTAIN ROBERT BURKE

"Father Kapaun gave you a good impression upon first meeting and if you lived to be a hundred, your opinion would never
change. I met him in late November, 1950, after five days of
torturous marching in bitter cold weather. Upon arriving at
a small valley completely exhausted, half-frozen, half-starved
and thoroughly disheartened, and possessed with the idea that
death would be so welcome, much better than our present existence, at this very critical point as we approached the house
where we were to be interned, the sun appeared and soon the
clouds completely disappeared. The sun referred to was not the
celestial body but the warm, friendly greeting of this MAN of
God. With a big, broad grin he extended his hand and said, 'My
name is Kapaun, glad to have you share our paradise.'

His calm, easy manner and winning smile soon relaxed us and
his words of encouragement gave us new hope and the clouds

of dismay and disappointment soon disappeared and our heavy hearts became lighter, our aching feet and numb fingers and tired bodies didn't seem to hurt so much now. His help in getting us fed and bedded down were just a few of the many kindnesses and considerations displayed by him that night. We all knew that this man was a real friend. We weren't wrong, because in the tough times that followed we could always look to our priest for guidance, leadership and encouragement. He kept our spirits bright and our morale high. He gave us many a laugh when laughter was hard to come by, with his witty remarks and his methods for obtaining more chow to supplement our starvation ration. We very affectionately honored him with the title 'best thief in the compound.' He was forever sticking his neck out to 'borrow' extra food, to visit the men further down the valley and give them moral support in these very trying times."[10]

DR. SIDNEY ESENSTEN

"I was a battalion surgeon of the 2nd Battalion, 27th Regiment, 25th Division, captured by the Chinese on November 27, 1950. I then met Father Kapaun about two weeks later when we joined a group of prisoners who were captured earlier in November, from the 1st Cavalry Division. We were imprisoned in a long valley, about a half mile to three quarters of a mile wide and about three miles long. The prisoners lived in the Korean farm houses up and down this long valley. Doctor Clarence Anderson, who was captured with Father Kapaun and I, was allowed to care for the sick and wounded in this first area of imprisonment. The officers were segregated from the enlisted men. The officers were held at the most distant part of the valley. Doctor Anderson and I would go throughout the valley everyday checking on the sick and wounded, and eventually, we would always end up at the officer's section. He and I would always look up Father Kapaun because he always wanted to know how the enlisted men were doing, as he knew most of the men from the 1st

Calvary from having served with them. We would always give him detailed reports as how they were doing, how their mental attitudes and morale were doing. Father Kapaun used to do many things in the Officer Compound. He would always go out and chop the ice out that covered the stream which provided water. He also would clean up after any man who was sick with dysentery and dirty their clothes. He would wash their clothes in this freezing cold stream. He would always volunteer to clean out the latrine, as that was one of the dirtiest details we had to do. And, he always volunteered to make runs to the head of the valley to pick up the few supplies the Chinese provided us.

He did this primarily, because he could then stop on the way to talk to the enlisted men, as they would always line up whenever they knew that we were coming through on a run to the head of the valley. He would greet everybody and help their morale and provide quick services and quick prayers, and he would always make sure to sneak off and come into the hospital section to help with the morale of the sick and wounded that we had. He was a constant morale builder for the troops. Their morale was always improved after he had passed through. He would have preferred living in the enlisted men's compound, providing help there, but of course, the Chinese refused this in this first prison area. Therefore, his contribution was mostly in personal leadership, morale leadership, plus the things he did personally for the men."[11]

CAPTAIN ROBERT E. BURKE

"Later, by February and March, the majority of us had turned into animals, were fighting for food, irritable, selfish, miserly, etc. The good priest continued to keep a cool head, conduct himself as a human being, and maintain all his virtues and ideal characteristics. When the chips were down, Father proved himself to be the greatest example of manhood I've ever seen in my life. At trying times like these, the men are separated from the boys, the weeds from the wheat, and, although not every man slipped into primitive and savage existence, our good priest stood head and shoulders above everyone. When most of us were down on our backs and a siege of dysentery swept the area, our benevolent padre would go out into the sub-zero temperatures at 5:30 searching for small twigs and pieces of wood to build a fire and carry water to fill the pans he diligently made of old pieces of sheet iron and then remove dirty trousers from the men who no longer could control their natural functions. After boiling this clothing and getting it dry, he would dress the pathetic hulks of skin and bones. The faint heart would become a little more audible, a spark of life would light up in their hollow eyes and the 'death stare' would vanish as the corner of their mouths would turn up and a smile would appear on their tortured faces. A movement of the Adam's apple on a scrawny neck would give away the lump in the throat that comes when one experiences a sentimental moment; one would swallow hard and with tears in the eyes, would manage to offer, 'Thanks, Father.'

Gestures like this repeated morning after morning, washing clothes, bathing the body and a few well-chosen words (he always knew just the right thing to say at the right time) nursed countless men back to health and today these men are home with their mothers and fathers, their sweethearts, their wives and children, their families. I'm sure these families and loved ones all know the story. Every man is proud to say, 'I knew Father Kapaun—he saved my life, he made me fight to stay alive when dying was so simple; it was easier to die than live in those days; death was a welcome relief. We owe our present happiness to that heroic man who gave his all, who sacrificed himself for his fellow man, who worked himself to death.'"[12]

POWS MARCHED FROM SOMBAKOL BACK TO PYOKTONG (CAMP 5)

On January 21, 1951, Chaplain Kapaun, along with the close to five hundred Sombakol prisoners who could walk, were marched out to return to Pyoktong. For many, this was their third death march in freezing temperatures in just three months. In an astonishing move, the Chinese kept about 275 of the worst of the sick and wounded behind in Sombakol, where they would remain another seven weeks in the care of Dr. William Shadish and a medic named Sergeant Charles Schlichter. An impossible task, less than 10 percent of these men survived. When they were finally force-marched to Camp 5 on March 13, only 109 were left to endure the weeklong trek. Only three dozen of these prisoners made it to Camp 5 alive, and within days, that number dropped to twenty-four. A statistic no one should have to hear. An atrocity.

Despite this aberration, decades later, Pentagon analysts said the camp at Sombokal, now dubbed "Father Kapaun's Valley," had far fewer deaths of POWs than the other camps of the same period. Many former POWs, including Mike Dowe, William "Moose" McClain, and William Funchess, claim the credit belongs to Father Kapaun.

CAPTAIN JOHN W. THORNTON
US NAVY HELICOPTER PILOT

"Faith was thus a powerful, versatile weapon that was very soberly recognized as such by captive and captor alike. It was why so many of the arguments, debates and great pressures were focused by the Communists in this particular area of the prisoner psyche. Those POWs who insisted on answering to, relying upon and having trust in a higher authority could obviously not sublimate themselves to another lesser authority. The communists could not tolerate this and sought to stamp it out by every possible means. But most of the time, their efforts would backfire. Reinforced by the horrors of captivity perpetrated by avowed atheists, prisoner resistance was only hardened. For those of the deepest faith who looked beyond this world to an eternal peace, death itself became no kind of effective threat. If prolonged agony at the edge of death was then counter-prescribed by our captors, the confidence that God would bear us along through it all made the torture endurable. Either way, faith was an impenetrable bulwark for those who clung to it. In death, we would be spiritually unbeaten. For the living, there would be yet another reason, another example of why and how we should fight back.

Obviously, none of the faithful were willing to die. Faith was not a license to perish with a whimper and a prayer. We were simply able to die if we had no other choice. And the choice was God's. It was His judgement to make. Perhaps the most inspiring aspect of faith was its universal presence within a group as diverse as our prisoner population. It could be found among the white, Anglo Saxon, Protestant Americans and the Englishmen. It could be found among the Catholics. It could be found among the Black and Jewish Americans. It could be found burning fiercely in the hearts of Muslim Turks. It, like the cross of the Mampo-gin Church, was there for all to behold and it refused to be destroyed. This universal nature of faith was personified by one man who could never be forgotten by any prisoner who ever knew or had merely heard of him. He was a young Army chaplain, a Catholic priest named Father Emil J. Kapaun."[13]

15

PYOKTONG

By the spring of 1951, about a half dozen POW stockades near the Yalu River had been hastily set up and were operated by the Chinese army. The largest was Pyoktong (later named Camp 5), which had been set up in January and was positioned on a few acres of barren peninsula protruding into the deep cold waters of the Yalu. If a prisoner did make the swim across the mile-wide river, he would find himself in Manchuria and be sent right back. The crude camp was divided into several compounds: one for officers and sergeants, and two enlisted men's compounds that kept white soldiers separated from African Americans, and one for Turks. The men were not allowed to wear their rank, give or take orders, salute, or interact with men in the other compounds. Talking was kept to a minimum, and prayer groups or any kind of religious service or gathering were strictly forbidden. The Chinese guards and political officers were extremely adept at keeping their prisoners under their control, as they knew that without morale and high spirits, the prisoners would feel isolated and alone and, even worse,

DOD

Rare photo of Pyoktong, North Korea, along the Yalu River. The village was comman-deered by the Chinese for use as a large POW camp, later known as Camp 5. Photo taken around 1951.

selfish. The Chinese believed that soon enough these lost souls would be putty in their hands.

WILLIAM FUNCHESS MEETS FATHER KAPAUN

The enemy had lost Funchess' paperwork and didn't realize he was an officer, so he was placed in the enlisted compound. This was early February 1951. Funchess walked up to a dirty soldier with a big beard tending a fire and was pleasantly greeted by this man who said his name was Chaplain Emil Kapaun and he was melting snow. He asked Funchess if he would like a hot cup of water and Funchess excitedly answered, "Yes, sir."

Funchess and the chaplain from the Midwest became fast friends. They both had much experience on farms and with agriculture, and Father Kapaun taught Funchess how to utilize any scraps of metal they could find into pots for boiling water and other simple devices to make their miserable existence better. Funchess admired the chaplain's bold descriptions of slipping through the barbed wire at just the right time to care for the enlisted men as well as the officers. Kapaun was a king scrounger who raided Chinese warehouses for corn, millet seed, and even soybeans, all of which he distributed evenly among his fellow prisoners. A couple of weeks later, the Chinese realized Funchess was an officer and transferred him to their compound. What a bonus for Funchess, as he could now meet up with Kapaun more often and help out any way he could. Little did Funchess know they would be roommates in Father Kapaun's hour of need and he would care for the chaplain as best he could.

This fortuitous and lasting friendship stuck with William Funchess all throughout his life. Having eaten snow and a few gulps of contaminated water over the past three months, he recalls that offering of water from Father Kapaun was the best drink he ever had.[1]

PETER BUSATTI

"I next saw Father when we arrived at Pyoktong. This last meeting with him I shall never forget. It was early morning, about 7:00 or 8:00 am. We were standing outside a hut. Father Kapaun walked over to me and asked, 'How do you feel, Pete?' I was amazed that he remembered my name. He said these words which remain in my mind up to this day: 'Pete, you won't have to worry too much now.' I asked why and he said, 'Because you'll be going home very soon.' I laughed because it seemed so preposterous. I said, 'It's OK, Father, I'm not scared, because you're around, and if I die, I might get to heaven.' He patted my shoulder and told me that was a good attitude and hoped that I would be the same after I arrived home. Some other fellows gathered around and our conversation ended. I couldn't get his words out of my mind. I prayed to God that Father was right, though it did sound fantastic to me."[2]

FELIX McCOOL

"Father Kapaun would hold evening devotions for all of us, and would always preface it with: 'Gentlemen, Evening prayer!' An immediate hush would fall and everyone would listen to the 'Our Father Who art in Heaven,—give us this day our daily bread.' Here everyone would remember bread as we had known it. I remember how my mother used to say, 'Sonny, don't waste your bread for someday you may be in need!' The prayer would continue to the Catholic ending and then to the Protestant ending. He was for all of us and showed it in all his actions.

One day I asked Walt Mayo, the boy from Boston College: 'Say old man, is there a Catholic priest here in the camp? I haven't been to confession for a long time and it doesn't look as if I will.' Mayo replied: 'Look over there in that burned out building. You'll see a man rummaging around in the debris. That's Father Kapaun. He was the Chaplain in the outfit that I was captured in.'

I looked and saw the priest he was talking about. He had a black patch over one eye and a stocking cap over his ears. It was bitter cold. I approached him and said, 'Father!' He looked up and smiled. His eyes were watering from the blackened soot or from emotion, as he said to me:

'Look here in this cellar. There is a water crock. We can keep water in that and have it boiled and sanitary. Maybe so many men won't die from drinking filthy water.'

The crock had a dead rat in it but that wasn't anything to us. It could have been a dead Korean and not made any difference.

'Wait a minute, Father,' I said. 'I'll drop down into the hole and pull it out for you, as you don't look as if you can do it.'

I dropped into the hole but it was too small for the crock to come out as the bombing had twisted the cellar out of shape. I looked up; the sky was cold, clear blue and his face was framed in the hole, looking down with a woe-begone expression. I assured him:

'It isn't so bad. Pull off some of these boards and dirt, so I can maneuver the crock through the hole.' He began, but the dirt started falling into the hole nearly covering me up. Then catastrophe—a large rock started to fall. He tried to stop it by deliberately placing his foot in its path. It bruised him horribly, and may have been the start of the clot that later formed in his leg. The rock came crashing through and hit the rim of the crock, cracking off a portion. What a disappointment for him! He called Hank Petticone. Between them they were able to clear the hole so that I might get out. We worked the balance of the afternoon carefully removing the debris and were finally able to remove the crock. It wasn't as good as we had hoped, but it served the purpose. Father Kapaun would boil water and place it in this container so that the sick could have a drink of pure water. The well men had to fend for themselves, but could always mooch a drink off Father by giving him some sticks to burn.'"[3]

"HE COULD TURN A STINKING MUD HUT INTO A CATHEDRAL"

"Other survivors of Camp No. 5 remembered the soft-spoken priest calmly making his self-appointed rounds ministering to the sick and wounded of all faiths. They saw him volunteer for work details that would take him to other compounds where he would slip into the fetid huts and hear confessions and anoint the dying. His captors took Father's rosary away from him, so he made one of wire, and at night gathered the Catholics and led them in that comforting litany. Ailing Protestants would look up and see the gray-eyed priest standing beside their pallets reciting the Lord's Prayer and they would join in with him.

The saintly chaplain labored ceaselessly at the corporal works of mercy in the valley where wind rushed down from barren mountains. It was exhausting work to bury dead POWs in the rocky ground, but he always made sure he was on the burial detail. When the frozen chunks of earth covered the emaciated body, he would say the prayer for the dead. When men became sick and helpless from dysentery, Father washed their reeking clothes and, while others bickered over whose turn it was to clean the latrines, a detested chore, he would sneak out and do it. In his soiled and ragged fatigues, with his scraggly beard and his odd woolen cap made of the sleeve of an old GI sweater pulled down over his ears—he looked like any other half-starved prisoner. But by his very presence he could for a time turn a stinking mud hut into a cathedral."[4]

FELIX McCOOL

"Once I saw [Kapaun's] helmet liner laying in the yard and I asked him about it. It had the Cross marked on the front in white lettering. A representation that the wearer was a Chaplain. He said, 'Mac, if I wear it that would only antagonize the Chinese, so I won't. But by the fact it is laying on this garbage heap causes every man to see it and remind them of their God. You know Mac, I often wonder just how many silent prayers are said by this old heap of trash. God moves in mysterious ways,' he said.

The helmet liner lay through the cold weather and the spring rains, rolling and turning in the wind and rain; I could see it from the door. He left us to go to his God, but the old liner lay there. I finally kicked it around the house and broke it up, tearing the cross from the broken parts, and hid it. I brought it home and sent it to the Father Kapaun Memorial Fund…"[5]

COMMUNIST INDOCTRINATION BEGINS

"On 1 April 1951 the Chinese assumed complete control of the camp and the North Koreans departed. Pyoktong became Camp No. 5. All the inmates were assembled to listen to an introductory speech by a senior Chinese officer. It lasted for four and a half hours and began in terms as follows:

'Everyone in the aggressive force is guilty of crime and no

leniency is required. The United States aggression is a good reason for exacting a blood debt. But surrendered soldiers are, nevertheless, treated humanely by the Chinese People's Volunteers who will not exact their blood debt, as is their right, providing you show yourselves willing to learn the truth. Those of you who refuse to cooperate will be regarded as war criminals, not entitled to the benefits of our Lenient Policy. To help you learn the truth a new daily program has been arranged. Henceforth you will be allowed to study for eight hours every day...'

The speaker insisted that South Korea had started the war, that the Americans had intervened unlawfully, that the prisoners should be eternally grateful for being spared their lives and allowed the opportunity to learn the truth. Under the circumstances only criminals would be ungrateful and, by implication, would be treated as criminals if they were unappreciative of the chances they were being given.

Squad leaders were then assigned to each hut to ensure that all prisoners strictly observed the regulations—basically coerced to be overt informers.

By 9 April, barracking and booing during lectures and discussion had become fairly commonplace and ribald catcalls greeted the Chinese speakers from unseen voices amidst the large assemblies. It was exceedingly difficult for the Chinese to identify the culprits, though they attempted to do so by posting lookouts at suitable points. Many prisoners slept through the assemblies, having already found the means of getting round the subsequent discussion periods. It was all very easy...

Eventually the Chinese identified the resisters by a well-tried and characteristically Maoist trick of 'letting a hundred flowers bloom.' During lectures the prisoners were encouraged to voice their honest opinions on the running of the camp and the content and methods of their political education. The prisoners were embarrassingly frank, thus allowing the Chinese look-outs to identify the speakers."[6]

POWs at one of the prison camps attending indoctrination sessions from the Chinese communists. Taken some time after Father Kapaun died, between late 1951 and 1953.

CHINESE POLITICAL OFFICERS
COMRADE SUN AND D.P. WONG

"The Chinese tutors sent to North Korea to initiate a new stage in the POW experience were extremely intelligent and spoke fluent English (with an easy command of slang); most had been educated in the United States. The minds of most of the self-confident, determined indoctrinators had been sharpened at the University of California and the University of Chicago. At Camp 5, according to navy helicopter pilot Lt. John Thornton, a man named Sun 'ran the whole educational program.' His command of the English language was good, 'not the King's perfect English,' said Thornton, 'but very understandable and legible and probably as well as I do without the accent.' Sun usually stayed in the background, but he brought with him on April 1, 1951, a large group of instructors, including 'Dirty Pictures' Wong and 'Snake Eye' Ding, as the GIs dubbed them. There were even a few female lecturers. A considerable band of indoctrinators was necessary because Camp 5 was by far the largest POW camp, eventually containing almost three-quarters of the American POWs in North Korea. It was here that the Chinese would make their most determined effort to influence and 'educate' their captive audience. Wong, who received his nickname once the Americans learned he collected lewd photographs (deemed 'Dirty Pictures'), gathered virtually all the prisoners of Camp 5 into a large barn that first day of April 1951. He lectured them on what they could expect, and gain, from conscientious study. The soldiers fidgeted and called back and forth to each other. Very few paid attention to Wong, who then burst out:

'You are the aggressors and if you don't accept the lenient policy and change your views, we have dug a hole which we are going to throw you in. You capitalist warmongers do stink. We are quite right in burying you. A person who does not accept our doctrine is not a human being because he is not for the masses and a man that is not for the masses does not deserve treatment any better than you give an animal. As an animal, we have a right to eliminate you. You will learn the truth and we don't care if it takes one year, two years, ten years, twenty years; we don't care if you die here because we will bury you and bury you deep so that you won't stink.'

The prisoners, both artillery captain Frederick Smith and marine warrant officer Felix McCool remembered, shut up. They knew he was serious, as was his government."[7]

LIEUTENANT MIKE DOWE

"As our bodies weakened, the Reds stepped up the pace of their propaganda assault upon our minds. Hour after hour we sat in lectures while Comrade Sun, a fanatic little Chinese who hated Americans with an insane hatred, assailed our rotten, capitalistic Wall Street civilization. Then we'd have to comment upon the great truths revealed by Comrade Sun. A few bold men, in reckless despair, commented in unprintable words of contempt and were thrown into a freezing hole or subjected to other severe tortures sometimes resulting in death. Some veiled their ridicule. 'According to the great doctrines taught us by the noble Stalin, Lenin, Marx, Engels, Amos and Andy...' they would read aloud in the 'classes.' Father was not openly arrogant, nor did he use subterfuge. Without losing his temper or raising his voice, he'd answer the lecturer point by point, with a calm logic that set Comrade Sun screaming and leaping on the platform like an angry ape."[8]

"'When our Lord told us to love our enemies,' Kapaun once said, 'I'm sure He did not have Comrade Sun in mind.'

Although they did not punish him directly, the Chinese took two of his close friends away and tortured them. Their hands were tied behind their backs and they were hoisted by ropes until their wrist joints were dislocated. They were forced to make statements accusing the Father of slandering the Chinese and advocating resistance to their study program. When they were returned to the hut, unsure of their reception, the two officers were greeted by Father Kapaun, who told them, 'You never should have suffered a moment, trying to protect me.' The expected public trial never took place. It became clear that the Chinese were afraid of the priest and were worried that if he was maltreated the whole camp of 4,000 men would rise up against them."[9]

"The communists ignored the provisions of the Geneva Convention for the duration of the war, including Article 34 which states that prisoners of war 'shall enjoy complete latitude in the exercise of their religious duties, including attendance at the service of their faith.' Furthermore, Article 35 says that 'chaplains who fall into the hands of the enemy power...shall be allowed to minister to the prisoners and to exercise freely their ministry among prisoners of the same religion.' During 1951 three American chaplains arrived at Camp 5 and two died within a short time. The third, Father Kapaun, whom we have met before, was not permitted to take part in any religious activity, but he did anyway, despite being branded by the Chinese as a troublemaker and reactionary."[10]

"Speculation was that the Chinese feared Father Kapaun's influence, and that if he was punished for speaking up during class, it might turn the entire camp on them. But later, when the priest was caught stealing wood from a fence, he was stripped to the waist and made to stand in the cold for hours."[11]

Walt Mayo recalls: "By March 1951, Father had a full-fledged beard and was using a sleeve from a GI wool-knit sweater for a stocking cap. His face was drawn and he was very thin. We used to kid him by saying he looked like one of the old, bearded Patriarchs. Every evening he went to the five houses in which the officers lived and offered evening prayers. He prayed for our daily material and spiritual needs, for our deliverance and liberation and for the enemy, the Communists, that they be delivered from that terrible scourge and false philosophy. He went on like this until April. In their indoctrination program the Chinese would yell and scream about American capitalists and warmongers. Father would sit on the mud floor of the farm house and in a soft, calm voice, refute their statements one by one. They taunted him by saying:

'Where is your God now? Ask Him to get you out of this camp. See if He can feed you. You should thank Mao Tse-Tung and Stalin for your daily bread. You cannot see or hear or feel your God, therefore, he does not exist.'

Father would reply: 'One day the good Lord will save the Chinese and free them from the scourge that has set upon them. The good Lord, as He fed the thousands on the mountains, will also take care of us. Mao Tse-Tung could not make a tree or a flower or stop the thunder and lightning.'

He also told them that his God was as real as the air they breathed but could not see, as the sounds they heard but could not see, as the thoughts and ideas they had and spoke but could not see or feel. After a while, they let him alone since they were afraid of his arguments. He would shame a lot of the English-speaking interpreters (knowing they were missionary-trained) by chastising them when they said religion exploited the masses, etc., and asking them if their missionary teachers had done such things as they alleged. Our guards told the enlisted men that he was an agitator and a capitalist propagandist and to have nothing to do with him. The men, God bless them, told the Chinese off in their own inimitable way. The Chinese obstructed Father in every effort to conduct services, but he always managed."[12]

"The Communists ridiculed him, you know, denigrated him, and came out with such stuff like, 'Don't ask God for your daily bread.' You know, 'Ask Mao Tse-tung. He's the one who provides your daily bread.' And Father Kapaun would respond with such little things like, 'Well, if this is an example of God's daily bread then God must be a terrible baker.' And that sort of left them hanging in mid-air."[13]

ST. PATRICK'S DAY

"By mid-March 1951 the food situation was becoming desperate. The men were becoming weaker, their strength drained by pellagra, beriberi and the perpetual diet of millet and corn which became so nauseating they could hardly bring themselves to swallow it. They searched everywhere for green weeds to boil in their hunt for vitamins. Their bodies began to swell as the first stage of death by starvation approached. The night before St. Patrick's Day, Father Kapaun called the men together and prayed to St. Patrick, asking him to help them in their hour of need. The next day the Chinese brought them a case of liver, the first meat they had had, and issued kaoliang instead of millet. The liver was spoiled and kaoliang is sorghum seed, used as cattle feed in the States, but to the prisoners the food was a

Godsend. Later he prayed for tobacco and that night a guard walked by and threw a little bag of dry, straw-like Korean tobacco in their room."[14]

MARCH 25, 1951—FATHER KAPAUN DELIVERS AN ECUMENICAL SUNRISE EASTER SERVICE

"On Easter Sunday, Kapaun openly defied Communist ideology by celebrating an ecumenical sunrise service in the ruins of a burned-out church. Holding a makeshift crucifix, Kapaun wore his priest's stole, the purple ribbon signifying his pastoral office, and recited the Stations of the Cross. Most of the men in the officers' compound attended, including Catholics, Protestants, Jews, and atheists. While the Chinese guards watched nervously, Kapaun ended the service by leading the men in song; 'America the Beautiful' echoed from the surrounding mountains, still blanketed by snow. The officers sang at the top of their lungs, hoping the music would reach the other prisoners at Pyoktong. 'There was nobody there,' recalled Sid Esensten years later, 'who did not feel the thrill of the music, the meaning of the words, the solemnness of the occasion, the goose pimples up and down their bodies and the feeling that this brought them much closer to home than they had felt for many, many months.'"[15]

From Matthew: "For I was hungry and you gave me no food, I was thirsty and you gave me no drink, a stranger and you gave me no welcome, naked and you gave me no clothing, ill and in prison, and you did not care for me. Then they will answer and say, 'Lord, when did we see you hungry or thirsty or a stranger or naked or ill or in prison, and not minister to your needs?' He will answer them, 'Amen, I say to you, what you did not do for one of these least ones, you did not do for me. And these will go off to eternal punishment, but the righteous to eternal life.' Such is the Gospel of The Lord."

★ ★ ★

Walt Mayo witnessed the service: "It was Easter, April, 1951, a cold, raw day, with the wind blowing from Manchuria over the Yalu. The ice was just breaking on the reservoir. Father had Easter Sunrise Services with the Rosary, Memorare, Stations of the Cross, Mass Prayers, and readings from the Bible and hymns. I will never forget that service as long as I live. Father was limping and had a cane, plus a black patch over one eye that had become infected. About 85 officers were sitting on the steps of a bombed-out church in our area. The steps were all that was left of the church. Catholic, Protestant and Jew were there, plus some that had no religion at all, but were starting to find one. There were very few officers whose eyes were not damp by the time it was over. The Chinese raised a stink with Father about it but he told them that they profess freedom of religion and after a while they dropped it.

Father had his ciborium and corporal, plus his stole and holy oils. He heard many a confession during these months. He held Catholic services on Sunday and then Protestant services. He ministered to all and neglected no one. He rarely complained and when he did it was always about some injustice suffered by someone else. He corrected those who were using profanity and helped to cure many of that habit."[16]

CARL KOPISCHKIE

"I still remember, so vividly, our first Easter Service, which Father Kapaun arranged and conducted and at which we assembled to worship God and give thanks for the Resurrection of our Lord, Jesus Christ. The singing of the Lord's Prayer by Bill Whiteside sent chills up and down my spine. The sermon given by Father Kapaun was inspiring and gave us a renewed hope and faith and made us realize that even though we were confined behind barbed wire with armed guards stationed around us, that our faith in God would eventually lead to our release."[17]

APRIL 1951

"After the Easter Services, we noticed that Father was limping badly and had difficulty moving around. We asked him many times what the matter was, but he would always smile and say that it was just old age creeping up on him. After he became sick and was lying prostrate, slowly starving, with such pain in his leg that only God knows how he suffered. People would seek his advice, but he never complained. When Father realized that his last illness was upon him, he asked Nardella to continue the religious services, especially saying the Rosary and missal prayers in the prison camp. Nardella promised."[18]

"I went down to the house and into the room. He was lying on the floor with his head propped up and eating. Doctors Esensten and Anderson were there with Captain Ralph Nardella and W.O. Felix McCool. Father was breathing heavily and talking strangely but rationally. His face was contorted with pain every few minutes and we were all pretty much scared. He kept talking about different subjects for about half an hour. He recognized everyone. Then Father's face was contorted and the pain must have been terrific because he started to cry. About a minute later, he looked up, the tears still rolling down his pain-racked face, and told us the story of the Seven Maccabees in the Old Testament:

"There was an emperor who had an old woman brought up before him. He told her to renounce her Faith or he would torture and kill her. She replied that he could do anything he wanted, but she would not renounce it. The emperor then had her seven sons brought in and said he would kill them if she did not do as he said. She still refused and he then put them to death one by one. The old woman was crying and the emperor asked her if she was crying because she was sad. She replied that her tears were tears of joy because she knew her sons were in heaven."

Father then looked at us and said he was crying for the same reason. He said that he was glad he was suffering because Our Lord had suffered also and that he felt closer to Him. By that time, we were all crying, everyone in that room, who had seen scores of people die in the past few months and who thought they were pretty hard.

Doctors Anderson and Esensten went out of the room for a minute and I went with them. They said Father was all right except that he had become overtired, and the leg had started to cause a great deal of pain. About that time, a Chinaman, and English-speaking officer, and a short, fat Communist, came running into the room and told us they were going to take Father to the hospital."[19]

Around this time Father Kapaun wrote his last words on a brown paper towel—it is a memorized version of the Catholic Prayers for the men to use in private services. It was kept protected by fellow POW Captain Eugene Shaw, who smuggled it out at the war's end. Dated May 18, 1954, Shaw mailed the prayers to Emil Kapaun's parents in Kansas with a letter explaining the contents:

"Dear Mrs. Kapaun, Just three years ago Father Emil Kapaun passed away at Pyoktong, Korea while he was a prisoner of war. I was among the group who was with him before and during his captivity. I did not know him prior to being captured but I was a member of the same unit. After our capture Father Kapaun and I slept side by side for several months and I got to know him well. Many nights we would talk together about our homes and he would tell me of the good things you would cook for him and what a wonderful Mother you were. Of course, he spoke of his Father also but he would always dwell on things regarding you.

I am not a Catholic but I know he had as many who were not as he did that were, who loved him for the great Christian he was. While we were together he wrote out a set of prayers for me and to the best of my knowledge it was his last writing. I want to give you these prayers because you are his Mother and will appreciate them more than anyone else could hope to do. Several people have asked me for them to use in publications but I felt that if they were released for that purpose then you should be the one to do so.

My deepest regards and may God bless and keep you. Respectfully, Eugene Davis Shaw."

Father Kapaun's last writing (written on a paper towel):

"Prayers to be learned by Heart

"1. In the Name of the Father and of the Son and of the Holy Ghost, Amen.

"2. Our Father Who art in Heaven, hallowed be thy Name. Thy Kingdom come. Thy Will be done on earth as it is in Heaven. Give us this day our daily Bread and forgive us our trespasses as we forgive those who trespass against us. And lead us not into temptation but deliver us from evil. Amen.

"3. Hail Mary, full of grace, The Lord is with thee. Blessed art thou among women and blessed is the fruit of thy womb; Jesus. Holy Mary, Mother of God, pray for us sinners now, and at the hour of our death. Amen.

"4. Glory be to the Father and to the Son, and to the Holy Ghost. As it was in the beginning, is now, and ever shall be, world without end. Amen.

"5. I believe in God, the Father Almighty, Creator of Heaven and Earth. And in Jesus Christ, His only Son, our Lord. Who was conceived by the Holy Ghost, born of the Virgin Mary, suffered under Pontius Pilate, was crucified, died, and was buried. He descended into Hell. The third day He arose again from the dead. He ascended into Heaven, sitting at the right hand of God the Father Almighty. From thence He shall come to judge the living and the dead. I believe in the Holy Ghost, the Holy

Catholic Church, the Communion of Saints, the Forgiveness of sins, the Resurrection of the body, and life everlasting. Amen."

MIKE DOWE

"The week after Easter he began to limp, hobbling along on a crooked stick. The next Sunday, as he read the service for the first Sunday after Easter, as he reached the line in the Epistle: 'And this is the victory that overcomes the world, our Faith,' his voice faltered, and we caught him as he fell. Beneath his tattered uniform his right leg was dreadfully swollen and discolored. For weeks, we knew, he had been suffering terrible bone aches, a by-product of hunger, that came upon men at night with such fearful pain that they would scream and beat the ground in agony. The communist 'doctor,' a brain-washer posing as a medical man, pronounced the usual diagnosis by which they sought to convince us—or themselves—that we were an evil, immoral and decaying race. Father, he said blandly, had syphilis. Doctor Anderson and his medical companion, Captain Sidney Esensten, knew it for what it was—a blood clot blocking circulation to the leg. They applied hot packs, and slowly the swelling began to subside. Soon Father could walk again, though he was so weak and shaky he would often fall. Then a fearful dysentery seized him, and as he so often had done for us, we cared for him as best we could. And he beat that, and got on his feet again.

Then one raw, cold day he arose, a walking ghost, to give the last sacrament to a dying man. The next day his eyes were bright with fever and his breath came in a hoarse rattle. He had taken pneumonia, and soon was in delirium. Thinking back upon it, I believe that period of semi-consciousness was the only happy time he knew during his captivity. Around him there seemed to gather all the people he had known in his boyhood on the farm in Kansas and in his school days. Babbling happily, sometimes laughing, he spoke to his mother and his father, and to the priests he'd known in the seminary. Even in his delirium, his unbreakable spirit manifested itself in sallies of humor. Finally, he sank into a deep and quiet sleep, and when he awoke, he was completely rational. The crisis had passed. He was getting well. But the Chinese did not intend that he should live."[20]

FATHER KAPAUN REMOVED TO DEATH HOUSE

In descriptions of Pyoktong's prison camp hospital, the word "hospital" is frequently in quotation marks as survivors of the camp well knew that you were lucky to walk out alive. The Chinese doctors did help where they could but their practice of medicine was far different than those trained in the West. Fortunately for the POWs, several experienced doctors were among the population and they were able to guilt trip the Chinese guards and officials that proper medical care was the right of all people—especially prisoners—in their time of need. To demonstrate this, the American and British doctors were often consulted for the medical care the Chinese guards and officers needed. This gave credence to the Communist doctrine of showing "leniency" to their captors. But still looming large over the situation was the fact that any prisoner in the camp deemed a "troublemaker" or a leader in any way that inspired their fellow prisoners not to succumb to the tireless indoctrination sessions was purposefully and deliberately withheld from treatment or sustenance so that they could declare their death as from "natural causes." So on the hospital grounds was a single-room building about 20 x 20, known as the "death house." A morgue for those not yet dead but fully conscious to suffer a sick and twisted torment right out of an Edgar Allan Poe nightmare. Without food or water, the Communists were simply hastening a "natural death" for propaganda purposes. But not helping the sick and wounded is still killing that prisoner—no different than shooting them in the head. They weaponized food, water, and medicine, just out of reach, as torture before death.

★ ★ ★

Walt Mayo sadly recalls: "First of all, we did not want to let Father go because we were taking care of him and he was getting better. However, the Chinese said he must go. The hospital was a place where they took people to die. Only about five officers out of sixty had ever come back from there. The Chinese hated him because he had such an influence over all the prisoners. He was a power for good and they hated and feared any power but their own, not to speak of a power exercising good. We refused, argued, threatened, pleaded, but to no avail. About half an hour later they came down with a makeshift stretcher. Father knew as soon as this Chinaman named Ku appeared, that he was going to the 'hospital.'"[21]

Ku insisted, "He goes! He goes!" and Father Kapaun protested no more. He handed his prayer book to Ralph Nardella saying, "You know the prayers, Ralph, keep holding the services. Don't let them make you stop." To Mike Dowe, he said, "Don't take it so hard, Mike. I'm going where I've always wanted to go. And when I get there, I'll say a prayer for you."

Walt Mayo continues: "As they were putting this makeshift stretcher on the ground and telling us to hurry, Father gave me his ciborium, corporal and a list of people he baptized. He said he was keeping his stole and holy oils because he probably would have use for them at the 'hospital.' We carried him out of the room and put him on the stretcher. There were two English-speaking Chinese interpreter officers, Sun and Ku. All of us were so mad we would have strangled both of them were it not for Father. We were all crying. Six of the officers were going to carry him on the stretcher. As they raised him up on their shoulders, Father said to me, 'Walt, if I don't come back, tell my Bishop that I died a happy death.' We all told him that he would be back with us soon but he sort of smiled and shook his head and asked us to say a few prayers for him.

Standing there watching Father being carried off down the

hill on that stretcher, I realized I would never see him alive again. I also realized that he knew that more than anyone else."[22]

DEATH ALONG THE YALU RIVER

Father Kapaun was taken to the death house and laid out in the unlit room on a dirt floor too filthy to even imagine. Fellow prisoner Jack Stegall somehow was able to check in on Kapaun and noticed some cracked corn in a bowl was still untouched and out of reach from his ailing chaplain. After a couple of days, on May 23, 1951, Father Emil Kapaun was now praying for his fellow man from heaven—not once thinking of himself. The guards ordered two prisoners to remove his body and bury him in the mass grave nearby, hoping Father Kapaun would be quickly forgotten. The Communists were afraid of him even in death. Little did they know the American burial detail went out of their way to ensure Father Kapaun's remains would not get mixed with the hundreds of others still accumulating. To this very day, the Communists are still afraid of him and the rest of the world is blessed to learn the story of his return home.

Epilogue

CHRIST IN BARBED WIRE

By late 1951, the officers had been relocated to Camp 2 and met new arrival Gerry Fink. After much searching, Fink found a solid piece of oak that he began carving into the body of Christ. Cherry wood was used for the cross. As Fink worked on the twenty-two-inch corpus, he was noticed by a guard who inquired whether the figure was the face of Chaplain Kapaun. Fink casually explained that the bearded face was not that of Father Kapaun, but Abraham Lincoln, whom the Communists considered to be a kindred spirit because he "freed the slaves" and therefore was no capitalist. Being that a "nonreligious" symbol could be permitted, Fink was allowed to continue. The face he was really carving was, of course, his interpretation of Christ on the cross.

The primitive tools were not quite sufficient for the final touches. At one point, Fink waited until the command quarters were empty and broke a window to collect the glass shards, which proved to be an excellent medium for sanding and smoothing the corpus. Fink said he couldn't really carve a crown of thorns so small, so he asked Funchess how they could fashion a crown of thorns to resemble barbed wire once the corpus was complete. Funchess procured a pair of tin snips and they were able to configure simple radio wire into a crown of thorns made to look like barbed wire.

By mid-1952, the pièce de résistance was finished. The cross is almost four feet high and the frail and slender corpus about two feet long. The expression on His face is perhaps the most touching of all, for it captures the common sorrow that both Christ and Father Kapaun share—a sorrow that all prisoners understood and that showed in the lines of their faces. It inspired and electrified all in the camp who saw it. Padre Sam Davies, an Anglican priest from the British forces, blessed the crucifix, and the men dubbed the masterpiece "Christ in Barbed Wire." They suspended it from the ceiling of their quarters to use at all religious services until the end of the war. Miraculously, it was never confiscated.

END OF KOREAN WAR

By July 1953, the rugged 150-mile landscape of the Demilitarized Zone (DMZ) along the Korean border was a barren wasteland of ditches, outposts, bomb craters, and blood-soaked ridges long devoid of any recognizable vegetation. Even worse was the buildup of weaponry on both sides that proved each side was going nowhere. A stalemate was inevitable. No soldier wanted to be the "last guy killed" over a dispute on whose dirt was whose. On July 27, 1953, after months of negotiations, the shooting stopped in Korea.

REPATRIATION—FALL 1953

For many anxious Americans and our allied nations, the day finally came that a truce had been signed and that "Operation Big Switch" would oversee the exchange of prisoners. In Kaeson, on the border between North and South, "Freedom Village" was

US ARMY

Private Joe Ramirez, who survived two and a half years as a POW, hugs his mother with a million-dollar smile on the tarmac of the Houston airport.

US AIR FORCE/COURTESY WILLIAM FUNCHESS

After a thousand days as a POW, William Funchess returns home a hero to his wife, Sybil, whom he says wore a red dress. They had been married just prior to the Korean War. They raised three children while he taught agriculture studies at Clemson University for many, many years. He passed away in 2021.

constructed to welcome our repatriated soldiers. Doctors and officials were ready with an abundance of amenities to bring the emaciated and broken men back to the Western world. The press was there too. Over the radio, millions listened with acute attention as radio announcers read the names and stories of the heroes who had survived. For about four thousand households, hearing the name of their loved ones brought great joy and relief. But for about the same amount of families, the silence was deafening and deeply disappointing.

When word came of the armistice, the Communists arranged to have cameras focused on the men as they were informed. The Communist leaders had heralded to the world that the prisoners would be released. They anticipated that this would be excellent propaganda, but of course this never happened.

THE CIBORIUM

Apart from the crucifix, the POWs from Camp 2 also planned to bring with them a smaller cross, the chaplain insignia that had been painted on Father Kapaun's helmet liner and rescued by Felix McCool; the tools Captain Fink had used to carve the crucifix; and the ciborium Father Kapaun used at Mass and Communion on the battlefield, and which had been present at the famous Easter Service. A ciborium is a receptacle designed to hold the consecrated Eucharistic bread of the Christian Church. It is shaped like a goblet, or chalice, having a domed-shaped cover, and is typically made, or plated, in a precious metal. The last thing many of the POWs remembered of their friend Father Kapaun was seeing that gold ciborium glitter in his hand as he was carried on the stretcher to the hospital. When he died, the prisoners wondered what had become of the sacred cup.

In April 1952, Captain Nardella was outside the building at Camp 2 when the camp commander's daughter walked by and, in her hands, was Father Kapaun's ciborium now filled with marbles. He tried to get from her but she cried and had to make a hasty retreat.

Captain Nardella strongly opposed such desecration and attempted to convince the Chinese that the gold cup was not just personal property or a symbol of the Crusades or anti-Communist propaganda but a relic of universal faith. He pleaded that the cup be placed in a safe place until the prisoners were released. Nothing further was seen of the ciborium. "And then at the very last moment before our release," Captain Nardella said, "it was given to me personally." Finally their captors yielded. More important even than the precious artifacts, the POWs carried the memory of the spiritual hero of Korea who did more than any other man for the POWs, and they were determined his influence would not die.

Throughout his imprisonment, Captain Gerry Fink was a source of stability, humor, and encouragement to his fellow POWs. He was a rock. When Operation Big Switch took place in August 1953, the surviving POWs were finally returned home. Major Tom Harrison's Fink-built leg was confiscated by the Chinese along with the secret documents bearing administrative records of that camp, which were in a "hidey-hole" in the leg. The records had been duplicated, however, and were brought out in a hole in the grip of his crutches. A third copy came out in the cane of an army captain, and William Funchess smuggled POW data scribbled on a dollar bill and in a Gideon pocket Bible. Most importantly, Funchess's record-keeping changed the official date of Father Kapaun's passing to May 23, 1951—giving the Kapaun family and the Wichita Diocese the first sign of much-needed closure.

And the Christ in Barbed Wire came out too.

"I had to negotiate with the Chinese to get it out," said Nardella. "Ever since the crucifix was made, I used it, suspended from the ceiling, during our services. Some Chinese showed it respect. Others, who had no Christian contacts, just gaped at it. The communists were unwilling to let me bring it along. I had to haggle and argue to get it out. They referred it to 'higher headquarters' before I got permission. There was no answer until the very last minute," said Nardella.

AP/WIDE WORLD PHOTO/FATHER KAPAUN GUILD

This exquisite crucifix was carved by Jewish Marine Corps fighter pilot Major Gerald Fink and dubbed "Christ in Barbed Wire." To smuggle it out of the POW camp when the war ended late August 1953, the POWs cut it into three pieces and wrapped it into fake leg splint bandages. It thus came with them on the POW trains headed for the border of South Korea where Freedom Village awaited. The crucifix was reassembled on the train and carried proudly to freedom by (left to right) Warrant Officer Felix McCool, USMC, Army Captain Joseph O'Connor, and Captain Ralph Nardella—all Catholics.

Not taking any chances, the POWs disassembled the cross in two pieces and removed the corpus. Knowing the guards never checked a POW's bandages, they wrapped the three pieces like splints on the POWs' legs with dirty rags and then "limped" out to the trucks waiting to take them to a train station. Once they were transferred onto boxcars headed south, the POWs reassembled the Christ in Barbed Wire in order to emerge victorious with a symbol proving they had never lost faith.

The sublime crucifix was brought into Freedom Village on the last day of the prisoner exchange by four close friends of Chaplain Kapaun: Captain Ralph Nardella of Norfolk, Virginia; Captain Joseph O'Connor of Spring City, Pennsylvania; Lieutenant Paul O'Dowd of Berkeley, California; and Warrant Officer Felix McCool, Marine, of Glendale, California.

Garbed in baggy blue POW suits, the quartet walked as a unit, with Nardella carrying the crucifix, a privilege accorded him by common consent, as he had taken over religious services after Father's death. The Communist captors had hated this layman just as much as they hated the priest. Nardella had been captured about the same time, and was with the priest-hero almost to the day he died. When Father realized that his last illness was upon him, he asked Nardella to continue the religious services, especially saying the Rosary and missal prayers in the prison camp."[1] Nardella not only kept his sacred promise but walked the crucifix and the story of Father Kapaun right into a throng of waiting reporters more than willing, eager, and able to share the remarkable story with the world.

"But among the sorely distressed were Enos and Elizabeth Kapaun. These dear parents loved their son deeply. He was always the ideal boy, the reverent son, one who during his life had never given them a moment of worry. As a student, as a priest, as a soldier, he had kept in close touch with his parents through the medium of numerous letters. Because Father Kapaun had not written them since October 1950 (almost two years had elapsed), they were quite certain that their son was dead. Yet day after day they went to the rural mailbox that was just a few feet away from their home on a Kansas farm road, always confident that there would be some message of hope. During Operation Big Switch, finally came that dread telegram:

I am writing you concerning your son, Chaplain (Captain) Emil J. Kapaun, reported missing in action... Chaplain Ka-

FATHER KAPAUN GUILD

*Wooden crucifix Christ in Barbed Wire mounted on brass plaque by the Catholic Dio-
cese of Wichita. Looking at it are Bishop Mark Carroll and former POW Lieutenant
Ralph Nardella, who helped smuggle the crucifix out of their North Korean POW camp.*

paun died May 5, 1951, at Pyoktong, North Korea… [His
date of death was later amended to May 23.]

At long last, Mr. and Mrs. Kapaun were consoled by the
thought of the Crucified Christ all during their long agony of
waiting. Christ indeed had placed a heavy cross on their shoulders because the death of their chaplain son was the first in their
immediate family. The clouds of sadness and sorrow were to be
dissipated by one of the most unusual memorials ever given to
mortal man. Because Father Emil had "spoken, acted and looked
like Christ," his grateful family of soldiers decided to carve a

crucifix in hallowed memory of their chaplain—conceived and completed in a North Korean prison camp. The other prisoners of all faiths and beliefs and of no belief gave Gerry Fink and now Father Emil's parents their full cooperation. Admiration for their priest friend and respect for his memory bound them together as one family."[2]

The crucifix was initially installed on the wall of the St. John Nepomucene Church in Pilsen. Later a controversial decision was made to hang it in a glass case in the foyer of Kapaun-Mt. Carmel High School in Wichita, Kansas, where it remains on public display to this day. But no matter the physical location of the Christ in Barbed Wire, Enos and Elizabeth Kapaun were no doubt comforted and pleased to hear a steady stream of stories that emerged over the years from the many veterans and ex-POWs who hailed the chaplain's deeds and actions from the rooftops—Emil Kapaun was a hero among heroes and a saint to many whether they met him or not.

GERALD FINK WRITES OF
FATHER KAPAUN AFTER THE WAR

I do not desire any credit for my work. Could I have done the crucifix in precious metals it would not the less take away from the memory of Christ or lend more to the memory of Father Kapaun, "a man the world should know about." I am extremely humble in the face of Father Kapaun's memory and the life that he led. Here was a man given to live, as "God intended men to live." His self-sacrifice, his love of his fellowmen, and even his love of his enemy marked him more saint than man. I did not know him as well as others, yet to have lived under his influence is like having bathed in the light of graciousness. As a priest of the Catholic Church, he gave to all what I am sure your Holy Father in Rome has come to expect of all his field representatives (that is to put it in my own phraseology).

With the trials and tribulations that beset our men in the hands of the Reds, with the unending onslaughts they made to shake our faith in God, with the cruelty which only man can show to man, with the hunger, the pestilence, with the deprivation all were subjected to, with the dejection, and the complete destitution we were faced with—with all these things that added to the crucible of fire that all men's souls were tested in—Father Kapaun withstood them, and showed the way and the light of the Lord. I cannot add more to this story other than to say I bear him love for showing us how a man must face his adversities. If the meek shall inherit the earth, it will be because people like Father Kapaun willed it to them. I am a Jew, but that man will always live in my heart. He was a man among many who were not. I saw the biggest, huskiest and toughest men crack under the strain. Father Kapaun not only served Christians well but he served everyone else with equal goodness and kindness. Never thinking of himself, he was always doing something for others. He represented to me saintliness in its purest form and manliness in its rarest form.

The crucifix carved in POW Camp 2 in Pin-Chon-Ni is one of the most extraordinary in existence. It seems to invoke the message young Emil Kapaun wrote in a letter sent from seminary school to Mr. and Mrs. E. Melcher on February 21, 1938:

I'm sending a little remembrance for your wedding. When I asked Father to bless the crucifix, he asked me what I was going to do with it. I told him to whom I was sending it, and he said:
Good, tell them to hang it up in their living room where

everybody will see it. And tell them to say some prayers together before the crucifix either in the morning or evening. If they continue this practice, God will bless their home and their work as Christ promised: "For where there are two or three gathered in My name, there am I in the midst of them." I wish them a very happy and fruitful life.

Be sure to send me your new address. As ever, Joe G. (Alias—Emil)

Afterword

THE PATH TO SAINTHOOD

As related by Scott Carter of the Father Kapaun Guild

"The process of Canonization is the procedure used by the Catholic Church to recognize individuals as saints. The Church has a rich history of venerating and honoring saints whose lives are considered exemplary and worthy of emulation by the faithful. The Canonization process is complex and involves several stages, including Beatification and Canonization.

So why does the Catholic Church create saints? Perhaps the better question is, why does the Catholic Church name saints? In the broad sense, a saint is simply anyone who is in heaven. We become saints by accepting God's grace and living accordingly. The Church does create saints, but only in the sense that it is a conduit for God's grace. A person is baptized and receives the gift of God's divine life through the sacraments. This allows one to live a life of faith, hope and charity, along with the other virtues. It allows one to know and love Christ, and in turn to love other people, and to become more and more conformed to Christ, so that when one dies, the soul is ready to dwell with God in heaven, there to await the resurrection of the body. Thus a new saint is made. This is the natural work of God through the Church.

The process of Canonization is in reality the process of recognizing or naming Saints. The term means to include someone in the official canon, or list of saints. While most Catholics and even non-Catholics are aware of certain aspects of it, the details of the whole process are confusing to even the most devout. This process is lengthy and involves many steps, usually taking decades, even centuries. Yet Catholics hold the process in high esteem; we love our saints!

Before diving into the process, it's important to understand the purpose of all this time and effort. There are many reasons for it. The saints are the heroes of the faith. The Christian calling can be challenging, and we need inspiration and help along the way. Robust theological arguments and homilies are important and necessary for our faith, but sometimes we need encouragement on a more human level; seeing those theological principles lived out—seeing God's grace truly alive in a person—that is inspiring.

Certainty is another element of it—certainty that a saint is actually in heaven. It wouldn't do to hold up for exemplification someone whose life doesn't lead others to truly live the Gospel, not to mention to pray to them. The Church tries very hard to be clear about her teaching so as to remain faithful to Christ and to help men and women apply the principles of the Gospel to the age in which they live. Saints are authentic examples of this; they are sure models for how to follow Christ and live the Gospel in a unique time and age. This is not to say that a saint was perfect on earth, for none of us are, but they always sought to turn from their sins and seek the Lord's forgiveness, teaching us how to approach our own shortcomings.

Confidence in prayer is another aspect. When people pray through a saint's intercession, there should be some assurance that they will be led to Christ, and not away from Him. No matter if our prayers are answered in the way we desire or in another way according to God's Providence, if we can be certain a saint is in heaven, then we can be confident they bring our prayers to Christ.

For all these reasons, the Church examines deeply a candidate for sainthood, and it does so both from earthly and supernatural perspectives, in order to have a moral certainty about their holiness before advancing them along each step. Only God creates saints, yet we believe that with the light of the Holy Spirit, the Church can certainly and infallibly declare that certain people are in heaven.

For many centuries, Canonization was an unofficial process, and there wasn't a strict canon of saints, per se. Saints were mostly made by acclaim of the faithful—the *sensus fidei*. Over time, Bishops became more involved to help authenticate the process, until the Pope and his Curial Court began overseeing the task in the tenth to twelfth centuries. Today Papal Decree is the only official way to name a Saint, although he is supported by the Dicastery for the Causes for Saints, whose purpose it is to do the heavy lifting for him. The process is adjusted from time to time as needed.

There are four steps along the path of Canonization: Servant of God, Venerable, Blessed, and finally the ultimate goal: Saint.

SERVANT OF GOD

At its core, Canonization truly is a grassroots process, even if there are many Canonical steps and tests to pass along the way. No cause gets started if there is not a groundswell of people clamoring for it. The sense of the faithful is a real thing. The candidate must have a reputation for holiness that is widespread. People must want to imitate their example. They must share their story with others. They must pray asking the person's intercession. And all of this must be consistent and lasting. That is why the Pope has instituted a five-year waiting period before any cause may officially begin: if the fervor dies out, then it's not worth pursuing, at least until the fervor is rekindled.

Once enough momentum is built up, a petition to begin a cause for sainthood may be brought forward. This petition must come from a competent authority, most likely the bishop of the diocese where the potential saint lived or died, or the superior of the religious order to which they belonged. First an inquiry is made in the diocese to ensure there are no major objections to the cause moving forward. Then the petition goes to the Dicastery for the Causes of Saints in Rome (formerly the Congregation for Causes of Saints) to see if there is any information that would prevent the cause from moving forward. Finally, the same is done with the national bishop's conference, where a vote also takes place to ensure the general support of the Church. If the candidate passes all of these preliminary tests, the candidate can be called a Servant of God. This title was declared for Father Kapaun by Pope John Paul II in 1993.

VENERABLE

Once a candidate is named a Servant of God, the real work begins. The supporting diocese or religious order conducts a thorough investigation into the life of the Servant of God. This includes collecting their own writings (journals, class notes, letters, homilies, books or other published items), and anything written about them in newspapers, magazines or books. Now it would also include digital content. The investigation also includes tracking down as many people as possible who can share detailed insight into the life, character and actions of the Servant of God. All of this information is compiled and sent to Rome, where a Postulator, who is chosen to assist the cause, condenses the information into a still-lengthy Positio (position or statement) that makes the case for each candidate.

This investigation is trying to prove one of three things: martyrdom, heroic virtue, or an offering of life. These are the paths forward to the next step in the process. Traditionally there were two paths forward: martyrdom and heroic virtue. In 2017 Pope Francis instituted a new path: the offer of life. If any of these can be proved, the candidate can advance on the path to sainthood.

Martyrdom is the most ancient path, and it is reserved for those who were killed in hatred of the faith. A person whose martyrdom is approved is fast-tracked to being named Blessed, which takes place in a Mass called a Beatification.

Heroic virtue is the next path forward, and it is reserved for people who have exhibited an extraordinary level of virtue for at least ten years prior to their death. This includes the theological virtues of faith, hope, and charity, both toward God and toward neighbor, as well as cardinal virtues of prudence, justice, temperance, and fortitude, along with other virtues connected to them, such as patience and chastity, for example. Heroic means that these virtues have become habits that enabled the candidate to perform their actions with uncommon promptitude, ease and even joy.

While we rightly think of Father Kapaun's life as heroic, according to the criteria of the Dicastery for Saints, it was really the last year of his life that was this way. Before that, there is a lot of testimony that he was a good but rather ordinary priest. In the end, there is a sense of beauty about this, showing us that any of us, if we practice at our virtue, can become extraordinary with God's grace.

Thankfully, there is another path to Venerable, and that is the offer of life. This is reserved for a person who lived a life of virtue while alive, and in imitation of Christ, freely parted with his or her life for others. As Christ himself said at the Last Supper: "Greater love has no man than this, that a man lay down his life for his friends" (Jn 15:13). This differs from martyrdom in that it does not have to be proven that the candidate was killed in hatred of the faith. In Father Kapaun's case, many of his fellow prisoners of war testify that he indeed was killed in hatred of the faith, and this was presented to the Dicastery for Causes of Saints, but they have recommended that with the available evidence, the offer of life would be the best path to use. There are multiple points where it can be demonstrated that Father Kapaun offered his life willingly for the sake of his men.

After the Positio is prepared and presented by the Postulator to the Dicastery for the Causes of Saints, it undergoes review at two different committees: the historical and theological consultors. The historical consultors check the information collected for accuracy and also adequacy, judging if there is sufficient evidence to review. The theological consultors then review the information to see if the candidate meets the stringent theological requirements to pass each path to sainthood. If so, then the cause goes for a vote with the official members of the Dicastery, bishops and archbishops who have the authority to make recommendations to the Holy Father. If they vote in the affirmative, the Holy Father is presented with the case and alone has the final authority to declare the candidate Venerable.

BLESSED

Up to this point, the process has focused on the life of the Venerable Servant of God while on earth. Now it takes a turn to what has occurred after death: a miracle must be attributed to the candidate's intercession before he or she may progress to Blessed. In looking for miracles, the Church is looking for supernatural confirmation that the deceased is interceding for us in heaven. That's because while we can examine a person's life to the best of our abilities, only the Lord sees the heart and truly knows the holiness of a man or woman (cf. 1 Samuel 16:7). Although a miracle is granted primarily for the sake of the person it blesses, it also acts like a supernatural stamp of approval from God that the intercessor is indeed in heaven with Him. These miracles are unrelated to any miracles the candidate worked while on earth, and only can be reviewed if they take place after death. It shows the depth of the Church's desire for certitude when it comes to saints. A miracle could in theory take many shapes or forms, and sometimes they do, but most often it revolves around a medical issue. In the practical sense, these are the easiest to prove. Just as the cause is reviewed thoroughly, so too is an alleged miracle. A group of medical and scientific consultors review it, checking for any possible medical or scientific explanation or intervention that might be the actual reason for the cure. That's not to say that the Church doesn't believe that God and the saints often intervene through ordinary means such as the work of doctors or medicine—perhaps even with some extraordinary circumstances coming together in an unusual or providential way—but it is very strict when it comes to official miracles.

Therefore, the Church usually looks for three telltale signs in any alleged miraculous healing. First, there is no clear medical explanation for the healing. Treatment wasn't solving the problem, or if some treatments were given, they don't explain the full extent of the healing. Second, the healing was immediate and lasting. This doesn't always have to be the case, but it helps. And finally, there must be a clear link to prove the intervention of the Venerable Servant of God. The person who received the miracle or people close to them must have asked for the candidate's intercession. Perhaps a novena was made, or they touched the candidate's remains or an item they frequently used. Perhaps there was another sign from the potential saint, such as the healing taking place on a day related to the candidate's life. Regardless, it must be shown that the candidate for sainthood was the cause of the miracle and not another saint.

If the medical consultors pass the alleged miracle, it once

again goes to a vote from the Dicastery itself, then again to the
Pope. If approved, a Beatification Mass is held, usually within
the candidate's home diocese, where the Holy Father's decree is
read and the Blessed is included in the liturgy for the first time.
This is a very important event, and it marks a significant shift
in the process for sainthood. Up to this point, devotion to the
candidate is primarily considered private. Although public events
might take place, the candidate cannot be included in any official liturgical prayers. After Beatification, public veneration may
take place on a local level: the Blessed's feast day is celebrated
each year with the proper prayers at Mass written for his or her
intercession. Churches and buildings may be named for them,
and statues or images may be included in churches. All of this
is at a local level, usually within the diocese or region where
they lived or worked. It is not universal or even infallible until
they are declared a saint.

SAINT

The step from Blessed to Saint mimics that of Venerable to
Blessed. Another miracle is required to advance the final step to
sainthood, and this miracle must take place after the candidate
is Beatified. As for Beatification, another review is conducted,
another vote is taken at the Dicastery for Saints, and the Holy
Father makes the final approval. At this point, a Canonization
Mass is held, usually in St. Peter's Square in the Vatican, and
usually with multiple saints being recognized. Interestingly, the
Canonization Mass is one of the few times that the Pope exercises his gift of infallibility, officially and preserved from error
by the Holy Spirit proclaiming that a person is a saint in heaven.

The Canonization of a saint is a significant event for the Catholic Church and its followers. It represents the recognition that
the individual has lived a life of exemplary holiness and service
to God and the church. The Canonization process is important
because it ensures that only those individuals who meet the rig-

orous criteria are recognized as saints. The Canonization of a saint is also an occasion for celebration and worship. The naming of a new saint inspires the faithful to emulate the heroic virtues of the candidate, and the saint is honored in liturgical celebrations and devotions. The Canonization of a saint is an opportunity for the Catholic Church to renew its commitment to spiritual renewal and evangelization.

Most importantly, the Canonization of a saint is an expression of the universality of the Catholic Church. The Church recognizes saints from different times, cultures, and regions, reflecting the diversity of the Catholic community. Saints serve as role models for the faithful and embody the virtues of sacrifice and charity. With this in mind, one can only speculate the value and impact on the world stage that Father Kapaun's message and story would accomplish were he to be officially named a Saint."[1]

STATUS OF FATHER KAPAUN'S CANONIZATION

While the Father Kapaun Guild can't say for certain how the Church will proceed with Father Kapaun's cause for sainthood, the Catholic Diocese of Wichita has investigated and made their case that Father Kapaun should be named Venerable based on the fact that he willingly and repeatedly offered his life for the sake of his men. The Positio with this information has been submitted to the Dicastery for Saints; their review and a Papal judgement will be required to name him Venerable. If that time comes, there are several potential miracles that could be presented, one of which would hopefully lead to his Beatification.

FATHER KAPAUN ACCOUNTED FOR

After Chaplain Kapaun passed away in May 1951, it was widely believed that he was placed in a shallow grave on the far shore of the inlet of the Yalu River, where already close to one thousand POWs had been buried as best they could by their fellow soldiers. This was in Camp 5, Pyoktong, North Korea, right along the Yalu River—the borderline with China. In 1954, the year after the prisoner exchange, both sides also negotiated an exchange of remains from those who had died—mostly on the battlefields—but some from the prison camps as well. The Chinese added to their war crimes by cruelly removing most if not all the dog tags, which are standard identifying tags that can survive for decades underground when left on a body. The dog tags were either kept by the Chinese or discarded. Nearly four thousand sets of remains were returned to US custody, and after being taken to Japan for analysis and identification, most were positively identified and sent to their home states. Over eight hundred could not be identified and were interred as Korean War Unknowns in the National Cemetery of the Pacific in Hawaii, also referred to as the Punchbowl.

From Pyoktong, about one hundred remains were sent to the Hawaii National Cemetery for internment. Little did anyone know the full story that Father Kapaun had not been buried in the mass graves, and that his remains—nearly completely intact —were among the batch sent to Hawaii.

Even with advances in DNA testing accelerating every year since the 1980s, it was still not easy to get DNA from skeletal remains—you have to drill into the teeth or bone marrow. The next problem was that the Defense Department POW/MIA Accounting Agency has a backlog of thousands of MIAs just from World War II alone, which meant all those unaccounted for were in a queue for testing after they were disinterred. Testing on Korean War remains, including Kapaun's, did not even begin until 2019. Imagine the excitement among those Department of Defense lab workers and investigators when they appeared to have a DNA match with Emil's brother, Eugene, who thankfully provided his DNA to the Department of Defense several years before his passing in 2010. Not wanting to make a mistake on such an important fact-finding mission, they double- and triple-checked the DNA results alongside dental records, a collar bone match to an X-ray taken in the 1940s, height and age analysis, and circumstantial evidence—all before making the confirmation official. They had identified a US soldier from the Korean War who not only was posthumously awarded the Medal of Honor but was on the path to Catholic Sainthood as well.

FATHER KAPAUN COMES HOME

Father Kapaun's remains were flown from Hawaii to Wichita, Kansas, on September 25, 2020, where he received a hero's welcome unlike any other. After being driven to Pilsen, Kansas, he was placed in the very same church where he had been baptized over one hundred years prior. Behind the church, in a cemetery, lie his parents, Bessie and Enos, Msgr. Sklenar, and other Kapaun family members. Kapaun's funeral services were held September 29 in an arena filled to capacity. Among the attendees were his fellow veterans and ex-POWs, Mike Dowe, Paul Roach, and Herb Miller, the man whose life he had saved on that dark day in November when they were defeated at the Battle of Unsan. The homily was delivered by the Bishop of Wichita, Carl Kemme, and remarkable speeches were made by Father Emil's nephew Ray Kapaun and retired Army Chaplain Matthew Pawlikowski on behalf of former POW Mike Dowe. A horse-drawn caisson with full military honors then escorted his body to the crypt where he now rests and is displayed within the Cathedral of the Immaculate Conception in downtown Wichita—home of the Father Kapaun Guild.

THE CASE FOR MARTYRDOM

This speech written by Mike Dowe for Father Kapaun's funeral services, is not only fitting and profound but speaks volumes about what those men went through in battle and as POWs and will have a deep impact on our military, our country and on geopolitical events well into the future. The speech was read by Mike's close friend Chaplain (Colonel) Matthew Pawlikowski (Ret.). It is presented here in its entirety:

MIKE DOWE SPEECH DELIVERED
SEPTEMBER 29, 2021

I bet I'm the only one here who can truthfully say that he or she spent several months sleeping beside a saint. But I'm getting way ahead of myself. Let me go back to the fourth of November 1950...

We had defeated the North Korean army and on 2 November my platoon had just reached the Yalu River at Sinuiju bordering China. I received orders from Battalion to keep my troops off the dam so as not to provoke the Chinese from entering North Korea to attack us. Little did we realize that the Chinese had already infiltrated into North Korea by the tens of thousands and that the shelling we heard way off to the Southeast was the 1st Cavalry being hit by the Chinese at Unsan, where Father Kapaun—along with Doc Anderson—would two days later volunteer to stay behind in their perimeter to take care of the wounded, while the unwounded broke out and made their way south to friendly lines. Meanwhile, after a forced march back to Anju, we were pushed up to the Chon-Chon River on a road that was not even on our old WW2 Japanese maps. There, we were to cover the withdrawal of the remnants of a ROK Division that had been decimated on the border by the ChiComs— The Chinese communists. We set up the roadblock on the 3rd of November and, sure enough, on the fourth we fought wave after wave, their bugles blaring. When we were out of ammo and I only had three men left in my platoon (my buddy Bill Funchess had ten left in his) "Lewis Rocky Rockwerk," the great company commander of Charlie Company 1st of the 19th Inf.—who was one of the "Battling Bastards of Bastonge" in WW2—ordered us to withdraw, but the enemy simply came around the hill and grabbed us. Until then we didn't know for sure that we were fighting Chinese and after recovering the bodies of prisoners tortured and mutilated by the North Koreans, capture was not an option. That night they took us to a school house where we were joined by the men from the Cav perimeter. I was unaware at the time that Father Kapaun was among them.

The ChiComs turned us over to the North Koreans for what was to be a death march of a couple of weeks to our first POW camp. Those who were able to, had to carry the wounded, for if anyone dropped back, so did a Chinese guard—there would be a shot, and that American solider was dead. While the North Koreans kept telling the men not to pay attention to our officers just take care of yourselves, it was necessary to continually organize and urge people to carry the stretchers we made from rice bags and poles that we cut. One of the officers who kept helping with the organization of the stretcher-carrying, despite the North Korean shouts, I later recognized to be Father Kapaun.

It was a couple of weeks after when we reached our intended destination, Pyoktong on the Yalu River. Our bombers arrived at the same time and, to our cheers from a hillside overlooking the town, firebombed and completely destroyed the town. As dusk settled we were assembled to march back to the southeast. I asked the name of the fellow who picked up the rear of the stretcher I was carrying.

"Kapaun" he said putting out his hand.

"Father I said I've heard of you!"

His reply was "Well Please don't tell my bishop. He doesn't know I'm here." And we got a much needed chuckle.

After walking for several days we were led into a Valley in which the soldiers had just driven out all the residents. There we were to spend from November through January, one of North Korea's coldest winters, in bitter twenty to forty below zero temperatures in our summer clothes. The wounded were dropped off next to the road and the enlisted men scattered in

the huts along the creek to the head of the valley where the officers were placed. Nothing stopped Father Kapaun and Doc
Andy [Anderson] from visiting and caring for and cheering up
the wounded as best they could without any supplies. Since the
daily ration we were given was but several hundred grams of
millet (birdseed) or cracked corn, neither of which our systems
could adequately digest, Father set the example as a FOOD thief,
praying for help to Saint Dismas, the GOOD thief, who was
crucified beside Christ. With the food Father would pilfer, he
would sneak down the valley in the evening with a container
and pockets of the grain he had stolen on ration runs or from
the native corn cribs and distribute it to the GIs. He would give
them a puff on his pipe (who knows what was in it since he was
out of tobacco)—talk to them about the importance of main-
taining their faith in God, their country, and each other—and
then he would move on to the next hut.

At the same time Father was doing this in Sim Bac Tu (the
Korean name), or Happy Valley (the Pentagon name) or Father
Kapaun's Valley (the name we GIs gave it), there were two other
similar POW camp valleys: Mining Camp and Death Valley.
The fact that the death rate was many times higher in the other
two camps than in Kapaun Valley can only be attributed to the
way Father Kapaun instilled the will to live among the troops.
By February, Pyoktong was repaired enough for the Chinese to
consolidate the three valleys and take over the administration of
the POWs from the North Koreans. In Pyoktong Father continued to sneak past the guards, away from the officer's compound
(again at the top of the hill) and pop into the GI huts that were
along the road down to the Yalu. The death rate kept growing
as the POWs continued to weaken (less than a thousand of over
2000 POWs survived that winter) and the burial detail was the
worst detail. The POWs who died during the night would be
placed outside their hut and the frozen corpses carried down to
the Yalu and across to an island where—using an entrenching

tool—enough ice would be scratched up to create a space to put the corpse and cover it with ice. Father Kapaun would volunteer for these horrible details—bring any good clothing back with him, wash it—and distribute it to the living in his rounds. In the officer's camp where he slept, Father Kapaun added to his fame by getting up around 6 am, in that freezing cold, stoke the cooking fires, and after heating water come around waking us up with:

"Hot coffee everyone!"

And man did that hit the spot. In March they introduced kaoliang beans into our diet. Father would parch them, put them in a GI sock, and soak them in boiling water. Let me tell you that was delicious coffee. Father confounded the ChiComs who tried to lecture us. He made implements and pans for cooking and boiling water and distributed them. In fact in one such endeavor, chipping at a piece of metal a splinter flew into one eye blinding it. It did not slow him down. He made a black patch for his bad eye and took off on his rounds sneaking past the ChiCom guards to minister to the GIs. With his straggly beard, eye patch, and hat pulled over his head made out of a GI sock, he looked a lot more like a pirate than one who could bring the comfort and peace he did to all the GIs. All religions and all nationalities. He would cheer them up—give them hope—give them a puff on his pipe—say a prayer—and sneak on to the next hut.

When it comes to the question of miracles, I have to tell you about my good friend and company executive officer Dick Haugen. For a short while Dick had been having discussions about religion with Father. When Dick knew he was fading from dysentery, pneumonia and the terrible conditions we were all in due to starvation and neglect—he asked us to get Father. Father was off on his rounds, and before we could find him, Dick passed away. It was well over an hour later when Father was located and brought back to our hut and told that Dick had been asking for him. Father sat down on the floor next to Dick, put

Dick's head in his lap—and Dick came back to life while Father administered the last rites; Dick then immediately died a happy death. Yes, most of us who survived that winter owe a great deal to Father, and many of those who did not, died a happy death because of him.

A week after his famous Easter service—that was held in defiance of the screaming ChiComs with the guards emplacing their bayonets at the end of their rifles—Father didn't even seem to realize that bayonets existed—it was a couple of weeks later, as he was again giving his forbidden weekly sermon, that he collapsed. He had a blood clot in his leg and now it was our turn to take care of him. A couple of weeks of rest and hot compresses did the trick, but he no sooner recovered from the blood clot when he caught pneumonia. Most of us had that or some form of bronchial disease, and with our doctor's help, routinely recovered. Clearly the ChiComs were afraid of Father. And when they learned he was recovering decided to get rid of him in a way that wouldn't cause a riot. There have been many versions on how he died and I want to tell you the correct one: just how he was MARTYRED.

Guards came with bayonets fixed. Despite the protest of our doctors who insisted that Father was recovering, the ChiComs said they were taking him to the hospital. We ALL knew that the ChiComs were going to kill him and when those of us around him started to react Father personally calmed us. I was in tears when he said to me, "Mike don't be sad. I'm going to where I've always wanted to go and when I get there I'll be praying for all of you." He then told Ralph Nardella, "Ralph. You know the prayers. Keep the weekly services going." And Ralph did. When they took him away, Bob Wood, a close friend from West Point who knew Father well and told stories about "the priest who ran to the sound of the guns," was one of the stretcher bearers and had described what happened.

The hospital is about half a mile away on a hill just outside of

the POW camp. At the bottom of the hill was the little infir-
mary where sick call was held. At the top of the hill were three
buildings—a structure on one side housing the ChiComs medical
personnel—a long structure next to it that was the hospital ward
where patients were treated—and a structure about ten meters by
ten meters without windows—that was the death house. Patients
who were incontinent or otherwise difficult to treat were put in
there TO DIE without food or water—with vermin, maggots
and feces. Once dead their bodies were thrown into a canyon
behind the death house that became a mass grave. No one lived
more than a day in the death house. No one placed in it survived. A few GIs say they did but they survived the ward which
many mistook for the death house. When they reached the hospital Bob has often described how they were forced to leave Father Kapaun in the death house instead of the hospital ward. Bob
Wood said that as the ChiComs put them in there, Father said:
"God forgive them, for they know not what they do." The
guards closed the door and, in a day or so, he was dead. That is
how they killed him. Not because of politics. Not because he
was soldier. But because he was a shining light in the darkness
living out his fate as a Christian—they martyred him.

Years later when our graves registration team was allowed to
recover the remains from that mass grave, none were identified
as Father. Amazingly there was one person buried separately near
the death house instead of being thrown into the mass grave. And
this singular grave is mysterious. But the person who was buried
in that separate grave has only recently been positively identified
as Father Kapaun. He is with us here today in his entirety—minus
a couple of fingers—and no one has an explanation. Father Kapaun's was the only separate burial found at that location. And that
is the true story of his martyrdom. When I returned home after
the war, I wrote a magazine article about Father that some may
have read; and I was assigned to the Pentagon where I worked
on a number of POW related matters, one of which earned me a

commendation from Ike. That assignment was for the Eisenhower
Commission to formulate a code of conduct for our Armed Forces.
The Air Force took the position that after 30 days a POW knows
nothing of tactical value and should be able to do or say anything
that—in his estimation—enhanced his situation. They were trying to emulate the actions of a colonel and his crew who went to
Peking and broadcast false germ warfare confessions. That was a
big victory for the Chinese communists who are masters of propaganda and manipulating the media. I use the comparison of the
survival rate of Kapaun Valley with that of the Mining Camp and
Death Valley under like conditions. I presented the army position basing it on how instilling loyalty to God, country and each
other, the POW not only becomes a problem for the enemy, but
enhances his own chances of survival. The Army position won
out. The example of Father's work and life in the camp became
the basis of today's Code of Conduct for our Armed Forces. So
whether people know his name or not, Father has been shaping
the character of service members in all the branches of our armed
forces for the past 70 years. I hope after today, many more people will now know his name and the character of this amazing
saintly man that I have the pleasure of calling my friend, whom
I look forward to seeing in heaven: my friend...

United States Army Chaplain Father Emil Joseph Kapaun.

MILITARY DECORATIONS AWARDED
CHAPLAIN (CAPTAIN) EMIL J. KAPAUN

The Taegeuk Order of Military Merit on behalf of the Republic of Korea—July 27, 2021

Korean Ambassador for Peace Medal—2021

The Congressional Medal of Honor—posthumously awarded April 11, 2013

Bronze Star medal with "V" Device—Sept. 2, 1950

Distinguished Service Cross—Aug. 18, 1951

Legion of Merit Medal

Purple Heart Medal

Prisoner of War Medal

American Campaign Medal

Asiatic-Pacific Campaign Medal with 1 Bronze star

Combat Infantry Badge (CIB) for actions under fire

World War II Victory Medal—CBI Theater 1945-6

Army of Occupation Medal with Japan Clasp

National Defense Service Medal

Korean Service Medal with 2 Bronze Campaign stars

Republic of Korea Presidential Unit Citation and Chryssoun Aristion Andrias (Bravery Gold Medal of Greece) streamer—1st Cavalry Division

United Nations Korea Medal

Republic of Korea War Service Medal

The President of the United States of America,
authorized by Act of Congress, March 3, 1863,
has awarded in the name of Congress
the MEDAL OF HONOR to

CHAPLAIN (CAPTAIN) EMIL J. KAPAUN
UNITED STATES ARMY

for conspicuous gallantry and intrepidity at the risk of his life
above and beyond the call of duty:

Chaplain Emil J. KAPAUN distinguished himself by acts
of gallantry and intrepidity above and beyond the call of
duty while serving with the 3rd Battalion, 8th Cavalry
Regiment, 1st Cavalry Division during combat operations
against an armed enemy at Unsan, Korea, from November
1–2, 1950. On November 1, as Chinese Communist Forces
viciously attacked friendly elements, Chaplain KAPAUN
calmly walked through withering enemy fire in order to
provide comfort and medical aid to his comrades and rescue
friendly wounded from no-man's land. Though the Americans successfully repelled the assault, they found themselves
surrounded by the enemy. Facing annihilation, the able-
bodied men were ordered to evacuate. However, Chaplain
KAPAUN, fully aware of his certain capture, elected to stay
behind with the wounded. After the enemy succeeded in
breaking through the defense in the early morning hours
of November 2, Chaplain KAPAUN continually made
rounds, as hand-to-hand combat ensued. As Chinese Communist Forces approached the American position, Chaplain
KAPAUN noticed an injured Chinese officer among the
wounded and convinced him to negotiate the safe surrender

of the American Forces. Shortly after his capture, Chaplain KAPAUN, with complete disregard for his personal safety and unwavering resolve, bravely pushed aside an enemy soldier preparing to execute Sergeant First Class Herbert A. Miller. Not only did Chaplain KAPAUN'S gallantry save the life of Sergeant Miller, but also his unparalleled courage and leadership inspired all those present, including those who might have otherwise fled in panic, to remain and fight the enemy until captured. Chaplain KAPAUN'S extraordinary heroism and selflessness, above and beyond the call of duty, are in keeping with the highest traditions of military service and reflect great credit upon himself, the 3rd Battalion, 8th Cavalry Regiment, the 1st Cavalry Division, and the United States Army.

Acknowledgments

First Sergeant (Ret) Alan C. Gathercole.

Bob Brooks and Dale McKinnon—veterans who tirelessly run several historical Facebook pages including Korean War Pics and Stories and The Korean War's Chosin Reservoir.

Ted and Hal Barker at The Korean War Project who have dedicated their lives to recording everything about those who served in the Korean War as accurately as possible.

Father John Hotze, Episcopal Delegate, and Scott Carter representing the Father Kapaun Guild's Cause for Canonization for Emil J. Kapaun for The Catholic Diocese of Wichita. Reverend Carl Kemme, Bishop of Wichita.

Harriet Bina and the volunteers at the Father Kapaun Museum in Pilsen, Kansas.

Rob Knapp, President of Kapaun-Mt. Carmel Catholic High School in Wichita, Kansas.

The US Army Chief of Chaplains, Chaplain (Major General) Thomas Solhjem (Ret) and retired Chaplain (Major General) Paul Hurley and the Office of the Chief of Chaplains at the Pentagon.

US Army Institute for Religious Leadership (Chaplain School) at Fort Jackson, South Carolina. Many thanks to Marcia Mc-Manus, director of the Chaplain Museum.

Avi Arad, Glen Sharp, Andrea Sharp, Peggy Schuler Lockwood, Carole Funchess, Mark Funchess, Tami Connely, Alan Greenberg, Jim DeFelice, Colonel (Ret) and Mrs. John Buckley, David and Naomi Shapiro, Kelly Patton-Grissom, Jean-Guy Despres, Stephen Campanelli, Clint Eastwood, Father Matthew Pawlikowski, Daniel Cohen, William S. Burroughs, Forest Robin, Landon Williams, Ben Willhite, Jerry "The Illuminator" Taylor, Kerry Bullock-Scarvie, Mark Malicoat, Mark and Diane Robison, Adam Makos, Captain (Ret) Dale Dye and Julia Dye at Warriors, Inc., Dan King, Steve Gonzales, Alan Glazer, James Little, Robin Coon, Beth Young, Jessica Walter, Paula O'Connor, Cara Bray, Rebel Roy Steiner, Jr., Maggie "Ma Bu" Luckerath, Roma Downey, Paula Kear, Chase Kear, Kevin Willmott, Paul Manion, Brian and Viviana Pollack, Ray Ramos, Ken Scar, Carole Sklenar, Aaron Zell, Marvin Tajchman, Brittany Ramirez, Brigadier General (Retired) Joe Ramirez, Jr., Stan Finger, CSM Fred Manney.

Kimberly Kay Bosze, my love and partner who never wavered in her belief and support of me even when the chips were down. Keep the faith.

Mel Berger, agent extraordinaire, and his associates at the William Morris Endeavor Agency. Mel's immediate recognition of the magnitude of this story left him no doubt that this unknown author deserved a shot at pitching to top publishers. I am deeply grateful for his guidance.

Peter Joseph, Editorial Director at Hanover Square Press and editor of this book. Peter had an immediate reaction to the power of this story and I am eternally grateful to Eden Railsback and the team at Hanover Square Press and all those at HarperCollins who worked on this book.

Mark Malatesta, friend and writing coach to many a successful author. Many thanks and blessings to Mark and his wife Ingrid, who truly never gave up on me.

President Barack Obama, who presided over Chaplain Kapaun's posthumous Medal of Honor ceremony on April 11, 2013. This is when I first learned of Emil Kapaun.

Korean War veterans and ex-POWs: Mike Dowe, Bill Richardson, Bailey Gillespie, Joe E. Ramirez, Charles Ross, William Funchess, Paul Roach, Robert McGreevy, Bob Wood, Herb Miller, Jack Goodwin, and all former POWs from the Korean War. Thank you for relating your powerful stories.

Ray and David Kapaun (nephews of Emil Kapaun) and the entire Kapaun family. Ray Kapaun graciously accepted his uncle's Medal of Honor at the White House before a live TV audience. Nearly a decade later, the Kapaun family was stunned to learn that Father Kapaun's remains were positively identified after seventy years listed as MIA. The tributes, interviews and services given Emil Kapaun upon his return home to Kansas were humble, tearful and joyful all at once.

Ryan and Betsy Stansifer, Mary Lee Stansifer and Jim Collins, Karen Stansifer-Sabot and Jean Yves Sabot, and all their many wonderful children.

My parents, Professor Charles and Mary Ellen Stansifer, both from Wichita, who raised me from day one on the importance of education and learning from history.

Author's Note

This book would not be possible without the large contributions of two very different writers, both of whom served as pastors in the Catholic Diocese of Wichita about the same time. In 1951, the Reverend Arthur Tonne was incardinated into the Diocese of Wichita, Kansas, and served as the pastor at St. John Nepomucene Church in Pilsen, Kansas, for nearly 38 years. When the community learned of Father Kapaun's passing after the Korean War, Rev. Tonne immediately set out to write the first biographical account of him and conducted numerous interviews with friends and family and veterans, and simultaneously exchanged hundreds of letters with people who had a story to tell about Father Kapaun. In 1954, he published *The Story of Chaplain Kapaun: Patriot Priest of the Korean Conflict,* which contains page after page of Kapaun's letters in their entirety. Interest in Father Kapaun's story only grew, and it was clear the Wichita Diocese would someday in the future open a cause for Father Kapaun's canonization. So the letter exchanges and official interviews continued to be collected well after the book's publication all the way until Monsignor Arthur Tonne's passing in 2003. The original book has fallen into the public domain and some portions cited have been edited for content. While some writings and letters will be sourced to his book, others gathered after are kept in the Father Kapaun Guild archives and will be labeled below as either the date of the letter and who wrote it or noted as "FKG archives."

Also part of the Father Kapaun Guild archives is an unusual document that had been shelved for many years in the Chaplain Kapaun High School library in Wichita. It is an untitled, unfinished, and unpublished biography of Father Kapaun and was written by his close friend and fellow priest, Father Joseph Goracy. Goracy was pastor of the Pilsen parish for five years and, after the Korean War ended, had the unfortunate duty to tell Enos and Bessie Kapaun, in person, that their son, Emil, would not be coming home. This news affected everyone deeply. Father Goracy then wrote about a hundred pages for a Kapaun biography but in a more personal style than Rev. Tonne's book. It was written in first person like a memoir, with deep meditations on what Father Kapaun was doing and thinking throughout his life, especially in his last ten years. So many of these passages were inserted in chronological order here and are noted simply as: "Father Joseph Goracy."

Endnotes

PROLOGUE—A MAN OF GOD

1   Lt. William Funchess, interview by author.

2   Ibid.

1. AD ASTRA PER ASPERA

1   Rev. Arthur Tonne, *The Story of Chaplain Kapaun: Patriot Priest of the Korean Conflict*, Didde Printing, 1954.

2   Emil Kapaun, diary, Father Kapaun Guild (FKG) archives.

3   Father Joseph Goracy, FKG archives.

4   Father Edward Malone letter to Rev. Arthur Tonne, FKG archives.

5   Rev. Arthur Tonne interview with Eugene Kapaun, FKG archives.

6   Rev. Tonne, *The Story of Chaplain Kapaun*.

7   Ibid.

8   Ibid.

9   Ibid.

10   Ibid.

11   Ibid.

12   Ibid.

2. FOR GOD AND COUNTRY

1   Emil Kapaun, diary, FKG archives.

2   Donald F. Crosby, SJ, *Battlefield Chaplains: Catholic Priests in World War II*, University of Kansas Press, 1994.

3   Father Kapaun letter, FKG archives, April 26, 1943.

4   Father Joseph Goracy, FKG archives.

5   Crosby, *Battlefield Chaplains*.

6   "The Chaplain," *US Army Field Manual*, Department of Defense, 1944.

7   Crosby, *Battlefield Chaplains*.

8   Father Joseph Goracy, FKG archives.

9   Rodger R. Venzke, *Confidence in Battle, Inspiration in Peace: The United States Army Chaplaincy, 1945–1975*, vol. 5, Office of the Chief of Chaplains, Department of the Army, 1977.

10   Father Joseph Goracy, FKG archives.

11   Ibid.

12   Ibid.

3. ABOVE THE CLOUDS

1   Rodger R. Venzke, *Confidence in Battle, Inspiration in Peace: The United States Army Chaplaincy, 1945–1975*, vol. 5, Office of the Chief of Chaplains, Department of the Army, 1977.

2   Father Joseph Goracy, FKG archives.

4. THE CATHOLIC UNIVERSITY OF AMERICA

1   Father Joseph Goracy, FKG archives.

2   Ibid.

5. THE WILL OF GOD COMES FIRST

1   Father Joseph Goracy, FKG archives.

2   Ibid.

3   Rodger R. Venzke, *Confidence in Battle, Inspiration in Peace: The United States Army Chaplaincy, 1945–1975,* vol. 5, Office of the Chief of Chaplains, Department of the Army, 1977.

4   Father Joseph Goracy, FKG archives.

5   Ibid.

6   Ibid.

7   Ibid.

6. OCCUPIED JAPAN—1950

1   Jim Draskovich letter to Bishop Gerber, FKG archives, December 17, 1996.

2   Rodger R. Venzke, *Confidence in Battle, Inspiration in Peace: The United States Army Chaplaincy, 1945–1975,* vol. 5, Office of the Chief of Chaplains, Department of the Army, 1977.

3   Father Joseph Goracy, FKG archives.

4   Ibid.

5   Ibid.

6   Venzke, *Confidence in Battle.*

7   Father Joseph Goracy, FKG archives.

8   Robert G. Wixom letter to Rev. Arthur Tonne, FKG archives, January 18, 2001.

9   Richard E. Mack, *Memoir of a Cold War Soldier*, Kent State University Press, 2001.

7. THE PUSAN PERIMETER

1   War Diary, 1st Cavalry Division, July–December 1950. Declassified records from the National Archives and after-action reports from 1st Cavalry Division Headquarters during the Korean War.

2   T. R. Fehrenbach, *This Kind of War: Korea 1950–1953*, Macmillan, 1963.

3   Rodger R. Venzke, *Confidence in Battle, Inspiration in Peace: The United States Army Chaplaincy, 1945–1975*, vol. 5, Office of the Chief of Chaplains, Department of the Army, 1977.

4   Combat medic Bailey Gillespie, interview by author.

5   Donald Knox, *The Korean War—An Oral History: Pusan to Chosin*, Harcourt Brace Jovanovich, 1985.

6   Lt. William Funchess, interview by author.

7   Venzke, *Confidence in Battle*.

8   Ibid.

8. TOMORROW WE ARE GOING INTO COMBAT

1   Father Joseph Goracy, FKG archives.

2   Rodger R. Venzke, *Confidence in Battle, Inspiration in Peace: The United States Army Chaplaincy, 1945–1975*, vol. 5, Office of the Chief of Chaplains, Department of the Army, 1977.

3   Capt. (Dr.) Jerome Dolan interview with Rev. Francis X. Rogue, FKG archives.

4   Lt. Mike Dowe, interview by author.

5   War Diary, 1st Cavalry Division, July–December 1950. Declassified records from the National Archives and after-action reports from 1st Cavalry Division Headquarters during the Korean War.

6   *A Saint Among Us: Remembering Father Emil J. Kapaun*, Father Kapaun Guild, 2005.

7   Venzke, *Confidence in Battle.*

8   Chaplain Arthur Mills letter to Rev. Arthur Tonne, FKG archives.

9   Donald Knox, *The Korean War—An Oral History: Pusan to Chosin*, Harcourt Brace Jovanovich, 1985.

10 Emil Kapaun letter to Father John M. Sklenar, FKG archives, August 12, 1950.

11 Venzke, *Confidence in Battle.*

12 Ibid.

13 Father Joseph Goracy, FKG archives.

9. THE BATTLE OF TAEGU—AUGUST 5–20, 1950

1   Capt. (Dr.) Jerome Dolan interview with Rev. Francis X. Rogue, FKG archives.

2   William "Moose" McClain letter to Joseph A. Pottebaum, FKG archives.

3   Father Joseph Goracy, FKG archives.

4   Capt. (Dr.) Dolan interview with Rev. Rogue.

5   William Clark Latham, Jr., *Cold Days in Hell: American POWs in Korea*, Texas A&M University Press, 2012.

6   Donald Knox, *The Korean War—An Oral History: Pusan to Chosin*, Harcourt Brace Jovanovich, 1985.

7   Ibid.

10. THE BATTLE OF TABU DONG—SEPTEMBER 1–18, 1950

1   Lt. Walt Mayo letter to Rev. Arthur Tonne, FKG archives.

2   Capt. (Dr.) Jerome Dolan, letter to the editor, *Saturday Evening Post*, September 15, 1951.

3   Daniel M. Cohen, *Single Handed: The Inspiring True Story of Tibor "Teddy" Rubin—Holocaust Survivor, Korean War Hero, and Medal of Honor Recipient*, Berkley Publishing Group, 2015.

4   Letter to Rev. Arthur Tonne, February 15, 1954, published in Rev. Arthur Tonne, *The Story of Chaplain Kapaun: Patriot Priest of the Korean Conflict*, Didde Printing, 1954.

5   Bill Richardson and Kevin Maurer, *Valleys of Death: A Memoir of the Korean War*, Berkley Publishing Group, 2010.

6   War Diary, 1st Cavalry Division, July–December 1950. Declassified records from the National Archives and after-action reports from 1st Cavalry Division Headquarters during the Korean War.

7   Richard E. Mack, *Memoir of a Cold War Soldier*, Kent State University Press, 2001.

11. NO BULLET GOT ME YET

1   War Diary, 1st Cavalry Division, July–December 1950. Declassified records from the National Archives and after-action reports from 1st Cavalry Division Headquarters during the Korean War.

2   Rodger R. Venzke, *Confidence in Battle, Inspiration in Peace: The United States Army Chaplaincy, 1945–1975*, vol. 5, Office of the Chief of Chaplains, Department of the Army, 1977.

3   War Diary, 1st Cavalry Division.

4   John P. Gannon letter to Capt. (Dr.) Jerome Dolan, FKG archives.

5   Rev. Arthur Tonne, *The Story of Chaplain Kapaun: Patriot Priest of the Korean Conflict*, Didde Printing, 1954.

6   Father Joseph Goracy, FKG archives.

12. THE CAPTURE OF PYONGYANG

1   Donald Knox, *The Korean War—An Oral History: Pusan to Chosin*, Harcourt Brace Jovanovich, 1985.

2   Pvt. Patrick Schuler letter to Rev. Arthur Tonne, FKG archives.

3   Capt. (Dr.) Jerome Dolan interview with Rev. Francis X. Rogue, FKG archives.

4   Capt. Joseph O'Connor letter to Rev. Arthur Tonne, FKG archives.

5   Capt. (Dr.) Dolan interview with Rev. Rogue.

6   Witnessed by Mike Dowe, William Funchess, Herb Miller, and about eight thousand troops in attendance that day.

13. THE BATTLE OF UNSAN

1   Rodger R. Venzke, *Confidence in Battle, Inspiration in Peace: The United States Army Chaplaincy, 1945–1975*, vol. 5, Office of the Chief of Chaplains, Department of the Army, 1977.

2   Rev. Arthur Tonne, *The Story of Chaplain Kapaun: Patriot Priest of the Korean Conflict*, Didde Printing, 1954.

3   Ibid.

4   Ibid.

5   Daniel M. Cohen, *Single Handed: The Inspiring True Story of Tibor "Teddy" Rubin—Holocaust Survivor, Korean War Hero, and Medal of Honor Recipient*, Berkley Publishing Group, 2015.

6   Lt. Walt Mayo letter to Rev. Arthur Tonne, FKG archives.

7   Ibid.

8   Rev. Arthur Tonne interview with James Petergall, FKG archives.

9   Sgt. Samuel Cleckner letter to commander at Fort Benning, FKG archives.

10   Robert Morrison letter, FKG archives, January 16, 2001.

11   War Diary, 1st Cavalry Division, July–December 1950. Declassified
      records from the National Archives and after-action reports from 1st
      Cavalry Division Headquarters during the Korean War.

12   Venzke, *Confidence in Battle*.

13   Lt. William Funchess, interview by author.

14   Ibid.

14. FATHER KAPAUN'S VALLEY

1   Lyle Otineru, "Honor and Courage: The United States 8th Cavalry
      at Unsan, North Korea, 30 October–4 November 1950," Master's
      thesis, Hawaii Pacific University, 2010.

2   Bill Richardson, interview by author.

3   Daniel M. Cohen, *Single Handed: The Inspiring True Story of Tibor
      "Teddy" Rubin—Holocaust Survivor, Korean War Hero, and Medal of
      Honor Recipient*, Berkley Publishing Group, 2015.

4   Lewis H. Carlson, *Remembered Prisoners of a Forgotten War: An Oral
      History of Korean War POWs*, St. Martin's Press, 2002.

5   Lt. Mike Dowe, interview by author.

6   William L. Maher, *A Shepherd in Combat Boots: Chaplain Emil Kapaun
      of the 1st Cavalry Division*, Burd Street Press, 1997, and White Mane
      Publishing, 2022.

7   Robert Morrison letter to Rev. Arthur Tonne, FKG archives, January 16, 2001.

8   Rodger R. Venzke, *Confidence in Battle, Inspiration in Peace: The United
      States Army Chaplaincy, 1945–1975*, vol. 5, Office of the Chief of Chaplains, Department of the Army, 1977.

9   Lt. Walt Mayo letter to Rev. Arthur Tonne, FKG archives.

10   Robert Burke letter to Rev. Arthur Tonne, FKG archives.

11   Dr. Sidney Esensten letter to Rev. Arthur Tonne, FKG archives, November 14, 1989.

12   Rev. Arthur Tonne, *The Story of Chaplain Kapaun: Patriot Priest of the Korean Conflict*, Didde Printing, 1954.

13   John W. Thornton, *Believed to Be Alive*, Naval Institute Press, 2012, originally published in 1981.

15. PYOKTONG

1   Lt. William Funchess, interview by author.

2   Peter Busatti letter to Rev. Arthur Tonne, FKG archives.

3   Rev. Arthur Tonne, *The Story of Chaplain Kapaun: Patriot Priest of the Korean Conflict*, Didde Printing, 1954.

4   John H. Joyce interview with Rev. Arthur Tonne, (the last paragraph he quotes Lt. Mike Dowe), FKG archives.

5   Felix McCool, Aileen Marckmann, and Scott Marckmann, *Let's Face It: Memoirs, Speeches and Writings of a Career Marine and Two-Time Prisoner of War*, CreateSpace Independent Publishing Platform, 2014.

6   Cyril Cunningham, *No Mercy, No Leniency: Communist Mistreatment of British Prisoners of War in Korea*, Pen & Sword Books, 2000.

7   Raymond Lech, *Broken Soldiers*, University of Illinois Press, 2000.

8   Lt. Mike Dowe interview, FKG archives.

9   Phillip D. Chinnery, *Korean Atrocity! Forgotten War Crimes 1950–1953*, Pen & Sword Books Ltd., 2009.

10   Ibid.

11   Daniel M. Cohen, *Single Handed: The Inspiring True Story of Tibor "Teddy" Rubin—Holocaust Survivor, Korean War Hero, and Medal of Honor Recipient*, Berkley Publishing Group, 2015.

12   Rev. Tonne, *The Story of Chaplain Kapaun*.

13   Lt. Mike Dowe, interview by author.

14   Chinnery, *Korean Atrocity!*

15   William Clark Latham, Jr., *Cold Days in Hell: American POWs in Korea*, Texas A&M University Press, 2012.

16   Rev. Tonne, *The Story of Chaplain Kapaun.*

17   Carl Kopischkie letter to Rev. Arthur Tonne, FKG archives, February 27, 1987.

18   Rev. Tonne, *The Story of Chaplain Kapaun.*

19   Ibid.

20   Lt. Mike Dowe, interview by author.

21   Rev. Arthur Tonne interview with Lt. Walt Mayo, FKG archives.

22   Ibid.

EPILOGUE—CHRIST IN BARBED WIRE

1   Rev. Arthur Tonne, *The Story of Chaplain Kapaun: Patriot Priest of the Korean Conflict*, Didde Printing, 1954.

2   Ibid.

AFTERWORD—THE PATH TO SAINTHOOD

1   Scott Carter, interview by author.

Select Bibliography

South to the Naktong, North to the Yalu by Lt. Col. Roy E. Appleman, US Army, (Ret.). Washington Center for Military History, U.S. Army, 1986

Disaster in Korea: The Chinese Confront MacArthur by Lt. Col. Roy E. Appleman, US Army, (Ret.). Texas A & M University Press, 1989

Faces of Holiness: Modern Saints in Photos and Words by Ann Ball. Our Sunday Visitor Publishing, 1998

The Sword of the Lord: Military Chaplains from the First to the Twenty-First Century. Edited by Doris L. Bergen. University of Notre Dame Press, 2004

Remembered Prisoners of a Forgotten War: An Oral History of Korean War POWs by Lewis H. Carlson. St. Martin's Press, 2002

Korean Atrocity! Forgotten War Crimes 1950-1953 by Philip D. Chinnery. Pen & Sword Books Ltd., 2009

Catechism of the Catholic Church translated into English by the United States Catholic Conference. Doubleday, 1997

Communist Propaganda Techniques by John C. Clews. Frederick A. Praeger, Publishers, 1964

Single Handed by Daniel M. Cohen. Berkley Publishing Group, 2015

Battlefield Chaplains: Catholic Priests in World War II by Donald F. Crosby. University Press of Kansas, 1994

The Korean War: A History by Bruce Cummings. Modern Library, 2010

No Mercy, No Leniency: Communist Mistreatment of British and Allied Prisoners of War in Korea by Cyril Cunninigham. Pen & Sword Books, London, 2000

The Legacy of Custer's 7th U.S. Cavalry in Korea by Edward L. Daily. Turner Publishing Company, 1990

1st Cavalry Division: Korea, June 1950 to January 1952 by the 1st Cavalry Division Association. Turner Publishing Company, 1994. Edward L. Daily, Board of Governors President, 7th U.S. Cavalry Association.

Fighting on the Brink: Defense of the Pusan Perimeter by Brig. Gen. Uzal W. Ent (Ret.). Turner Publishing Company, 1996

This Kind of War: Korea 1950-1953 by T.R. Fehrenbach. Macmillan, 1963

MacArthur by Richard B. Frank. Palgrave Macmillian, 2007

KOREA P.O.W.- A Thousand Days of Torment by William H. Funchess. South Carolina Military Museum, 2002

Korean War Remembered: POW, 1013 Days in Hell by SFC Bailey Gillespie. Joy and Bailey Gillespie, 1993

The Korean War: The Story and Photographs by Donald M. Goldstein and Harry J. Maihafer. Brassey's, 2000

I Remember Korea: Veterans Tell Their Stories by Linda Granfield. Clarion Books, 2003

The Coldest Winter: America and the Korean War by David Halberstam. Hyperion, 2007

Q Clan: The First Summer of the Korean Conflict, June-September 1950, A Lieutenant's Memoir by Ralph Derr Harrity. Dorrance Publishing Co., 2005

The Korean War by Max Hastings. Simon & Schuster, 1987

Douglas MacArthur: American Warrior by Arthur Herman. Random House, 2016

War in Korea by Marguerite Higgins. Doubleday, 1951

This Place Called Kansas by Charles C. Howes. University of Oklahoma Press, 1987

On To The Yalu by Edwin P. Hoyt. Military Heritage Press, 1984

The Pusan Perimeter by Edwin P. Hoyt. Military Heritage Press, 1984

A Celebration of Life: A Prisoner of War's 54-year Journey Since the Korean War by Cecil Mark Inman. Xulon Press, 2006

The Korean War - An Oral History - Pusan to Chosin by Donald Knox. Harcourt Brace Jovanovich, 1985

Cold Days in Hell: American POWs in Korea by William Clark Latham, Jr. Texas A&M University Press, 2012

Broken Soldiers by Raymond B. Lech. University Illinois Press, 2000

Memoir of a Cold War Soldier by Richard E. Mack. Kent State University Press, 2001

A Shepherd in Combat Boots: Chaplain Emil Kapaun of the 1st Cavalry Division by William L. Maher. Burd Street Press, 1997

Formidable Enemies: The North Korean and Chinese Soldier in the Korean War by Kevin Mahoney. Presidio Press, 2001

Lives of the Saints by Richard P. McBrien. HarperCollins, 2001

Korean War Atrocities Subcommittee Report - Senator Joseph McCarthy, chairman. US Congress, 1954

Let's Face It: Memoirs, Speeches and Writings of a career Marine and two-time Prisoner of War by Felix McCool. With Aileen and

Scott Marckmann. CreateSpace Independent Publishing Platform, 2014

Truman by David McCollough. Simon & Schuster, 1992

The Korean War - The essential Bibliography Series by Allan R. Millet. Potomac Books, 2007

The War for Korea, 1950-1951: They Came From the North by Allan R. Millet. The University Press of Kansas, 2010

"Honor and Courage: The United States 8th Cavalry at Unsan, North Korea 30 October–4 November 1950." Master's thesis by Lyle K. Otineru for a Master of Arts in Diplomacy and Military Studies, Hawaii Pacific University, Fall 2010

In The Shadow Of The Greatest Generation by Melinda L. Pash. New York University Press, 2012

Voices from the Korean War: Personal stories of American, Korean and Chinese Soldiers by Richard Peters and Xiaobing Li. The University Press of Kentucky, 2004

Wichita 1860-1930 by Jay M. Price. Arcadia Publishing, 2003

Valleys of Death: A Memoir of the Korean War by Colonel William (Bill) Richardson. With Kevin Maurer. Berkley Publishing Group, 2010

The Dragon Strikes: China and the Korean War: June-December 1950 by Patrick C. Roe. Presidio Press, 2000

When Hell Froze Over: The memoir of a Korean War combat physician who spent 1010 days in a communist prison camp by William Shaddish, M.D. With Lewis H. Carlson. iUniverse, 2007

A Moment In Time: A Korean P.O.W. Survivor's Story by William W. Smith as told to Charlotte Smith. Gazelle Press, 2008

The Story of Chaplain Kapaun by Father Arthur Tonne. Didde Publishers, Emporia, Kansas, 1954

The United States Army Chaplaincy 1945–1975—Confidence in Battle, Inspiration in Peace, Volume V, by Major (Chaplain) Rodger R. Venzke. Published by the Office of the Chief of Chaplains, Department of the Army, Washington, D.C. 1977

The Captives of Korea: An unofficial white paper on the treatment of war prisoners by William Lindsay White. Charles Scribner's Sons, 1957

A Saint Among Us: Remembering Father Emil J. Kapaun. Edited by Pat Wick and published by the Father Kapaun Guild, Wichita, Kansas, 2005

Index

Page numbers in italics refer to photographs.